JOHNSON'S LIFE OF LONDON

ALSO BY BORIS JOHNSON

THE DREAM OF ROME
LEND ME YOUR EARS
HAVE I GOT VIEWS FOR YOU

72 VIRGINS (Fiction)

THE PERILS OF THE PUSHY PARENTS (Poetry)

BORIS JOHNSON

JOHNSON'S LIFE OF LONDON

THE PEOPLE WHO MADE THE CITY THAT MADE THE WORLD

Harper
Press

This edition produced for The Book People Ltd, Parc Menai, Bangor LL57 4FB

Harper*Press*
An imprint of HarperCollins*Publishers*
77–85 Fulham Palace Road
Hammersmith, London W6 8JB
www.harpercollins.co.uk

Published in Great Britain by Harper*Press* in 2011

1

A catalogue record for this book
is available from the British Library

ISBN: 978-0-00-790855-4

Illustrations on page vii © Museum of London;
pages iii, 24, 47, 74, 305 © Getty Images

Typeset by G&M Designs Limited,
Raunds, Northamptonshire
Printed and bound in Great Britain by
Clays Ltd, St Ives plc

FSC
www.fsc.org
MIX
Paper from
responsible sources
FSC™ C007454

FSC is a non-profit international organisation established to promote
the responsible management of the world's forests. Products carrying the
FSC label are independently certified to assure consumers that they come
from forests that are managed to meet the social, economic and
ecological needs of present and future generations,
and other controlled sources.

Find out more about HarperCollins and the environment at
www.harpercollins.co.uk/green

For Marina

Contents

Sundry interesting London inventions have been interspersed in the text

London Bridge

Still they come, surging towards me across the bridge.

On they march in sun, wind, rain, snow and sleet. Almost every morning I cycle past them in rank after heaving rank as they emerge from London Bridge station and tramp tramp tramp up and along the broad 239-metre pavement that leads over the river and towards their places of work.

It feels as if I am reviewing an honourable regiment of yomping commuters, and as I pass them down the bus-rutted tarmac there is the occasional eyes left moment and I will be greeted with a smile or perhaps a cheery four-letter cry.

Sometimes they are on the phone, or talking to their neighbours, or checking their texts. A few of them may glance at the scene, which is certainly worth a glance: on their left the glistening turrets of the City, on the right the white Norman keep, the guns of HMS *Belfast* and the mad castellations of Tower Bridge, and beneath them the powerful swirling eddies of the river that seems to be green or brown depending on the time of day. Mainly, however, they have their mouths set and eyes with that blank and inward look of people who have done the bus or the Tube or the overground train and are steeling themselves for the day ahead.

This was the sight, you remember, that filled TS Eliot with horror. A crowd flowed over London Bridge, so many, reported the sensitive banker-turned-poet. I had not thought death had undone so many, he moaned; and yet ninety years after Eliot freaked out the tide of humanity is fuller than ever. When I pass that pavement at off-peak times I can see that it is pale and worn from the pounding, and that not even the chewing gum can survive the wildebeest tread.

The crowd has changed since Eliot had his moment of apocalypse. There are thousands of women on the march today, wearing trainers and carrying their heels in bags. The men have rucksacks instead of briefcases; no one is wearing a bowler hat and hardly anyone seems to be smoking a cigarette, let alone a pipe. But London's commuters are still the same in their trudging purpose, and they come in numbers not seen before.

London's buses are carrying more people than at any time in history. The Tube is travelling more miles than ever, and more people are riding on the trains. It would be nice to reveal that people are ditching their cars in favour of public transport; and yet the paradox is that private motor vehicle transport is also increasing, and cycling has gone up 15 per cent in one year.

As we look back at the last twenty years of the information technology revolution, there is one confident prediction that has not come true.

They said we would all be sitting in our kitchens in Dorking or Dorset and 'telecottaging' down the 'information superhighway'. Video link-ups, we were told, would make meetings unnecessary. What tosh.

Whatever we may think they 'need' to do, people want to see other people up close. I leave it to the anthropologists to come up with the detailed analysis, but you only have to try a week of 'working from home' to know it is not all it's cracked up to be.

You soon get gloomy from making cups of coffee and surfing the Internet and going to hack at that piece of cheese in the fridge. And then there are some profounder reasons for this obstinate human desire to be snuffling round each other at the water cooler. As the Harvard economist Edward Glaeser has demonstrated, the move to the city is as rational in the information revolution as it was in the Industrial Revolution.

By the time I get to cycle home, most of the morning crowds have tramped the other way. Like some gigantic undersea coelenterate, London has completed its spectacular daily act of respiration – sucking in millions of commuters from 7 am to 9 am, and then efficiently expelling them back to the suburbs and the Home Counties from 5 pm to 7 pm. But the drift home is more staggered. There are pubs, clubs and bars to be visited and as I watch the crowds of drinkers on the pavements – knots of people dissolving and reforming in a slow minuet – I can see why the city beats the countryside hands down. It's the sheer range of opportunity.

You can exchange Dante/Beatrice glances on the Tube escalator; you can spill someone else's latte and offer to buy them another; you can apologise when they tread on your toe, or you can get your dog lead tangled in theirs, or you can just collide with them on the pavement. You can even use the personal dating services in the evening paper or (I imagine this still goes on) you can offer to buy them a drink. These are some of the mating strategies of our species; but they have statistically a far higher likelihood of success in a city, because it is in the city where there are the numbers and the choice of potential mates – and the penalty for failure is much lower.

The metropolis is like a vast multinational reactor where Mr Quark and Miss Neutrino are moving the fastest and bumping into each other with the most exciting results. This is not just a question of romance or reproduction. It is about ideas. It is about the cross-pollination that is more likely to take place with a whole superswarm of bees rather than a few isolated hives.

You would expect me to say this, and I must of course acknowledge that many great cities can make all kinds of claims to primacy, but at a moment when it is perhaps excessively fashionable to be gloomy about Western civilisation I would tentatively suggest that London is just about the most culturally, technologically, politically and linguistically influential city of the last five hundred years. In fact, I don't think even the Mayors of Paris, New York, Moscow, Berlin, Madrid, Tokyo, Beijing or Amsterdam would quibble when I say that London is – after Athens and Rome – the third most programmatic city in history.

Around the world there are similar crowds of commuters, tramping similar pavements with the same grim-jawed mood of economic competitiveness. They are wearing a London invention – the dark suit, with jacket, trousers and tie, that was pioneered by eighteenth-century dandies and refined by the Victorians. They travel on devices that were either invented or developed in London: underground trains (Paddington to Farringdon, 1855) or buses, or even bicycles, which were certainly popularised if not invented in London.

If they have just got off a plane, that machine will have been guided through the sky by air traffic controllers who are trained to speak a language that emerged in its modern form in the London of Geoffrey Chaucer.

They may make use of a cash machine (Enfield, 1967) before entering a department store (which appeared in its modern form in Oxford Street in 1909). When they get home the chances are they will slump in front of a television (the first example of which was turned on in a room above what is now Bar Italia in Frith Street, Soho, in 1925) and watch the football (whose rules were codified in a pub in Great Queen Street in 1863).

You know, I could keep it up for quite a while, this tub-thumping list of London innovations, from the machine gun to the Internet to the futures market for Château Haut-Brion. But the city's contribution has also been spiritual and ideological. When Anglican missionaries fanned out across Africa, they carried the King James Bible, a masterpiece translated in London. When the Americans founded their great republic they were partly inspired by the anti-monarchical slogans of London radicals; and across the world there are governments that at least pay lip service to concepts of parliamentary democracy and habeas corpus that London did more than any other city to promote.

Darwinism originated in the English capital. So did Marxism. So did Thatcherism, come to that, and the anarcho-communism of Bromley resident Peter Kropotkin.

It was the vast pink patches of empire that did the most to allow Londoners to project themselves abroad, the Cambrian explosion of Victorian technology and energy. But the empire was no accident, and it was no sudden fluke that made London in 1800 the biggest and most powerful city on Earth. That imperial epoch was itself the product of centuries of evolution, and the Victorians inherited a conglomerate of advantages – a wonderfully flexible language, skill in banking, naval expertise, a stable political system – that previous Londoners had laid down.

A big city gives people the chance to find mates, money and food; and then there is one further thing that bright people come to London to find, one currency more dear to the human heart than money itself – and that is fame.

It was the eternal contest for reputation and prestige that encouraged Londoners to endow new hospitals or write great plays or crack the problem of longitude for the navy. No matter how agreeable your surroundings, you couldn't get famous by sitting around in some village, and that is still true today. You need people to acknowledge what you have done; you need a gallery for the applause; and above all you need to know what everyone else is up to.

It is the city that gives the ambitious person the scope to eavesdrop, borrow or just intuit the ideas of others, and then to meld them with his own and come up with something new. And for the less ambitious, it is a chance to look busy and ingratiate yourself with the boss in the hope of avoiding the boot – because if someone is 'working from home' then I am afraid they are a great deal easier to sack.

These are some of the reasons why people have chosen not to stay at home with the cat; that is why there is the drumming migration over London Bridge. For centuries people have been coming not in search of oil or gold or any other natural wealth – because London has nothing but Pleistocene clay and mud – they have been coming in search of each other, and each other's approbation. It is that competition for prestige that has so often produced the flashes of genius that have taken the city forwards – and sometimes the entire human race.

If you had come to London 10,000 years ago, you would have found nothing to distinguish the place from any other estuarial swamp in Europe. You might have found the odd mammoth looking lost and on the verge of extinction, but no human settlements. And for the next 10,000 years it was pretty much the same.

The civilisations of Babylon and Mohenjo-daro rose and fell. The Pharaohs built the pyramids. Homer sang. The Mexican Zapotecs began to write. Pericles adorned the Acropolis. The Chinese emperor called his terracotta army into being, the Roman republic endured a bloody civil war and then became an empire and in London there was silence save the flitting of deer between the trees.

The river was about four times wider than it is today, and much slower – but there was scarcely a coracle to be seen on the Thames. When the time came for Christ to preach his ministry in Galilee there were certainly a few proto-Britons living in a state of undress and illiteracy. But there were no Londoners. There was no big or lasting habitation on the site of the modern city, because there was no possibility of a settlement – not without that vital piece of transport infrastructure I use every day.

By my calculations, today's London Bridge must be the twelfth or thirteenth incarnation of a structure that has been repeatedly bashed, broken, burned or bombed. It has been used to hurl witches into the Thames; it has been destroyed by Vikings; it has been torched at least twice by mobs of angry peasants.

In its time the Bridge I use every day has sustained churches, houses, Elizabethan palaces, a mall of about two hundred shops and businesses as well as the spiked and blackened heads of enemies of the state.

The previous dilapidated version was sold in 1967 – in one of the most magnificent examples of London's protean talent for export – to an American entrepreneur called Robert P McCulloch. He paid $2.46 million for the structure, and everyone laughed behind their hands because they assumed that poor Mr McCulloch had confused London Bridge with the more picturesque Tower Bridge; and yet the Missouri chainsaw tycoon was not as foolish as he seemed.

The bridge has been re-assembled stone by stone in Lake Havasu, Arizona, where it is the second most visited tourist attraction after the Grand Canyon; and the fascination is deserved, I would say, given the utter indispensability of London Bridge in the creation of London.

It was the bridge which created the port; it was the toll booth on the north side that necessitated the guards, and the guards that necessitated the first housing. It was the Romans, in about 43 AD or soon thereafter, who built the first pontoon bridge.

It was a bunch of pushy Italian immigrants who founded London, and seventeen years later the boneheaded ancient Britons responded to this gift of civilisation by burning London to the ground, destroying the bridge, and massacring everyone they could find.

Boudica

Who goaded the Romans to invest

It must have happened about here, I reckon. It is a bright autumn day, and I have found what could well have been the heart of the earliest Roman settlement. It's just up from London Bridge, at the junction between Gracechurch Street and Lombard Street, with Fenchurch Street running off to the right.

There's a Marks & Spencer and an Itsu restaurant ahead, but according to all my books the space I am interested in is now occupied by a yellow box junction at the crossroads.

So I risk a few toots from the motorists by cycling on to the spot; and my mind empties as in a trance; and I no longer see the shiny new banks and accountancy firms, but half-built wooden homes, the smoke from a thousand new hearths shimmering over all and new unsurfaced roads and a forest in the distance; and just before I scoot away again I imagine what it must have been like to be in the hobnailed sandals of poor exhausted Suetonius Paulinus, the governor of the new province.

He had just marched as fast as his troops could go, down what is now the A5 from North Wales, down the Edgware Road, down Cheapside, and now he stood on the patch of gravel that served as the marketplace for the very first London. Before him there was a collection of London merchants, in a state of terror.

They knew what had happened to the people of Colchester in Essex – thousands of them sliced by sharp Celtic swords or skewered on pikes or burned alive in their wattle dwellings; the very temple of the deified Claudius sacked and burned to the ground, its occupants carbonised. They had heard all about the ferocity of the Iceni and their queen, Boudica. They had heard what a big and indignant woman she was, with her mane of red hair and her determination to avenge the rape of her daughters by Roman troops.

Help us, Suetonius, they begged the Roman general; and the miserable fellow shook his head. As he looked at early Londinium, he could see the ambition of the settlers everywhere. Colchester (Camulodunum) was officially the colonia or capital, but London was already the most populous centre, an entrepôt town, as Tacitus describes it, swarming with business folk and travellers of all kinds.

If Suetonius looked to his right, down to the bridge, he could see ships tied up at the dock: unloading marble from Turkey to beautify the sprouting new homes, or olive oil from Provence or fish sauce from Spain. He could see ships loading the very first exports of this country – hunting dogs or tin or gold or depressed-looking woad-stained slaves from the dank forests of Essex.

All around he could see the signs of the speculative money that had been poured into the town. Just in front of him, we now believe, was a new shopping mall with a portico 58 metres long, and he could see women with their heads covered, haggling by some scales, and pigs snuffling in rubbish. There were piles of fresh timbers being laid out, so that proper square Roman buildings could replace the primitive round huts of the earliest years. There were fresh hazel laths for the wattle, fresh clay for the daub. There were carpenters who had been hired for the work, not all of whom had been paid. The roads through London were already done to a professional Roman standard, nine metres wide and constructed of hard-rammed gravel, cambered at the side to allow rainwater to drain off into ditches.

There were about thirty thousand of these Londoners in an area roughly the size of Hyde Park, and when I say Londoners I don't mean cockneys, obviously. They weren't Brits: indeed, they would have been pretty contemptuous of the 'Britunculi' – the little Britons, as one Roman legionary was later to call them.

They were Romans, Latin-speaking traders in togas or tunics, from what is now France, Spain, Germany, Turkey, the Balkans – from all over the empire. They had expensive Roman tastes, for wine and red *terra sigillata* crockery, with its pretty moulded reliefs. Even in this misty outpost, they liked to lie back on their couches and toast each other in gorgeous glass goblets from Syria.

It all cost money, and they had got badly into debt; and that, at root, was the cause of the disaster that was about to enfold them.

I'm sorry, Suetonius said to the hand-wringing deputation, we can't stay; we can't risk it. He just didn't have the numbers. The Roman general's troops were knackered, their feet flayed by the march from Wales. He could call upon a maximum force of about ten thousand from the whole island. Boudica and the Iceni already had about one hundred and twenty thousand and more were flocking to the banner of revolt.

These legionaries were no wimps, mind you: Germans, Serbs, Dutch, capable of going for days on nothing but hard tack and water, and then throwing a pontoon bridge across a river. But they knew how Boudica's troops had carved up Petilius Cerealis and the 9th Legion, and understandably they didn't fancy it themselves. So Suetonius did what it pained a Roman to do more than anything else.

He ordered a strategic retreat, back up what is now the Edgware Road, taking with him everybody who could walk and who wanted to come. Those who stayed included the old, the infirm, and women who were scared of marching through the forests, and merchants who just couldn't face abandoning their investments.

For a few hours London had that eerie feeling of a Wild West town awaiting revenge: flapping awnings, and people peering through the casements at the deserted streets. We have some archaeological vignettes of the panic. In Eastcheap it looks as though someone grabbed a pot made in Lyons and then stuffed it with four finger-ring intaglio gems before grubbing it into the earth.

In a house in what is now King William Street, someone took seventeen coins, mainly bearing the head of Claudius, put them in a little red-glazed bowl and stuffed them in a corner. Others no doubt prayed, and sacrificed animals (we have the bones of a goat) and fondled the sooty little clay figurines of their household gods.

At length there was a rumble in what is now the Bishopsgate area.

Whooping down the branch-strewn track in their wickerwork horse-drawn war chariots came the Iceni warriors and their queen. She was a tremendous sight, according to Dio Cassius: very tall, with a harsh voice, and always wearing a multicoloured tunic, and with a great big one-kilo necklace – a torc – made of thick twisted strands of gold. She had a bosom so big that she was capable of using it to conceal her prophetic hare, an animal she would whisk out at the end of her bellicose speeches, and which she would invoke, depending on whether it ran to the left or the right, to foretell the outcome of battle. Within that bosom was a heart set on mayhem.

Far below the streets of modern London we are still unearthing the traces of the Boudican holocaust – a red layer of burned debris about forty-five centimetres thick. They set the first fires somewhere near Gracechurch Street, where Suetonius met the Londoners; and as the defenceless citizens ran from their homes the Celts chopped off their heads or slaughtered them in the Walbrook, the malodorous stream that ran between the two low hills – now Cornhill and Ludgate – that comprised early London.

They hanged, they burned and they crucified with a headlong fury, says Tacitus; while according to Dio Cassius they took the noblest and most beautiful women, stripped them and cut off their breasts and then sewed these breasts to their mouths so that they appeared to be eating them. They even profaned the graveyards, and evidence from excavations in the City of London seems to indicate that they exhumed the corpse of an old man and stuck the head of a young woman between his legs.

They went over the bridge and burned the buildings in what is now Southwark, while in the centre of town the buildings collapsed together in a single conflagration and a column of smoke rose to the heavens. Barely seventeen years after it was founded, London was destroyed.

By the time she had finished doing the same to St Albans, Boudica had killed seventy thousand people, claims Tacitus. That may be on the high side, but in proportional terms she was still more destructive of London and Londoners than the Black Death, the Great Fire, or Hermann Goering. In an act of incredible nihilism, she attacked the entire commercial infrastructure of Britannia – the very trade nexus the Iceni needed themselves.

They sold horses to the invaders; they depended on Roman custom. Boudica's late husband Prasutagus was almost certainly a Roman citizen – and so, by extension, was Boudica. You have to wonder why she was so furious as to act in this apparently self-defeating way. The answer is that the Romans had behaved with diabolical stupidity.

When Prasutagus died, he had hoped to keep his East Anglian kingdom in the family, by leaving half to his daughters and half to the Emperor Nero. Whether or not they were following the orders of Nero the matricidal despot, the Roman administration decided to expropriate all Iceni possessions. The chief tax collector or procurator was one Catus Decianus – an arrogant twerp – who sent his centurions to Thetford, where Prasutagus and Boudica had lived in their kraal of concentric ditches and ramparts.

They laid hands on the queen of the Iceni; they cudgelled her milk-white Celtic skin and raped her daughters, and then, most stupidly of all, they humiliated the Iceni elite by robbing them of their property and enslaving the relatives of the dead king. It was this humiliation, and the Roman greed, that enraged the Iceni, and the next question, therefore, is why did the Romans behave so badly? It is all there, surely, in the text of Tacitus. It was primarily an economic fiasco.

When Claudius invaded Britain in AD 43, he was a stuttering pedant in search of military glory, and he was going against historic Roman advice. Britain, said most Roman experts, was a dump, and a scary dump at that. When Julius Caesar had led his first inconclusive expedition, a century earlier, he had found the place so poor and wretched that there was nothing worth taking. Don't bother going beyond the existing northern boundaries, said the Emperor Augustus, it's like fishing with a golden hook: the prize isn't worth the tackle.

The Brits were said to swim in mud, and to have weird Maori-style tattoos of shapes and animals which they liked to exhibit on their half-naked bodies – like modern football fans – for all to see. Ovid said they were green. Martial said they were blue. Some said they were half-human and half-animal. Going to Britain was like a moon shot, in other words: you did it for glory rather than as an investment.

So when Claudius arrived on his elephants, and found himself accepting the surrender of British kings – with hardly any Roman losses – it must have been a tremendous moment for Roman pride. His general Aulus Plautius had expertly solved the problem that had defeated all previous inhabitants of this country, and built the bridge.

The bridge opened up the rest of Britain to people coming from the south coast, and soon London was a boom town. The population shot up; prices rose; people needed to finance the houses they wanted to build and the shops they hoped to open. So they turned to the financiers, and the bankers piled in.

Nero's tutor Seneca made a loan of forty million sesterces for commercial development in Britain, and when you consider that a legionary was paid only nine hundred sesterces a year, you can see that this was a huge sum of money. The trouble was that the British investments did not pay off – or not fast enough for the bankers. It cost a lot to build the gleaming white temple of Claudius at Colchester, and to finance the port and shopping arcade of London.

The repayments weren't enough; the loans were going bad and Catus Decianus the procurator started behaving like a real swine: whacking up the taxes on local people, kicking the natives out of their homes, and ultimately trying to despoil the Iceni of their land and property.

The position of the Britons is well summed up by the first ever image we have of Britannia, a carving from Aphrodisias in Turkey. It shows a bare-breasted woman being subdued from behind by Claudius in helmet and cuirass. She has a faintly cross-eyed expression, and in the words of Professor Miranda Aldhouse-Green of Cardiff University, 'one has the disturbing feeling that he is about to bugger her'.

To put it in today's language, the ordinary people of Britain were paying the price for a series of unwise property speculations, in which the borrowers and the bankers were both culpable. It wasn't the first time it had happened in the Roman Empire, and it wasn't the last time it was to happen in London.

In her own way, and at one remove, you could say that Boudica was the first banker-basher to hit the Square Mile. She was also at the beginning of what was to become a grand London tradition of female leaders. There is evidence that the early Britons were accustomed to strong female figures: Cartimandua, queen of the Brigantes, gave her menfolk a very tough time.

Then look at Elizabeth's great pre-Armada speech at Tilbury, all about having the body of a poor weak woman but the heart and stomach of a man. It's pure Boudica. Or look at Victoria, with her tartan cloak and brooch. There is more than a hint of the queen of the Iceni.

Or look, dare I say it, at Margaret Thatcher, with her blonde hair, staring eye, harsh voice and firm views about national sovereignty. These days we identify Boudica so closely with London-based national heroines that we get into a muddle about what actually happened.

If you go to Westminster Bridge, you can see the famous 1884 sculpture of the outraged bare-breasted battleaxe and her poor raped daughters, framed against the sky in their scythe-wheeled war chariot. On the pediment are some lines from 'Boudica an ode', a popular poem by the eighteenth-century poet William Cowper:

'Regions Caesar never knew
Thy posterity shall sway,
Where his eagles never flew,
None invincible as they'

Cowper's point is that Boudica had the last laugh on Rome. It was her 'posterity' – her British descendants – who went on to found an empire vaster than Caesar's. Which is all very patriotic and consoling, but completely untrue.

After she had sacked St Albans, Boudica went off to the Midlands where on some as yet unidentified plain she was finally and decisively routed by Suetonius Paulinus, whose troops, disciplined and refreshed, overcame odds of 20–1.

Boudica either died of dysentery or poisoned herself; and no, she is not buried under a platform at King's Cross station. Contrary to what Cowper says, her defeat was so total that her language was almost completely wiped out, and her Celtic posterity was driven very largely to the fringes of Britain, while the British Empire was eventually ruled in a language that owed much more to that of Suetonius Paulinus than to that of Boudica.

The greatest thing Boudica did for London was so to shock and infuriate the Romans that it became a matter of prestige to win the province back and to assert Londinium's status as an ever more glorious and important centre.

It was thanks to Boudica's banker-bashing aggression that the Romans rebuilt London – to an extent that archaeologists have only recently begun to appreciate – as one of the biggest and most populous cities of the northern part of the Empire. It was Claudius' quest for prestige that led to London's foundation, and one of the most impressive spurts of construction began when it was announced that the Emperor Hadrian was on his way.

Hadrian

He made London the capital

Clonk. They were rebuilding London Bridge in 1834 when workmen hit something on the bed of the river. It was green and slimy, but after they had got the mud off they could see it was a fine Roman head, 43 centimetres high and slightly over life-size.

It was an emperor, with a long straight nose and a slight frown and – aha – a beard and well-trimmed moustache. He wasn't as fleshy as Nero, and the beard was less bushy than Marcus Aurelius. It was a delicate sort of beard. It belonged to a Hellenophile aesthete and intellectual, one of the greatest administrators the world has ever seen.

He was called Publius Aelius Trajanus Hadrianus Augustus, or Hadrian. Born in 76 AD of Spanish/Italian descent, he had spent his career touring the Empire and bequeathing us some of the most colossal ruins of the ancient world – from the rebuilt Pantheon in Rome to the Temple of Zeus in Athens to the British wall that bears his name.

Someone had made this fine bronze head in his honour and stuck it in the marketplace; and then someone else had come and chopped it off and chucked it in the river. They didn't melt it down to make saucepans. They wanted to show active contempt. They wanted to humiliate the emperor and his sneer of cold command.

Ladies and gentlemen of the jury, it is probably almost 1700 years since this crime was committed, but I am going to produce for you individuals who had the motive, and the opportunity, to carry out this macabre offence ...

To understand the mystery of the decapitation of Hadrian, you must grasp that this bronze object was actually divine. It was the head of a god. Rome's first emperor, Augustus, had instituted the cunning system of the imperial cult, by which the emperor himself personified the majesty and divinity of Rome. If you were an ambitious local, and you wanted to get on in the Roman Empire, you became a priest in the imperial cult. That was why the first important temple of Roman Britain was the temple of the deified Claudius, and that was why Boudica took such pleasure in burning it down. It was a seat of local government, a symbol of power.

So when in 121 AD it was announced that the emperor – the living god – was actually coming to Britain, the news broke over London like thunder.

The Romans had almost panicked when Boudica torched the early settlements. Nero came close to abandoning the province altogether. But once she had been defeated, they decided it must not happen again. They poured money into the place, and from 78 to 84 AD the governor Agricola subsidised the building of squares and temples and grand housing of one kind or another. There were still uprisings, and pressure from the Celtic fringe, but in a sense the very threat of revolt was good for London. Thanks to the bridge, London was the centre of military operations, and that meant soldiers flush with cash.

The Londoners built baths at Cheapside and then at Huggin Hill, where they shocked purists by enjoying mixed bathing. There is an amphitheatre under the Guildhall, and you can go and have the spooky experience of standing on the spot where men and beasts were slaughtered, and you can inspect the bones of a female gladiator. In the sixty years between the Boudica revolt and the arrival of Hadrian, the Londoners Romanised fast.

They steadily took off their trousers and put on togas and started to get rather good at Latin – Tacitus says they spoke it better than the Gauls. They invited each other round to their dining rooms, painted a fashionable arterial red, to eat turbot on expensive Mediterranean silverware and to toast each other in Bordeaux or Moselle. It was the beginning of the London dinner party. 'The native Britons described these things as civilisation,' sneers Tacitus, 'when in fact they were simply part of their enslavement.'

London was already a loyal and growing outpost. But when they heard the Emperor was on his way, the citizens went into overdrive. It was like being awarded the right to host the Olympics: the place had to look its best – and that meant infrastructure investment. The Emperor was known to like sleeping in the barracks with the troops, so the London authorities seem to have erected a new barracks for his visit – a big square fort at Cripplegate – complete with the living quarters that he famously liked to inspect.

What looks like a governor's palace was constructed, a splendid place of courtyards and fountains, on the site of what is now Cannon Street station. They built a new forum, far grander than the patch of gravel on which Suetonius Paulinus had addressed the first Londoners, in an area partly now occupied by Leadenhall market. At the north end of this vast space they built a basilica – a mixture of a shopping centre and law courts.

If you go downstairs at the barbers at 90 Gracechurch Street you can see that this wasn't any old basilica. Look at that great chunk of brick and masonry that formed one of the piers of the structure and you get a sense of the scale. This was the biggest forum and basilica north of the Alps. The building was 164 yards long, and when you look at the model in the museum of London you are forced to adjust your preconceptions about our city's place in the Roman world.

When Hadrian arrived in AD 122 he found a big, bustling place, with a population of perhaps 100,000 and a ruling elite in a state of sycophantic ecstasy. They installed the emperor and his retinue in the smart new barracks and governor's palace. They showed him the upgraded baths and the renovated forum and, like the man from Del Monte, the emperor nodded his approval. Then there is no doubt that they took him to that great basilica, and somewhere near what is now Leadenhall

Market (we have found a big bronze arm from the neighbourhood) they unveiled their special sign of esteem – the statue, garlanded with flowers. The emperor beamed.

Then it seems highly likely that the Londoners had some sort of service; cowled priests of the cult of Hadrian gave thanks for his divine presence. They may even have slaughtered a cow or bull – right there in front of him – just to show how much they revered him. Or they might have slaughtered the bull to Jupiter. It didn't matter. They were both gods. It is one of the most attractive features of Roman London (and the whole Roman world) that for hundreds of years it was a place of religious and racial tolerance.

Somewhere near Blackfriars Bridge Londoners built a temple to Isis, an Egyptian goddess of motherhood, whose husband Osiris personified the annual flooding of the Nile. We also have proof that they worshipped Cybele, or the Great Mother – Magna Mater. This Cybele was supposed to have conceived a passion for a young man called Atys, and when Atys failed to respond to her advances, she became jealous. When she caught him having it off with someone else she drove him so mad that he castrated himself. I am afraid that respectable young Londoners would celebrate their devotion to Magna Mater by doing the same – and we know this for sure because the river near London Bridge has also yielded a fearful set of serrated forceps, adorned with the heads of Eastern divinities. Experts have no doubt as to its purpose.

There is even a theory that the cult of Magna Mater is remembered today in the name of the nearby Church of Magnus Martyr, noted by TS Eliot for its 'inexplicable splendour of Ionian white and gold'. Naturally it might seem repulsive to modern Christians that the name of this beautiful church should be contaminated by the memory of this savage Eastern cult of self-mutilation. And yet the worship of Magna Mater had more in common with Christianity than you might suppose.

What early Londoners liked about the story of Atys was that he may have died of his terrible self-inflicted injuries – but he then rose joyously from the dead. In traditional Greco-Roman religion there wasn't much of an afterlife, and the underworld was a cold and miserable environment, populated by gibbering shades. In a Roman society where many faced earthly lives of hardship and injustice, it is not surprising that these Eastern tales of rebirth became ever more popular. Indeed, not long after leaving Britain Hadrian was to start his own bizarre cult of a boyfriend of his called Antinous, who had mysteriously drowned in the Nile. Temples and oracles were founded in the name of Antinous; coins were struck of the sulky-looking youth.

His cult became so huge that some Londoners would certainly have been among his adherents, because it was essentially another resurrection and redemption story, like Atys and Osiris. But of all the Eastern cults in London, the most popular – especially with legionaries – was Mithraism. This was the story of Mithras, the son of a life-giving rock, who killed a bull and released its blood for – you've guessed it – the rejuvenation of mankind.

The important point is that all these religions co-existed more or less happily. Just as the modern Hindu can go from the temple of Ganesh to the temple of Hanuman, Roman Londoners saw nothing odd about having a temple of Isis at Blackfriars, a temple of Magna Mater at London Bridge and a temple of Mithras at Mansion House.

And then along came another Eastern religion. Christianity on the face of it seemed to have much in common with these other cults. It discussed a young man of surpassing moral virtue, who died and was reborn as God. It offered the promise of eternal life. But Christianity was like the Judaism from which it emerged (and like the Islam which emerged from them both) in that it did not tolerate – and Christians would not accept – the idea of any coexisting religion, whether it was Jupiter, Isis, Hadrian, Cybele or anyone else.

'I am the way, the truth and the life', said Jesus. 'No man shall come to the father except through me.' It took a long time before Londoners showed any interest in this bold monotheistic assertion, but in 312 AD the Emperor Constantine changed the course of history by making Christianity the state religion of the Roman Empire.

The pagans started to come under pressure. On 18 September 1954 there was a sensation in the world of archaeology – and pretty big news all round – when it was revealed that Professor W F Grimes had discovered the long-sought Temple of Mithras near the Mansion House. It was all astonishingly well preserved.

You could see the place where the bulls had been killed, and their steaming blood splashed to the ground. You could work out where the Mithraic torch-bearers had stood – Cautes with his torch pointed upwards, Cautopates with his torch pointed down. You could imagine the chanting congregation in the dark and smoky Mithraeum, all giving thanks and praise for the sacrifice of the animal. But as Professor Grimes studied the temple, he could see that something funny had been going on.

Significant objects appeared to have been buried in shallow pits beneath the nave and the aisles. There was a head of Mithras with his Phrygian snood; there was a statue of Serapis and a dagger-wielding hand. It wasn't long before the archaeologists had come up with a theory.

Sometime in the early fourth century AD, the Mithraist Londoners began to face persecution; then one day they could take the insults and the bullying no longer. Fearing that the game was nearly up, they had stolen into their temple and buried their most sacred objects.

Shortly thereafter their religious competitors broke in and smashed every remaining statue, kicked down the altar and destroyed the Temple of Mithras, just as they destroyed the Serapaeum of Alexandria and other mighty shrines. The religious pluralism of early London gave way to the monotheism of Yahweh.

Ladies and gentlemen of the jury, I put it to you that it was these same people who went to their forum, pulled down the idolatrous statue of the pagan man-god Hadrian, and threw it in the river. My hunch is that it was the Christians; and that they may even have had particular objections to Hadrian. If you read the early Church fathers such as Tertullian, or Origen, and the homophobic venom to which they were inspired by the memory of Hadrian and the cult of Antinous, you will see what I mean.

Christianity triumphed across the Roman world and the cult of the emperor was over. You don't have to go as far as Edward Gibbon, who blamed Christianity for the Fall of Rome (he claimed that its doctrine of meekness was antithetical to the Roman ancestral love of martial glory) to see that something had been lost.

That bronze head of Hadrian incarnated the authority of Rome, in divine form. Once it was clear the emperor was no longer divine – well, anybody could be emperor, or could try to be. From the middle of the third century on, the garrison of London was weakened by the demand for troops on other frontiers.

Units were constantly sent to support some of the myriad pretenders to the imperial throne, and the province became subject to terrifying raids from what are now Holland and Germany. Living standards declined in London; cows and pigs were housed on mosaic floors. After AD 402 no new imperial coinage entered London and from 410 the province was officially abandoned.

Roman Britain was a long time dying; and, as we shall see, the memory of that epoch was never entirely to fade in the imaginations of Londoners.

Hadrian's mission to the city was brief but not insignificant. He triggered a spurt of building that helped shape the city for hundreds of years. He formally turned London into the capital of the province, and relegated Colchester. He set up the physical schism between England and Scotland that endures to this day, and that has excited Londoners such as Samuel Johnson to satirical rudeness.

His rule embraced a spirit of religious tolerance that the city was not to recapture until the twentieth century. Sometimes I stop my bike at the remains of the Temple of Mithras, which have been removed from their original site and are now displayed on Queen Victoria Street.

Go and look at those enigmatic courses of stone and brick, once deep in a cellar, now out in the wind and rain. Imagine the poor Mithraists, fleeing in terror before the Christians. Think of their tears as they watched their sacred statues smashed to bits. It wouldn't have happened in our day, and it wouldn't have happened in Hadrian's.

What happened next is a terrible warning to all those liberal educationalists who believe that standards will always keep rising. Wave after wave of invaders so shattered the old Roman system that civilisation all but collapsed. Londoners forgot their Latin. They forgot how to read; they forgot how to repair a bridge. Between the years AD 400 and 850 we find no traces of any human occupation of Southwark. There is only one conclusion: that pontoon bridge of Aulus Plautius, repaired and reinforced by generations of Londoners, had decayed and toppled into the river. The vital link was gone. There were still some hairy-looking Londoners living around what is now Covent Garden – peasants and swineherds – but the population had plummeted.

In AD 800 Baghdad had a million people, a glorious circle of scholars and poets, and a library of thousands of books on everything from algebra to medicine to watch-making. By the same year London had returned to barbarism. They were neither Roman nor Christian, until in the early seventh century a man was sent from Rome to try to rescue the situation. His name was Mellitus, which means 'honeyed', and you have a job to find Londoners who have heard of him.

Mellitus

He brought back Christianity and got the bum's rush

'Mellitus?' said the guide with a faint air of surprise. I felt as if I had gone into Waitrose and asked for something quaint – like a hogshead of mead. But Vivien Kermath is one of the accredited red-sashed guides of St Paul's Cathedral. She knows her stuff.

'Of course,' she said. 'Mellitus. AD 604. He built the first of several churches there have been on this site. Come this way.'

'Wait a minute,' I said. 'There isn't any physical evidence of the original building, is there?'

'No,' said Vivien, 'but we have an icon of Mellitus.'

'An icon?' I boggled.

We walked slowly through the great church of Christopher Wren, past memorials of Nelson and Wellington. We passed the spot where Lady Diana Spencer consecrated her ill-fated union to the Prince of Wales. We passed the list of former deans, including John Donne, and his illustrious predecessor, Alexander Nowell (1560), the Londoner who first worked out how to bottle beer – 'probably his greatest contribution to humanity,' said Vivien.

Right at the far eastern end of the church we came to the American memorial chapel, and there – perched above an illuminated book recording the names of the 28,000 Americans who gave their lives in the Second World War – is Mellitus.

To be accurate, it is a rather recent and brightly painted icon-style portrait of how Mellitus might have looked, presented to the cathedral by the Greek Orthodox Church.

I stared at his long thin nose and his deep-set brown eyes, and tried to think myself back into the mindset of this valiant Christian saint, this Roman abbot who had been sent here on his dangerous mission more than 1400 years ago.

Behind Mellitus was London, tightly walled and neatly roofed, with an anachronistic dome of St Paul's bulging to heaven. Showing off, I deciphered the Greek quotation on Mellitus' open Bible.

'And he who sat upon the throne said, behold, I make everything new.'

To make everything new. That was the mission of this Roman bishop to London. Fat chance.

Having paid my respects to the icon, I went out and stood on the steps of St Paul's, and imagined the terrible scene that greeted him.

Roman London had waxed and waned over the years since Hadrian left. Some buildings fell into disrepair, but other notable structures were erected, including the two-mile wall that can still be seen, intermittently girdling the city, and which we think was built in around AD 200.

And then in the third century the Roman Empire entered a period of sustained inflation and chaos. London began to suffer. Lines of supply became too long. Civil servants went unpaid. Morale fell. By AD 410 the Saxon raids had become so terrifying that Londoners issued a desperate appeal to the emperor, Honorius – who deserves to go down in history as the man who gave this country a deep childhood rejection complex.

Sorry, said Honorius, no can do. The legions could not be spared. In 446 the Londoners tried one last time, begging for help from the great general Aetius.

'The Saxons drive us into the sea, and then the sea drives us back into the arms of the Saxons! It's a massacre,' they wailed.

It was no use. London was forsaken, no longer deemed to be part of the empire. Rome readopted the crushing verdict of Augustus, that our country was not worth the bones of a single legionary.

Nothing now stood in the way of the most powerful Germanic tribes, and over they came – Hengist, Horsa, the lot of them, and the Romano-Londoners were put to the sword or driven to the Celtic fringes of the country. When Mellitus arrived at the place where I now stood, on what is now the crown of Ludgate Hill, he saw a post-apocalyptic landscape, a scene to bring despair to a proud Roman heart.

In my mind's eye I erased the buses and the tourists, and I levelled the banks and the Costa coffees, and I could see London as it appeared in 604. The baths and the amphitheatre were wrecked, and swine were kept in the atria of the old villas. The secret of the hypocausts was lost to Britain, and it would be centuries before Londoners rediscovered central heating.

The governor's palace had tumbled to the ground, and huge tracts of the city – where once tens of thousands of ambitious Roman Londoners had lived and dreamed – were covered in black earth. Archaeologists are divided as to whether this dark soil indicates some catastrophe, or whether the land had simply been turned over to farming.

Such people as remained were called names like Cathwulf and Ceawlin and, let's face it, folks (or volks), they were essentially German. They had taken off the togas that Agricola had taught them to wear, and they wore trousers. Yes, the barbarians wore the trousers in London now. Yet it was worse than that; almost three centuries after Constantine's conversion to Christianity, they now believed in the bosky German pantheon, and that their rulers were descended from Woden, to whom, every November, they made prodigious sacrifices of cows and pigs, so that the month was known as 'blodmonath'.

In the words of Rowan Williams, when Mellitus arrived in London, 'he found almost no relic of the Christian presence.'

The bishop had a plan. He gazed about himself there on the top of Ludgate hill, and his eye settled on a dilapidated Roman temple. That would do, he thought.

His mission had been conceived in AD 591, when Pope Gregory had been mooching about a slave market in Rome. He spotted some male slaves with fair skin and golden hair. Where do that lot come from? he asked.

They are English, the auctioneer replied – or '*Angli sunt.*'

Gregory clapped his hands and made a famous joke: '*Haud Angli, sed Angeli!*' ('Not Angles, but Angels!') And tell me, he asked, are they Christian?

Unfortunately not, said the auctioneer. Right, said Pope Gregory. We'll see about that.

First he sent Augustine, in 596, and Augustine had a remarkable coup. King Aethelberht of Kent was himself a pagan, but his wife Bertha had Christian leanings. Soon Aethelberht was won for Christ, and Augustine appealed for reinforcements. Business was brisk, he reported back to Rome, but he needed more props. Vestments, altar decorations, chasubles, religious texts – that kind of thing. Get them over here quick, he urged the Pope.

Gregory sent Mellitus and a handful of others, together with a celebrated letter on how to convert the heathen Brits. Whatever you do, said Gregory, don't rush it. Don't try to wean them off their pagan festivals and sacrifices. Let them enjoy it; let the fat and gravy run down their chins – but just tell them it is all to the glory of God. And don't tear down their temples, Gregory advised. Just build new huts on the side of the old shrines.

Somewhere on the site of what is now our cathedral, the Roman Mellitus persuaded Saeberht, the nephew of Aethelberht, to let him construct a church. In the ruins of what had been a temple of Diana, he built a simple wooden nave, and dedicated it to St Paul.

Christianity was back in the soil of London – but only precariously.

Sometime around 616 or 618 both Aethelberht and Saeberht died, and Christianity lost its two most important Saxon patrons. According to the Venerable Bede, the son of Aethelberht, Eadwald, behaved particularly badly. He immediately reverted to paganism and announced that he was shacking up with his father's wife – not the sort of thing to tell Pope Gregory.

As for the sons of Saeberht, they mocked the good Mellitus. They spotted the new bishop of London giving the host – the body of Christ – to communicants in his little wooden church.

'Give us some of that bread, O Mellitus,' said the pagan Saeberht boys.

'Well,' said Mellitus, 'you can have some bread but only if you believe in Christ and let me lave you with holy water.'

'Lave us?' said the Saeberht boys. 'We don't want to be laved. Just give us some of that bread.'

'Sorry,' said Mellitus. 'You can't have one without the other. If you want the bread, you have to believe.'

At that point, alas, the uncouth youths abused the bishop roundly and he was driven out of London, never to return.

In the end Mellitus' legacy was to prove astonishing. The building originally founded by Mellitus was to become the symbol of national defiance during the Blitz, and to this day the glimpses of St Paul's are so sacred to Londoners that they are protected by elaborate viewing corridors. No building may impede the sight of the dome from Richmond Hill, Primrose Hill and other high spots around the city.

And yet when Mellitus was kicked out, paganism remained so strong in London that it was not until 654 that Cedd succeeded as second bishop and resumed the see of London. 'Long time no see!' as he doubtless put it in his first sermon.

I thought of Mellitus one evening in 2010 when I had the honour of meeting the Pope. I stood on the tarmac at Heathrow, a representative of this modern metropolis with its myriad races and beliefs; and I felt vaguely that I should offer some apology or explanation for the irreligiousness and hedonism of my fellow Londoners.

I felt like some woad-painted, butter-haired, betrousered Saxon savage, forced to explain himself and his city to this effulgent vision from Rome. At last the Pope appeared from his Alitalia jet, evidently exhausted but still somehow glowing – like a sugared almond – in his white vestments and scarlet slippers.

'It all goes back to 410,' I said, when we were on a sofa together in the Royal Lounge.

He looked at me keenly, as though trying to remember what had happened at teatime.

What I meant, I babbled, was that the decision of Honorius was of huge psycho-historical importance for this country. Britain was unlike so many other parts of the Roman Empire in that we underwent a complete reversion.

A city that had once been entirely Roman and entirely Christian had lapsed, had lurched back into the arms of paganism and sin.

And if time had allowed, I would have gone on to blurt my feeling that there would always be a sub-tectonic paganism and wildness about London; and that our fifth-century experience of a sundering from Rome – and a betrayal by Rome – would always leave us with a subconscious mistrust of any great continental scheme for a religious or a political union.

I was about to tell him of my theory that the umbilical severing by Honorius was a partial explanation for everything from Henry VIII to the British refusal to join the Euro.

Luckily for the Holy Father, I had only embarked on a couple of sentences when a cavalcade of cardinals came to take him to his hotel.

'Very interesting!' he said.

* * *

It is easy to laugh at poor Bishop Mellitus, hounded out of London by the ungrateful pagans, but in recapturing the city – and the country – for Christianity, we could surely argue that he was a figure of decisive historical importance.

Imagine if he had never been able to found that frail wooden Church of St Paul's, or to replant the tender bloom of faith in the blackened soil of post-Roman London. Imagine if the British elite had continued – to this day – to swear by brooks and glades and rocks and not by Jesus Christ. The British Empire would frankly have had a very different flavour. So would the story of the United States of America. We would be talking about 'one nation, indivisible under Woden', and instead of Christmas or Thanksgiving, I expect we would all be complaining about the excessive commercialisation of Bloodmonath.

This fantasy will of course be dismissed by believers in a divine Christian plan, but for the next three hundred years after Mellitus the pagans were never far away, and their methods were vicious.

Of Mellitus' church there is no sign today, and indeed there is no trace of early Saxon habitation in the old Roman London. The Saxons moved out west to huddled settlements at Aldwych and Covent Garden, and up the Thames came the enemy.

One man can take much of the credit for beating them off, and for reoccupying and rebuilding the ancient city. After centuries of decay, he was sufficiently literate to revive the memory of Rome.

Alfred the Great

He restored London and suffers from being a dead white male

It was only a hundred years ago that Britain could claim to be the greatest power on Earth. Royal Navy Dreadnoughts roamed the seas. Statues were raised in honour of the founder of the Navy, an axe-wielding, cross-gartered fellow with a flowing beard and deep-set eyes beneath a kind of Santa Claus hat.

Every child in England knew his name, and at one festival in his honour Lord Rosebery made a speech in which, among other superlative compliments, he hailed Alfred as 'the ideal Englishman, the perfect sovereign, the pioneer of England's greatness.' E A Freeman, the Whig historian, later called him 'the most perfect character in history.'

Alfred has not only a claim to be the father of the navy, and therefore of Empire and the entire supremacy of the Anglo-Saxon world – still just about alive at the beginning of the twenty-first century – but he also revived learning in a benighted land, he beat off a sadistic pagan enemy, he united his country and will go down as a man who saved London from oblivion.

And yet today Alfred is almost ludicrously unfashionable. His images are being lost or covered up; his statue in Wantage is regularly vandalised. Children are taught nothing about him: it is as if we are determined to send him back to the Dark Ages from which he rescued us.

In so far as we have relics of Saxon London before Alfred, they are dispiriting stuff. There are broken-toothed combs carved from the shoulder bones of sheep. There are pewter baubles you might expect to find at Camden Lock Market, except not so good.

There is the splotchy-glazed primary school pottery, and when you sit in one of the conjectural wooden dwellings in the Museum of London you have the impression of hippy squalor. There is no brick, no stone, no frescoes, no mosaic and certainly no public sanitation of a kind the Romans had used.

Perhaps some Anglo-Saxon historians will insist that we are talking of a golden age – but you have only to squat in that reconstructed hut to smell the smoke in your matted hair and the aromas of the pigs, and soon you feel a Dark Age dankness seeping up your ankles, to be followed by the chilblains and the pustules and an overall life expectancy of thirty-two.

The population had fallen cataclysmically since the days of Hadrian – to perhaps a few thousand. Londoners owed a distant allegiance to Essex or to Offa, the brutish and illiterate king of Mercia. They had moved out of the old Roman city, apparently because of some superstitious dread of the ruins.

Still, it seems there was something to be said for Lundenwic, the area they settled around the Strand and Aldwych. We have found pots that show there was busy trade with Merovingian Europe. In the 1980s, excavations around Covent Garden found a street with about sixty houses in it.

In the words of the Venerable Bede, London was still 'a mart of many nations resorting to it by land and sea'. In spite of its decline, London at the beginning of the ninth century was still probably the richest and most important place in the country – in a not very hotly contested field. Things were about to get a good deal worse.

There is a sense in which you could say that the Anglo-Saxons had it coming. They were, after all, predators themselves. They were Germans, blond-haired toughs from the plain between the Elbe and the Weser, and they had behaved so aggressively towards the existing population

– killing them and kicking them out wherever they could – that the Byzantine historian Procopius got the impression that Britain was actually two countries: a place called Brettania, opposite Spain, and Brettia, a more Germanic place opposite the mouth of the Rhine.

Even during the reign of Alfred the Saxons continued to persecute the Romano–Celtic Britons, driving them west to Wales and Cornwall. Alfred's maternal grandfather was a royal butler called Oslac, and it was one of Oslac's boasts that his family had killed all the British they could find in the Isle of Wight.

The Saxons had been merchants of genocide, and in the years before Alfred was born they got their comeuppance. Some say the raiders were driven by a population boom in Denmark, where the habit of polygamy had produced many younger sons of second wives, all casting envious eyes on the sheepfolds of England. Whatever the reasons, the Vikings came to Britain, sailing up the rivers in their sneaky, flat-bottomed craft and disembarking with hideous ululations.

Captured Saxon kings suffered the rite of the 'blood eagle', which in its milder version meant carving an eagle on the back; but which properly involved hacking the back ribs from the vertebrae of the still living victim, reaching into the thorax and pulling out the lungs, draping them artistically over the spread ribs so as to form 'the wings of an eagle'.

They conducted other forms of human sacrifice. They sacked churches because a church, to them, was just another building, if one more likely to contain gold. The desperate kings of Wessex and Mercia tried to bribe them to go away. The Vikings took the gold and swore dreadful oaths that they would go – and ratted on the deal. In 842 it seems from *The Anglo-Saxon Chronicle* that there was a raid on London, 'with a great slaughter'; but the real disaster took place in 851.

A fleet of 350 ships under Rorik sailed up the mouth of the Thames. First they stormed Canterbury. Then they sailed further on, landed on the north bank of the Thames – and Lundenwic was sacked. The women were raped. The men were killed. The blood flowed in rivulets into the Thames.

The man who would one day avenge this disaster was then only three or four. He was growing up in a huntin', shootin', fishin' and prayin' environment on the estates of royal Wessex. He was the son of Aethelwulf, the son of Egbert, the son of Eahlmund, the son of Eafa, the son of Eoppa, the son of Ingild – in other words, he was a proper Saxon toff.

The only trouble was that his parents had already had four sons – Aethelstan, Aethelbald, Aethelbehrt, Aethelred – and a daughter, called, you guessed it, Aethelswith. Alfred began with the advantage of the snappier name (it seems to mean something like elf-wisdom).

His biographer – a sycophantic monk called Asser – tells us that the young child beat his elder siblings in a poetry-memorising contest. One can imagine the disgust of all the older Aethelkiddies at the sight of this golden-haired Little Lord Fauntleroy, prattling away in front of his beaming mother.

Even more important in his development, Alfred was singled out by father Aethelwulf for a treat. Aethelwulf was in theory a descendant of Woden, lord of the pagan gods, but he was a devout Christian, so God-fearing that shortly after the Battle of Ockley (or Aclea) in 852, he did a most peculiar thing. The Vikings were still circling England – the threat had not gone away – and yet he decided to take the five-year-old child across the sea and over the mountains on a pilgrimage to Rome.

Pope Leo IV welcomed the bearded Saxon in St Peter's basilica, and while flunkeys discreetly relieved the King of Wessex of his tribute – a four-pound gold crown, an ornamental sword and a purple-dyed tunic embossed with golden keys – the Pope came up with a fitting compliment for his visitor. Aethelwulf was created a consul. The highest office of the Roman republic, which poor old Cicero had flogged his guts out to achieve, was handed out like buttons to this obscure Germanic chieftain; and little Alfred was made the Pope's godson.

With treatment like that, it is no surprise that the Rome experience seems slightly to have gone to Aethelwulf's head. Father and son stayed for a whole year, living in the Schola Saxonum – a huddle of Saxon-style huts up against St Peter's, designed for the use of religious tourists from

England – and spending yet more of his country's cash on doing up Roman churches. Two years later, when Alfred was seven, they came again, on a second pilgrimage.

Not so long ago I took my daughter to Rome, and we walked around the Colosseum, which now appears pretty much as it must have done in Alfred's time. I looked up at the rain coming down like silver darts past its sooty arches, and thought how much vaster and madder it is than it appears in the photos. Imagine the impact of those buildings on his young mind – the scale of the Roman architecture. The whole of Saxon Southampton – the biggest commercial centre outside London – could have fitted comfortably into the baths of Caracalla.

Of course, much of Rome was as ruined as Roman London. But the impressive thing about little Alfie's godfather, Pope Leo, was that he was determined to erect Christian structures to rival the pagan relics. He built massive walls around the Vatican and what had once been the Mausoleum of Hadrian, now the Castel' Sant'Angelo. At the age when a child is most impressionable, Alfred the Great saw the remaking of a city, and understood something that had been all but forgotten in England – the idea of the city itself.

It was an idea the Vikings rejected with violence. They weren't interested in cities; they were interested in burning them.

In 860 they sacked Winchester, the capital of Wessex, and Alfred came to manhood engaged in an almost continuous struggle with the heathen. His father had died in 858, and one by one his older brothers now proceeded to die, none of them reaching the age of thirty. In 871 a twenty-three-year-old Alfred took the crown in wretched circumstances. The Vikings were out of control, and in 872 part of the Great Heathen Army decided to reoccupy the desolation of London, raping and pillaging anyone who happened still to be knocking around. It looks as if the Viking chief Halfdene even had a coin minted in London, just to show who was boss.

Alfred was driven to paying the Danegeld (not in itself a disgraceful strategy; it is still used, with mixed results, against the Taleban), and found himself eventually harried into the wilds of the Somerset marshes, a fugitive in his own country. There it was that he burned the cakes in the peasant woman's hearth, and in the words of *1066 And All That*, became Alfred the Grate. There too, legend has it, he and a servant disguised themselves in order to spy on the Danish camp.

To a degree that is almost embarrassing to modern taste, he had a Victorian public school spirit, a muscular Christianity, a fervent belief not just in God but that the mind can be trained to overcome the infirmities of the body. As he came of age he was perturbed by his sexual urges, and actually prayed for a disease that would distract him. The Almighty rewarded him with piles so sizeable that after a particularly agonising hunting trip in Cornwall he stopped at a monastery and prayed for another disease.

He then fell victim to a mysterious abdominal pain that afflicted him for the rest of his life, and which has been identified with Crohn's disease. Later on, when Alfred thought of himself as a G20-style world leader, he wrote to Patriarch Elias of Jerusalem inviting that learned authority to advise him on his intestinal grief. Elias sent back a disgusting series of remedies, including scammony for constipation, gutamon for stitch, spikenard for diarrhoea, tragacanth for corrupt phlegms, petroleum to drink alone for inward tenderness and the 'white stone' for all unknown afflictions.

It is not clear if or when Alfred really started to drink petroleum to cure his aching stomach, but most modern doctors agree that if he could survive the Patriarch's medicine, he could probably survive anything. Overmastering his innards, and perhaps with the fumes of four-star already shooting from his rear end, Alfred came roaring out of those marshes. He forged the Saxons into a 'fyrd', or standing army, organising a rota system so that each man would have time to go back to his fields. He changed the whole defensive approach, converting about thirty towns into fortified double-ringed 'burhs'. In 878 the Saxons clashed decisively with the Danes at Edington.

The armies closed like hoplites, first throwing their spears – between 1.8 and 2.4 metres long. Then it was a grunting, heaving affair of shield-boss against shield-boss; and if you look at the surviving Saxon stabbing swords – slender, evil-looking seaxes and scaramaxes – you can see why the Vikings did not like being at the sharp end. Gudrum the Viking was vanquished, and agreed, rather half-heartedly, to be baptised, with Alfred standing as his proud godfather.

Edington was the turning-point, the moment the Viking threat began to wane. But still the brutes would not entirely go away. In 882 it seems they raided London again, though who or what they were raiding is not clear. Perhaps the sad truth is that the settlement was so beaten up that there was no government to speak of – and yet London remained strategically crucial. It was still at the centre of the web of Roman roads, and if Alfred was to stop the Vikings moving around east and south east England, the simplest thing was to gain control of the crossroads.

In 886 he '*gesette*' London, says *The Anglo-Saxon Chronicle*. He besieged it, or he occupied it, and at any rate there was another conflagration (of whatever dwellings the Vikings had constructed) and a considerable loss of Danish life. A famous hoard of coins, found at Croydon, seems to indicate that now it was the turn of the Vikings to bury their goods and scram. Once he was in possession of the ancient Roman capital, Alfred was able to do as his godfather Leo had done in Rome. All those ideas he had absorbed, as a child-pilgrim, came pouring forth, and in the words of Asser, 'he restored the city splendidly and made it habitable again.'

He wanted a city with history, and like so many rulers before and since he was filled with the Dream of Rome, the Charlemagne-style desire to assert his own credentials as the heir to the great Roman Christian culture that had once ruled Europe; and so he decreed that the Saxons would overcome their Romano-phobia and move back inside the vast, mouldering pink-and-white walls.

From Cheapside down to the river he took a chunk of the old city, about 300 metres wide and 1000 metres long. He created a grid pattern of streets, still visible at Garlick Hill, Bread Street, Bow Lane and other places. Lundenwic was over, and Lundenburg was born. The old city became the new city, and the new city became the old city – as the name Aldwych (old market) reminds us.

New old London had two ports, at Billingsgate and Queenhithe, and trade began to flourish in the reconstructed wharves. We have turned up Norwegian ragstone hones and querns from Niedermendig in Germany. We have coins from Belgium, Normandy and Scotland, showing that London was recovering its identity as a multinational, multilingual kind of place.

Alfred created the framework for 150 years of stability and growth. Even more important than the physical reconstruction, Alfred's London embodied a huge new political fact. He put the city in the charge of a Mercian, Ealdorman Aethelred (whose name is supposed to survive in Aldermanbury), and London became the fulcrum and symbol of a new unity between Wessex and Mercia; and Alfred, himself married to a Mercian princess Eahlswith, was no longer just king of Wessex.

He came up with a new title. He was *rex Anglosaxonum* – king of the Anglo-Saxons, and he referred to his language as Englisc. When he died in 899, full of wealth and honour, he was described as '*cyng ofer eall Ongelcynn*' – King over all the English – and you can see the modern world's master-language struggling to emerge from that phrase, like the semi-human features of an Australopithecus.

Alfred left 2,000 pounds of silver in his will, an astonishing sum for the age, and perhaps a sign that the Anglo-Saxons had learned to profit from the defeat of the Vikings and the clearing of the seaways. He also goes down as one of the greatest educators this country has ever had, who used the spread of literacy and Christianity as a weapon against the illiterate Danes.

Alfred was a scholar, who personally translated Augustine, Boethius and the psalms into his own language. He was a law-giver and theorist of government, with his own *Domboc* of dooms. His Churchillian energy and self-confidence inspired him to redesign the very boats his sailors were using.

There may be some cynical modern historians who will tell you that Alfred's boats were not much cop, turning out to be rather heavy and sluggish. But he can claim to be the direct creator of an Anglo-Saxon naval supremacy that still exists, somewhat to the irritation of Beijing, in the furthest reaches of the Pacific Ocean.

He invented his own special Alfred clock – so that he could give up precisely half his hours to worshipping the Lord and half to earthly matters. After a great deal of experiment, he ordered his chaplains to gather together blobs of wax equivalent to the weight of seventy-two pennies. This block of wax was then to be divided into six very thin candles, each of them twelve inches long. Alfred had somehow worked out that each candle would burn for exactly four hours, and his plan was to have a permanent supply and burn them continuously, day and night, so that he could mark the exact passage of time.

Alas, the various tents and churches he occupied were so breezy that he found it very hard to keep his Alfred-o-meter going. Hmm, said Alfred, stroking his beard. We need something that lets the light through and keeps the wind off …

So he ordered his carpenters to make a wood-framed box, with side panels of horn so thin as to be translucent – and lo! The King had invented the lantern!

As it happens, modern scholars have struggled to replicate his candle-powered clock. They claim a thin twelve-inch candle burns out much sooner than four hours. That feels like pedantry. This was a man who not only beat back the Vikings and united his country; ships, clocks, lanterns – he had a string of major patents to his name.

So what has happened to us all, that we forget this soldier-scholar-polymath and saviour of his country? There is one statue in the Strand, near the Law Courts, which rightly commemorates his legal contributions – but absolutely nothing to remind Londoners of what he did for the city.

There used to be a plaque at his port of Queenhithe, until it got 'lost' by developers, and was only restored at the insistence of the excellent John Clark, lately of the Museum of London. 'One almost suspects *damnatio memoriae*,' says Mr Clark, 'or collective amnesia.'

Part of the answer may be that Alfred left no obvious physical legacy, no London touchstone. Those Saxon palaces, those churches

– not a brick or post of them survives. But we must also face the sad fact that he is in many ways so deeply uncool. There is something about his exhausting Christian virtue, his colossal energy and self-denial, that was probably more appealing to the Victorians than it is to us.

We modern sensualists are puzzled that a man should pray for piles to cure his sexual feelings. 'Even as the bee must die when she stings in her anger, so must every soul perish after unlawful lust,' wrote Alfred lugubriously, in an embellishment of his Boethius translation.

Novelists and Hollywood have struggled in vain to inject some sexual zing into his character. We must also accept that for much of the past century he was slightly too Teutonic to be a completely successful national hero. It was perfectly fine, in Queen Victoria's time, to note the strong connexions between the early English and the Germans. She was married to a German herself. After two world wars, the association had become less popular.

These days, I am afraid, he suffers not so much from being Germanic, but from being history's ultimate Anglo-Saxon. At the University of Alfred in Alfred, New York, the faculty decided in the 1990s that they would commission a statue of their eponymous figurehead. Alas, the move was instantly controversial, with Dr Linda Mitchell protesting that 'if the university is claiming a dedication to diversity, it would be foolish to choose a symbol so exclusive and effective in emphasising the dead white male power structure in history.'

Even in Winchester, the capital of Wessex, they have betrayed the memory of the old boy. Between 1928 and 2004 there was a seat of learning called King Alfred's College. It is now the 'University of Winchester.'

One Saturday morning in December, I decided to go in search of Queenhithe, the port Alfred commissioned in what had been the old Roman city. Surely, I said to myself, you can't get rid of a whole port. There must be something to see. I had just reached Upper Thames Street when the Almighty unleashed the biggest snowstorm the capital had seen for a hundred years, and I am afraid Queenhithe and all traces of Alfredian infrastructure were lost, along with everything else, in a white hell.

It was only a couple of weeks later, when the snow had cleared, that I finally found it. I was very pleased to have made the effort. There it is – an amazing square inlet in the shoreline of the Thames, surrounded now by red-brick modern flats and office blocks. Nobody was watching me, and in an instant I had hopped over the wall and was standing on Alfred's very shore. I looked beneath my feet, and my jaw dropped.

Queenhithe is where things wash up, and beneath my feet were thousands – hundreds of thousands of bones: white bones, brown bones – the jaws of sheep, the ribs of pigs, the femurs of cows, and jumbled among them were innumerable broken stems of white clay pipes and bits of coal and tile and pot. As I looked across I could see the snazzy restaurants on the South Bank, the Globe theatre complex. But I was standing on a midden of London history, stretching back to heaven knows when.

I understood how perfectly Queenhithe is protected from the current of the river, how ideal it must have been for loading and unloading, and I could see how Alfred's port had played its part in the recovery of mediaeval London; and I thought indignantly of those who have allowed the memory of Alfred to die, and the apathy of our age.

If it hadn't been for Alfred, London might have gone the way of Silchester and other abandoned Roman towns.

If it hadn't been for Alfred, there wouldn't have been an English nation, and this book would probably be written in Danish.

* * *

After a century of peace, the Danes were back, and it is a tribute to Alfred's legacy that London was the prize. The port was open, and trade with the continent had resumed, in bacon or wool (depending on whether a crucial manuscript refers to 'lardam' or 'lanam').

Alfred had put back the bridge, and though the Londoners who trudged across it were generally runtier and fewer than in Roman times, they had a healthy rustic menu: peas and roots for broth, eggs for scrambling, the odd blubberfish for blubberfish stew.

They had lost the luxurious wines and spices of the Roman Empire; they had lost the fine Syrian tableware. But London was the seat of the first democratic institution – the Saxon folkmoot, that met by St Paul's – and Londoners were making enough money to be well worth attacking.

In 994 the Danes arrived, and met stout resistance. For the next fifty years mastery of the city went one way and then the other. In 1014 the Saxons lost to Danish Sweyn Forkbeard; but later that year they came back and actually attacked their own bridge, so that their ships could get at the Danish-held town.

With the help of some Norwegian allies led by King Olaf, they tied ropes to the wooden posts and pulled it down – which is why a billion children have sung a rhyme to the effect that London Bridge is Falling Down. The following year Sweyn's son Cnut was on the scene, and by 1016 he had taken control.

In addition to being history's most evocative misprint, the half-Danish half-Polish Cnut has a fine regal record. The Danes no longer burned churches. They were Christians, so they built them. They didn't abolish the folkmoot. They had a Danish version, called the hustings (house-things).

In the most far-sighted of all his deeds, Cnut took his officials to a marshy place to the west of the Roman city, where the river bends and runs north–south. Here, on a flat called Thorney Island, he found a place to build a residence, and it was here – at least according to the guides of the House of Commons – that he put his chair on the shore and used the incoming tide to show his courtiers the limits of governmental power.

The spot is now occupied by the Palace of Westminster, where the point of his parable is so often forgotten.

Cnut was followed by Edward the Confessor in using Thorney/Westminster as the centre of royal and political authority, and the Normans were to go further still in the development of the rival site.

Ever since the story of London has involved that basic tension, between the politicians and the moneymen, between the cities of London and of Westminster.

It was during this see-saw period that Londoners got the idea that they had the right to 'elect' the King of England. They liked to think they had chosen Edward the Confessor, in 1042, by popular acclaim.

They even liked to think they had 'offered' the crown to William the Conqueror – a touching belief, under the circumstances, in their own democratic prerogatives.

William the Conqueror

The tower builder

It was a cold and clammy morning. A biting wind was coming up off the Thames. A huge glossy raven gave a metallic cark, and the white tower seemed to get bigger and more sinister as we came in under its eaves.

As we approached the monument of William the Conqueror, I gazed up through the thin mist at its chalky stones, and felt the savagery of the place. It wasn't so much the thought of the ghosts of Anne Boleyn and the other men and women slaughtered in the grounds – just over there, in fact, where a yellow-jacketed janitor was sweeping something up. Nor was I thinking of the corpses of children they found in the walls, or the thousands of headless bodies they discovered under the church.

Ever since it was made – at the behest of the Conqueror – the Tower of London has been a Lubyanka, an expression of power, a horrible bully of a building.

'It was a skyscraper for the times,' said the Yeoman Jailer, RSM Victor Lucas, as we cricked our necks to inspect its beautiful lines. 'Anglo-Saxon London had nothing on this scale.' Of course it was handy for controlling the Thames, and it put paid to the endless aquatic invasions that had destabilised London over the centuries. But its main purpose was surely symbolic.

It told the English that they had been beaten. They had been thrashed, licked, stuffed, conquered by a race of people who built great donjons and keeps on a scale that had never been attempted on the island.

The Normans didn't even build the tower with indigenous stone. They disdained the Kentish ragstone and shipped in limestone from Caen. Not only the design but the very substance of the building is an import, a colossal alien cuboid crash-landed amid the Roman ruins and the huddled Anglo-Saxon huts.

The whole thing was an insult, and it was also the most audacious fraud. This William – from whom today's aristocrats like to trace their descent – he wasn't even English. It was an act of usurpation.

He was born in Falaise, the son of Robert I of Normandy, in about 1028, and he was a bastard. That is, he was the illegitimate product of Robert's union with a tanner's daughter, and he had some difficulty asserting his claim to Normandy, never mind to the English throne.

Remember that in 1066 Harold Godwinson had been properly acclaimed as king; he had been named as the heir of Edward the Confessor. What was William to do with England?

He was a Norman, the descendant of Frenchified Vikings, who had been settled in that part of France since Rollo arrived there in 911. He didn't speak Anglo-Saxon. His only link with London was that he was the great-nephew of Emma, the wife of Ethelred the Unready, one of the most famously useless kings in English history. It is a tenuous connexion, and yet William was convinced that he was born to rule England. He set about doing so with frightening efficiency.

Having cheated a childhood assassination attempt (they stabbed the baby in the next-door crib), William grew up tall – well, about five foot ten, which was tallish for a Norman – with gingery hair and powerful arms that enabled him to shoot arrows from a horse at full gallop. He was a hearty eater, and in middle age he had acquired such a belly that his enemies said he was pregnant. He was a voracious student of the arts of hunting and war, so that by the death of Edward the Confessor he was psychologically ready for an expedition of Caesar-like audacity, a seaborne invasion that would change England and the world forever.

There is no need to repeat the essentials of the campaign: how Harold was faced with simultaneous threats from Danes and Normans; how he rushed back south from the battle of Stamford Bridge and got an arrow in his eye at Hastings. All this is well known (or blooming well should be) to the average ten-year-old. What is much less clear is how William clinched the deal.

It was one thing to proclaim yourself the conqueror of a small hill on the Sussex coast, but ever since Alfred had restored the city and its fortifications, London held the key to the kingdom. London was the fat spider at the centre of the web of Roman roads, and it took William a surprisingly long time to make himself master of the city. Indeed, the closer you study the story, the more you wonder whether Hastings was as decisive as all that.

Perhaps Londoners could have held out. Perhaps they could have changed the course of history – had they not behaved so badly, or been so badly led.

'London is a great city,' says the twelfth-century 'Song of the Battle of Hastings', 'overflowing with froward inhabitants and richer than the rest of the country. Protected on the left side by its walls and on the right side by the river, it neither fears enemies nor dreads being taken by storm.' In the end, it was the cynicism and divisions among Londoners that handed the city – and the country – to William.

For about a month after Hastings William hung around, hoping that London would just drop into his lap. There was a pro-Norman faction behind the walls, and indeed the court of Edward the Confessor had shown Normanising tendencies. But for the time being these pro-Normans were outnumbered by the pro-Saxons, who favoured the claims of one Edgar the Atheling.

You have to understand that London was at this stage a bit of a multi-culti maelstrom. In the last seventy years they had chopped and changed so often between English and Scandinavian rulers that by the time

William arrived at Hastings, London was milling with Anglo-Saxons and Anglo-Danes and Anglo-Celts and Anglo-Normans, to say nothing of the other international merchants in the city.

If you went into a shop and ordered a pound of offal, it is not at all clear what language you would be expected to speak. While Londoners bickered in their various tongues, William's troops got dysentery. He tried to bring matters to a head by attacking the south of the city, burning much of Southwark to the ground; and yet somehow the victor of Hastings was repulsed – which shows, perhaps, what the Londoners might have achieved had they possessed more discipline.

William retreated south and west, and eventually crossed the Thames as far away as Wallingford in Oxfordshire, before wheeling across to Berkhamsted in Hertfordshire. From there he issued a fresh invitation to the Londoners to pack it in – and again, the citizens delayed. By now it was late autumn of 1066, and disease and campaigning were surely taking their toll of the Norman army.

Behind the city walls the defences were organised by one Ansgar the Staller, who is named in some chronicles as the 'mayor' of London. The Staller had been injured at Hastings, and had been heroically carried into the city on a stretcher. For weeks, perhaps even months, Ansgar the Staller stalled away.

He might have stalled to victory had he not been let down by his allies. Edgar the Atheling – the Anglo-Saxon alternative – was supposedly backed by Edwin, Earl of Northumberland, and his brother Morcar. At the critical juncture they seem to have vanished back up north, taking their troops with them. Another Edgar backer, Archbishop Stigand, switched sides and went over to the Conqueror, and by December 1066 the Staller could stall no more.

Like Suetonius Paulinus, William marched down what is now the Edgware Road, but this time he turned right at (what is now) St Giles's Circus and established his HQ at Westminster. There he constructed 'siege engines and made moles and the iron horns of battering rams to destroy the City ... to reduce the bastions to sand and bring down the proud tower to rubble'.

It is not clear what Guy of Amiens means by 'the proud tower', but he is presumably referring to the remaining Roman fortifications. Ansgar and Co are said to have put up a vigorous resistance, with what little soldiery they had left. But William's knights were tougher. They 'inflicted much sorrow upon London by the death of many of her sons and citizens'.

William was crowned King of England in Westminster Abbey, on Christmas Day 1066. It is a measure of the extreme tension in the city that the ceremony very nearly ended in disaster.

The turncoat Archbishop Stigand was given the honour of placing the English crown on Norman temples (even though he had crowned Harold in the same year), and he turned to the English contingent and asked them, in English, if William was acceptable as their king. They shouted their assent – as well they might, given that they were surrounded by Norman knights.

Bishop Geoffrey of Coutances then put the same question in French, for the benefit of those in the audience who could not speak English. The Norman knights shouted *Oui!* so loudly that the guards outside thought there was some sort of revolt going on. They torched the neighbouring buildings, and the congregation fled – some to fight the flames, some to loot the houses. A handful of clergy and monks were left to complete the consecration of the King, who was trembling from head to foot. As for Ansgar the Staller, his lands at Enfield were confiscated and he went on to have a quiet career as a minister in Westminster Abbey.

There are many senses in which Norman rule in London was merely a continuation of what had gone before. The new king issued a famous Charter for Londoners, in which he greeted all the burgesses, French and English, in friendly wise, and assured them that all the laws of Edward would continue to apply. 'And I will that every child be his father's heir after his father's day and I will not suffer any man to offer you any wrong. God keep you,' said the benign new ruler. London's political system was kept intact, with the Saxon portreeve evolving into the Norman sheriff, and Londoners by and large retained the freedoms they had acquired in the reign of the Confessor. According to William of Poitiers, one of the more boot-licking Norman chroniclers, the English were absolutely thrilled to be conquered.

'Many English received by his liberal gift more than they had ever received from their fathers or their former lords ... He gave them rich fiefs in return for which they willingly endured hardship and danger. But to no Frenchman was anything given unjustly taken from an Englishman.'

It is not clear that the English saw it this way. William devastated the north of England, and on any objective reading the Norman Conquest was a cultural and political catastrophe for the Anglo-Saxons. Lands and titles were plundered and handed over to Norman noblemen. Many English aristocrats were driven to flee the country, some to Flanders, some to Scotland. Some turned up as soldiers in the Byzantine empire's Varangian Guard, some were sold into slavery.

By 1086 the Norman cuckoo had shoved almost all the Saxon fledglings over the side of the nest, and the English aristocracy retained a pathetic 8 per cent of its original landholdings. Half the country was owned by one hundred and ninety men, and a quarter by just eleven men. All were Normans. Lovely Anglo-Saxon crafts of embroidery and metal working were lost. Above all, a foreign language was imposed on the country, and French was to be used by the ruling classes for the next three hundred years.

As Sir Walter Scott pointed out, the subjection of the Saxons is visible in the language today, where we use an English word for a farm animal, and a French word for the cooked meat it provides. So the Saxon servants would take a cow and provide the Normans with beef, or they would take a pig and offer them pork, or a sheep and offer them mutton. Scott composed a little ditty, which he put into the mouth of someone called Wamba. It was 'Norman saw on English oak, On English neck a Norman yoke; Norman spoon to English dish, And England ruled as Normans wish.'

It was a humiliation, and I have always been fascinated by the politics of the Conquest. '*Et fuga verterunt Angli*', it says on the Bayeux tapestry

– and the English turned in flight. To any modern English-speaking person the message is clear: we, the English, lost. And the Normans conquered *us*, right?

I ask the Yeoman Jailer whether he thinks that we – the English – were conquered by foreigners. He pauses and then says judiciously: 'I think in the end, sir, that we conquered them. In a hundred years they were calling themselves kings of England.' I suppose that is true; but for three hundred years the language of the elite in England became French, and the Anglo-Saxons were ruthlessly pushed down the social scale.

When William died he was not buried in London, but in his Norman home of Caen. He had become so fat that they could not fit him into the sarcophagus, and when the officiating bishop tried to push down on the lid his body burst, releasing such appalling vapours from his ventral cavity that the congregation swooned.

It seems unlikely that he was mourned by any of the four thousand Anglo-Saxon lords who lost their land, because the sad truth is that the Conquest was a nightmare for the Anglo-Saxons; and yet it was terrific for London.

Suppose it had been William, not Harold, who had taken one in the eye at Hastings. Or suppose that Ansgard the Staller had won the battle of London. Without the Norman Conquest the city would never have had the unity and peace that goes with firm government.

The chronicler tells us that under the Conqueror a young maiden could travel the length of England without being injured or robbed, and it is security that is the paramount condition for trade. Merchants from Caen and Rouen came over to buy and sell, and London flourished under its famous charter. It is an indication of the city's favoured status under the Normans that it was not required to submit to the Domesday Book – even Winchester was eventually required to tot up its assets.

Norman London was to become emphatically and officially the capital of England – perhaps for the first time since the Romans. And William enshrined one reform that was crucial for the development of the city.

Edward the Confessor had originally moved the court from outside the Alfredian/Roman boundaries, because he wanted to oversee the rebuilding of the eighth-century West Minster monastery, which he turned into the Abbey. William not only decided to be crowned in the Abbey, but he established the Norman court – the centre of administration and justice – at Westminster.

So it was that London acquired its bicephalous identity, with the centre of political power at one remove from the centre of wealth.

Sometimes the moneymen have infuriated the politicians, and sometimes the politicians have egged on the mob against the moneymen. But for a thousand years London's commercial district has had easy access to government – and yet been apart from it; and that semi-independence has surely contributed to the City's commercial dynamism.

We have the Normans to thank for that, just as we can thank them for the rule of law, a series of socking great castles, and above all for adulterating the language so vigorously with French. If Harold had won at Hastings, or if Ansgard the Staller had held London, then we would never have been blessed with the hybrid language that was to conquer the world.

The success of that hybrid has been ascribed to the genius of our next great Londoner – the first in the series to have been actually born in the city.

* * *

Just before we come to Chaucer, we must consider an important detail about his pilgrims. Think of them all: the fornicating friar, the randy old widow, the cook with the ginormous zit, the drunken miller, the pretentious prioress. If they came from London or anywhere north of the river, there was only one route to get to Canterbury, and that was my daily commuter trek. London Bridge was still the only crossing, and in the years of England's Norman kings it was a very rickety affair.

We have seen that Olaf the Norwegian found it easy enough to pull it over with his rowers in 1014, and on ten occasions between that date and 1136 the bridge either collapsed or experienced a disastrous failure, and no wonder.

The population of the city had doubled between AD 1000 and 1200 – to more than twenty thousand. Across this wonky track went growing quantities of people and goods: wool from Dorset, wine from Deauville. It seems unlikely to have been more than six metres or ten metres across at the widest point, and there would scarcely have been room for two carts to pass abreast. Then in 1170 the decrepit Saxon piece of infrastructure faced a new load – a fresh rush of mediaeval commuters with their defecating horses and pounding heels.

Henry II had his row with Thomas à Becket about the power relationship between church and state. In one sense the argument ended decisively in Henry's favour, as Cheapside-born Becket's brains were splattered over the altar of Canterbury Cathedral. But in death the great Londoner was more powerful than in life. Henry made his penitential pilgrimage, and to the mediaeval mind that showed the triumph of God over the kings of the earth.

To mediaeval folk who believed in the literal truth of the licking tongues of hellfire, a pilgrimage of their own was a chance to win points with the almighty. Even greater numbers started to head for Canterbury. A priest called Peter de Colechurch, the chaplain of the church where Becket had been baptised, proposed a lasting solution.

What was needed, he told Henry II, was a stone bridge. The pilgrims and the holy blissful martyr deserved no less. Fed up with paying for repairs on the wooden structure, Henry agreed. The design appeared to be very expensive, so he announced a tax on wool and set up a monastic guild called the Brethren of London Bridge, who could raise cash through the sale of indulgences.

Even with these funding streams, the project proved almost too much for twelfth-century England. The river was 900 feet wide, strongly-flowing and tidal. The design required twenty stone piers, rising on vast ship-shaped stone starlings that rose from the river bed and jutted their prows into the current.

These days you would build a cofferdam, and pump the water out to allow the men to work on the bed of the river. That was beyond them.

Henry ran out of money and died; Peter de Colechurch was buried in the uncompleted foundations. Richard the Lionheart was too busy with the Crusades. After thirty years and the loss of one hundred and fifty lives, the project was finished by King John.

He did a cunning deal with the merchants of London. In exchange for loans to complete the bridge, they could have revenue from tolls and all future bridging rights over the Thames. These days we would call it a private finance initiative. London Bridge was completed in 1209, and was a huge popular hit. Houses and shops were built along it, with the eaves leaning together above the crowd. The congestion was so bad that sometimes it took the pilgrims an hour to cross.

On they struggled through the next one hundred and fifty years, with all the disasters of the Middle Ages – the little ice ages, the Black Death, the start of the One Hundred Years War with France.

They went to see the shrine of the martyr, because they believed he could help relieve them of their aches and miseries, but there were times when the people's feeling of oppression was so great that the consolation of religion was not enough.

GEOFFREY CHAUCER

The father of English – now the unofficial common language of humanity

It was Wednesday 12 June 1381, the time of year when England is almost at its loveliest. The brief candles were still on the chestnuts, and the evenings were getting longer as the midsummer climax approached.

A fat and slightly depressed author of about forty was sitting at the window of his flat and starting to feel alarmed. His wife was away, as usual, at the court of John of Gaunt, and we have some reason to suspect that her relations with the great prince were not beyond reproach. As for our hero, it was only a year ago that he had himself been implicated in a discreditable liaison, in the form of the 'raptus' of a young woman called Cecily Champain.

Whatever the exact connotations of this charge – from which he managed to exonerate himself by paying a fine – it cannot have done wonders for his reputation or his morale. He had a good job, as Comptroller of the Wool Custom and Subsidy of the Petty Customs, and had established a reputation as a poet. Indeed he still beats le Douanier Rousseau as the greatest artist ever to have been a customs officer. In addition to his £10 annuity from the King's uncle, John of Gaunt, his poetic gifts had somehow entitled him for the last seven years to a pitcher of wine a day – about a gallon. Even if he didn't quite drink it all himself, he knew, as the son of vintners, how to turn wine into money.

Geoffrey Chaucer was at the epicentre of fourteenth-century England, a merchant who had been a courtier since the age of fourteen, a trusted ambassador who knew the politicians as well as he knew the moneymen, a man of such tremendous bustle that he personally bridged the two cities, of London and Westminster. As he looked out of his apartment windows that summer evening, Chaucer saw events unfolding that threatened to turn his world upside down.

He lived in Aldgate, a curious castellated structure built above the old Roman gate at the north east of the ancient city. From one side of his pad, he gazed upon London, as it had grown under the French-speaking monarchs that had followed William the Conqueror; and in many ways there had been an embarrassing lack of technological progress since Norman times.

They might have had windows in their casements, but people still moved by horse and cart and used bows and arrows, and though they had knives and spoons, they had not yet got the hang of the fork. There was no plumbing, there was no hot water. It was still a universe of toothache and constipation. There was abject poverty and appalling infant mortality, and always the risk of plague, sent by heaven as a punishment for our sinful species. And yet the population was growing – up to as much as fifty thousand, though not yet back to Roman levels; and there was money in London, money on a scale never known before. For centuries the English had been trading with France and the Low Countries, and the money from wool had built great houses for the merchants in the fashionable village of Charing, between the Strand and Westminster.

Money gilded the tapestries of the merchants, and dressed their wives in silk, and the wealth of the mercantile class expressed itself in all the refinements of the age: the carvings on the headboards, the love poetry, the stained-glass windows with their etiolated bodies and their floppy slippers. In fact, some merchants became so rich that the nobility came to resent the signs of their wealth. In 1337 England's first sumptuary laws were promulgated – a ban on the wearing of furs by certain categories of society.

Money encouraged thieves, prostitution and strange entertainments, like the podicinists, the professional farters whose skill Chaucer found so amusing, and the tournaments, where Chaucer and others of his class would put on finely wrought armour and play quintain, tilting at targets mounted on a rotating beam, always being careful not to be clonked on the back of their heads as the beam whirled round.

Now the governing class of Britain faced exactly that – a terrific clonk on the back of the head, caused by their failure to watch the growing gap between rich and poor. Through the other window, out of town, Chaucer looked out over Essex, at the countryside where the bulk of the population still lived. Life out there was not, as a rule, much fun.

A fourteenth-century alliterative poet describes a man hanging on his plough, his coat of coarse cloth, his hood torn, his shoes broken, his mittens only rags. His four scrawny heifers can hardly move the plough, and his wife walks beside him with ice-cut bare feet and a baby wailing for her at the end of the furrow. By 1381, the past decade had been rotten for harvests, and successive plagues had devastated the villages.

Time and again, in Chaucer's lifetime, people were struck by a biblical horror, as buboes erupted in their armpits and groins. Children buried their parents with a regularity that almost matches sub-Saharan Aids. Over the period 1340–1400, roughly Chaucer's lifespan, the Black Death cut the population of England in half. To cap it all, these God-cursed peasants were told they had the honour of paying yet another tax to the state, supposedly to finance yet another attempt by the King to gain kudos on the battlefield in France. It was a poll tax, meant to fall equally on every head in the country.

It was grossly unjust. Assuming our wretched ploughman had to pay for his wife as well, and assuming he earned twelve shillings a year, he would have had to pay the same amount as Chaucer, who earned a hundred times as much. In May that year, a spark had been lit in the village of Fobbing in Essex, where they refused to pay the tax collector (they fobbed him off); and now the gorse was crackling with popular indignation.

The Peasants' Revolt was the first and in some ways the most important insurrection in English history. It was the first people's movement with a recognisably left-wing and levelling agenda, and the first of the radical programmes that have been such a part of London history. As Chaucer sat in his flat and looked out towards the fields of Mile End, he could hear a noise that drowned the summer murmurings of the bees and the doves. He could hear the voices of thousands of peasants as they prepared to camp outside the city.

Darkness fell; traitors stole forth. The Mayor of London, William Walworth, had given instruction that all the gates of the city should be closed, especially Aldgate. In the middle of the night an alderman called William Tonge is supposed to have disobeyed the order and let them in. If Chaucer had stayed in his flat, he would have heard them padding through the ancient gate. He would have heard the muffled oaths of people who wanted to destroy the world that had fostered his genius. Chaucer had nothing to gain from this revolution, and everything to lose; and yet there is a sense in which he was himself a radical, if not a revolutionary. In one fundamental respect he stood shoulder to shoulder with the rebels. After three hundred years of French dominance, he elevated and glorified the language spoken by the people of England.

In the words of William Caxton, the pioneering London printer who kicked off his career with *The Canterbury Tales*, he was 'the worshipful fader and first foundeur and embellisher of our Englissh'. It was now, in the later fourteenth century, that the bud unfurled to form the vast and intricate bloom of the English language.

Geoffrey Chaucer was born in Thames Street under what is now Cannon Street station. Followers of this story will note that this is becoming a popular venue for key London events: Hadrian may well have stayed here on his trip in 122, in the governor's house, and it is overwhelmingly likely – even if the area had been rebuilt dozens of times – that the scene of Chaucer's nativity possessed at least some traces of Roman masonry.

He was educated in the shadow of St Paul's, founded by Mellitus in 604 (and what a shadow it was by now, a colossal mediaeval cathedral, with a spire even taller than the building we see today). At the age of fourteen he entered the court of the Duchess of Ulster, as we can tell from an account book that records his uniform: short jacket, red and black stockings. He was only nineteen or twenty when he went campaigning in France, was captured at Reims, and was ransomed by Edward III for £16 – indicating that he was already a person of some consequence.

He went on to have a long career as a diplomat, an MP, a spy, a Clerk of the King's Works and above all as a courtier; and in the court they did not, as a rule, speak English. They spoke French. His very name, Chaucer, probably comes from Chausseur – the French for a shoemaker. What did Edward II exclaim when he picked up the garter dropped by a lady of his court, and gallantly tied it around his own calf? He didn't say, 'never mind, darling', or 'there you go, sweetie'. He said, '*Honi soit qui mal y pense*.' When John of Gaunt wanted to explain why he was giving a man and his wife an annuity, the record states that it was '*pour mielx leur estat maintenir*', the better to maintain their estate. And yet French was emphatically not the language of the buzzing crowd that passed underneath his chambers.

Some of the vaguely educated may have attempted a bit of parley-vous, but even if they did they risked being mocked for their accents, like the pretentious Prioresse, the madame Eglantine. 'French she spake full fair and fetisly, after the scole of Stratford-atte-Bowe', says Chaucer urbanely. She spoke French with a fine East end accent.

The story of the fourteenth-century is to some extent a tale of revolt against these hieratic class-redolent languages, French and Latin. In 1362 an Act of Parliament decreed that all legal pleas would henceforward be heard in English, and by now the countryside was humming with Lollardy, inspired by John Wycliffe and his English Bible. The Lollards didn't like prayers or sermons they couldn't understand. In fact, they didn't think much of any kind of clerical mediation between man and God.

When the fiery Lollard preacher John Ball was whipping up the peasants in Blackheath, he reached for rhyming English verse. 'When Adam delved an Eve span, who was then the gentleman?' he demanded. Some have looked at Chaucer's status – as a supremely well-connected merchant, married to the daughter of a Flemish nob – and wondered whether this decision, to mould the language of the proletariat into a new pentameter verse, was some kind of political act.

Is he giving a clue, some historians have wondered, as to his own anti-clerical feelings? Is he a Lollard, like some of the knights he knew? And others have said, no, they can't find any real evidence that he was anything but a good (if caustic) Catholic. One idea we can certainly rule out: even if it is true that there were people like Alderman Tonge, who were willing to collaborate with the peasants, Chaucer was surely not among them. What happened over the next three days was terrifying.

On Thursday 14 June, Londoners awoke to the Feast of Corpus Christi. But today there were no pageants or miracle plays; the streets were sunk in fear. On the outskirts of the city, houses were already burning. A mob under Wat Tyler swarmed up through Southwark and stormed the Marshalsea Prison. In Lambeth they burned all the records – hated symbol of the Latinate judgments of their superiors.

Tyler then led his men to London Bridge, where they broke down a brothel occupied by Flemish women and 'farmed' by the Mayor – not so much because they objected to the concept of a brothel, but because they disliked the Flemish. Then there was more treachery (and again, Alderman Tonge and his colleagues were suspected), as the keepers disobeyed the orders of Mayor Walworth and opened the chain and drawbridge of London Bridge.

Now the mob was getting into its stride. They broke open the Fleet Prison, attacked the Temple, to destroy more records, and then they set off down the Strand to what was the richest and most gorgeous residence in England, the Savoy Palace of John of Gaunt. With great thoroughness they burned the fine linen and the hangings and the carvings, and then accidentally or not they finished the whole job off with three barrels of gunpowder. The next day the xenophobic murders began.

In the Vintry – where Chaucer had been brought up – thirty-five poor Flemings were dragged from a church and beheaded, by a mob led by one Jack Straw. Another group entered the Tower of London itself – again as a result of internal betrayal – and killed Archbishop Simon Sudbury and various other worthies and tax-collectors. They cut off their heads, and stuck them on poles on London Bridge. Then they announced that all Flemings should suffer the same fate, and then, for the sake of balance, they went to rough up the Italian bankers of Lombard Street. The next day, Saturday, the burnings and beheadings continued until the afternoon, when suddenly the boy king Richard II announced that all should go to Smithfield for a parley.

It was one of those coin-turn events that could so easily have gone the other way. Imagine the young King in his elegant armour, ranged against Wat Tyler and the angry bulbous-nosed peasants of Kent. We are told that Tyler treated the King of England with insolent familiarity. He wanted the abolition of villeinage (a kind of serfdom, where you were compelled to farm the lands of your lord); he wanted to abolish the process by which you could be outlawed for a crime, and he wanted an end to the new taxation and wage restraint. Then he repeated the demands of John Ball, the proto-communist preacher, that there should be no more lordship save that of the king, that the Church should be stripped of its possessions and that there should be only one bishop left.

The King is said to have behaved with remarkable coolness, and seemed even to agree to these outrageous demands. But a fracas somehow blew up between Tyler and Walworth; and Walworth, Mayor of London, pulled the rebel off his horse and ran Tyler through with his sword.

Others of the King's retinue piled in and jabbed at the wounded man. There was a shout of anger from the crowd, and they might have shot the King with their arrows had the fourteen-year-old not spurred his horse to meet them and shouted, 'Sirs, will you shoot your king? I am your captain! Follow me!'

Spellbound by royal charisma, they all went to Clerkenwell, a few hundred yards to the north. The wounded Tyler was rushed to A & E at St Barts, but Walworth wasn't having any of it. He whisked him out and had him beheaded. Richard then stuck Tyler's head on London Bridge, in place of Archbishop Sudbury, and told the peasants to go home – which, amazingly, they did.

In London, the peasants' revolt was over. The King knighted Walworth on the spot.

It is surely impossible that Chaucer could have supported any aspect of what had happened. Even if he resented Gaunt's supposed carrying-on with his wife, don't forget that he had once written a poem for the great man, in memory of his dead wife Blanche. It must have been deeply shocking to learn – or even to see – that his house was burning. Chaucer was a well-travelled and cultivated man. He would have felt nothing but horror at the slaughter of innocent Flemings and the bashing-up of Italians.

How could he have sympathised with the rebels against the King and court on whom he depended? He didn't. And yet his only reference to the Revolt – this national disaster – has a bizarre jocularity.

In *The Nun's Priest's Tale* he is casting around for a way to describe a bunch of people pursuing a fox.

So hydous was the noise, a benedicitee
Certes he Jakke Straw and his meynee
Ne made nevere shoutes half so shrill
Whan that they wolden any Fleming kille
As thilke day was maad upon the fox.

Which means something like, so hideous was the noise, Lord have mercy on us, that Jack Straw and his mob never shouted so shrilly when they wanted to kill any Fleming they could find, as they shouted that day in pursuit of the fox.

It may seem a bit jaunty to compare Jack Straw's vicious pogroms to a foxhunt. But that of course is Chaucer's style: the deadpan detachment of the satirist. When old man January sees his wife being grossly embraced by a squire in a tree, Chaucer says; 'And up he yaf a roryng and a cry, as dooth the mooder when the child shall dye.'

The heartlessness makes us snort with laughter. That is surely Chaucer's motive: to amuse. Take Absolon, the ludicrous parish clerk in *The Miller's Tale*, who conceives a lust for Alison, a married woman.

I suppose you could argue that this portrait of this silly, golden-haired, twinkletoed, lustful cleric is meant to be an attack on an unreformed church. The punchline of the Miller's tale involves Absolon coming to Alison's window in the dead of night, and asking for a kiss.

Dark was the nyght as pich, or as the cole,
And at the window out she put her hole,
And Absolon, hym fil ne bet ne wers,
But with his mouth he kiste hir naked ers
Full savourly, er he wer war of this.
Aback he stirte, and thoughte it was amys,
For wel he wiste a woman hath no berd …

And so on. I am not going to put that into modern English. I think we all know the meaning of *ers*.

Call me juvenile, but even at a distance of 620 years I chuckle at Chaucer's prep-school climax to this shaggy dog story … And now we are getting to the heart of the matter. That's why Chaucer wrote in English – not because it was the language of revolt or of religious dissent. He didn't deploy the people's tongue because he wanted to make a political point, but because like all authors he wanted to reach the largest possible audience, and he wanted to make them laugh.

English was the language of bawdy, because it was by definition the vulgar language. It was the language of the people he wanted to amuse and it was the most amusing language to write in. All along the river-bank from Tower Bridge to the Fleet there were wharves where Londoners loaded and unloaded the goods that were making them rich. There was Galley quay where the Italian galleys arrived; then there was the Custom House, where Chaucer worked; then Billingsgate fish market; then the Steelyard, the walled enclosure of the merchants of the

Hanseatic League who dominated the trade with Scandinavia and eastern Europe.

Those Germans spoke to the cockney stevedores in English, and English grew in importance with the rise of the merchant classes. By the end of the fourteenth century the aldermen of London were political heavyweights, and the King could not do without their financial support for his military ventures – not when the poll tax had proved such a dismal failure.

The nobles might want war, but the merchants wanted peace, like capitalist cowards down the ages, and the merchants called the shots. Men like Sir Nicholas Brembre, a grocer and future Mayor of London, would lend one thousand marks at a time; but when Sir Nicholas and his chums decided not to stump up, as they did in 1382, the King had no choice but to call off his campaign. Thus was political power transferred to a rising class. The Peasants' Revolt failed, like so many proletariat insurrections, but a successful linguistic revolution took place nonetheless, and it was led, like all successful revolutions, by the bourgeoisie.

Chaucer's choice of English was a function of a power shift from King and court to the affluent moneymen of London. A 'gentleman' might not become an alderman, but the aldermen and sheriffs of London were increasingly keen on recognition; and, as ever, the sons and daughters of the nobility were willing to marry money.

As London's guilds or 'misteries' grew more powerful, so power was contested more bitterly between them. They weren't one homogeneous mass of wealth creators. They were divided with Sienese rivalrousness into grocers and drapers and mercers and fishmongers, and so on. The victuallers were engaged in chronic and bloody feuds with the drapers, and in the battle for power the factions of merchants would line up behind different nobles and indeed different royal houses.

In 1387 Richard II, Chaucer's ultimate patron, was almost deposed by a bunch of nobles (backed by the drapers) and some of Chaucer's allies, such as the poet Thomas Usk, were executed, along with top grocer and leading moneybags, Sir Nicholas Brembre. Chaucer seems at this stage to have been relegated to Greenwich, where he served as MP for Kent, and at one point he was given the unobtrusive job of deputy forester in Somerset, where he is thought to have concentrated on his poetry. With the return of Richard and Gaunt he was restored, taking up the grand-sounding post of Clerk of the King's Works, overseeing repairs to the royal palaces. But in 1399 it was all over.

Richard II was deposed by his cousin, Henry Bolingbroke (who was to become Henry IV, part one), and again, the London merchants were behind it. Like so many other kings and governments down the ages, Richard had decided to take on the moneymen. He decided to punish the City, for its role in the recent revolt, by interfering with its ancient constitution. He appointed a Warden to govern the place – infringing the charter of liberty bestowed on London by the Conqueror himself – and tried to restrict the term of the Mayor to one year.

The City wasn't having it. When Richard asked Henry who had come to arrest him, the usurper replied (or so Froissart tells us), 'For the most part, Londoners.' London merchants switched sides to protect their prerogatives.

Gaunt was dead. Poor weak King Richard II was starved to death, aged thirty-three, in captivity; and there are some who think Chaucer himself was put to death. Out of favour with the new regime, hounded by Arundel, the new archbishop, for the allegedly irreligious tone of *The Canterbury Tales*, he may have been quietly 'slaughtered' – to use the word of his friend and contemporary, Hoccleve.

It is a fascinating theory, but apart from that one word of Hoccleve, there just isn't enough evidence to support it. The new king had in fact just confirmed his pension, and throughout his career Chaucer had shown a feline ability to flit between the warring worlds of court and the guilds – and to take money from princes and merchants alike – without notably falling foul of anyone. He was buried in Westminster Abbey for his public service (not for his poetry); and yet his literary legacy was permanent.

He took two great linguistic streams, Germanic and Romance, and fused them. Accident, agree, bagpipe, blunder, box, chant, desk, digestion, dishonest, examination, femininity, finally, funeral, horizon, increase, infect, obscure, observe, princess, scissors, superstitious, universe, village: those are just some of the everyday words that Chaucer introduced to the language through his poetry. Let me offer one final reason why English was the natural vehicle for a poet interested in pentameter couplets: with two parallel streams of vocabulary it was uniquely rich in rhyme, and the pleasure and magic was often to take a Norman-French-Latinate word and find an English rhyme; or even more satisfyingly, you could take a sensible Latinate word and find a raunchy English pun.

Take the word *queynte*, which seems to come from the Latin *cognitus*, meaning clever or learned, and which happens to be a variant spelling for an Anglo-Saxon four-letter-word that looks like a Danish king.

One day Nicholas, the clever clerk from *The Miller's Tale*, takes advantage of the absence of a husband to go and visit a young wife: 'Whil that her housbonde was at Oseneye, as clerkes ben ful subtile and ful queynte; and prively he caught her by the queynte …'

What worked for poetry worked for everyday life. With a dual or hybrid nature, English gave its users a flexibility like no other. They could go for the Latinate topspin or the Anglo-Saxon smash. They could be pompous or they could be blunt. They could talk about remuneration or pay, economies or cuts, redundancies or sackings, and ever since Chaucer English has been like a gigantic never-quite-setting omelette into which fresh ingredients can be endlessly poured. The *Oxford English Dictionary* now has 600,000 words and the Global Language Monitor calculates that there are one million English lexemes.

To give you the relevant comparisons, Chinese dialects together can muster about half a million; Spanish 225,000; Russian 195,000; German 185,000; French 100,000 and Arabic 45,000. English is the international language of air traffic control, business, the UN and there is no other language capable of conveying 'the offside trap' with comparable succinctness.

Of course it makes us very proud that this grammar – honed and simplified by the despised medieval English peasantry – has become the grammar of the modern world. It pleases us to think that we invented it, we hold the copyright, and that we are somehow the best exponents of writing it. We laugh when we pick up a menu in Vietnam and discover 'pork with fresh garbage'. Tears of patronising joy run down our cheeks when a Japanese menu offers 'strawberry crap'; and yet any such feelings should be immediately qualified by the reflection that one in four eleven year olds is still functionally illiterate in London; and of the 1.4 billion people who speak English across the world, many have long since exceeded the average Briton in proficiency.

English has slipped the surly bonds of England and become Globish, a vast syncretic unifier of our human culture. The best we can say is that the whole adventure really got going in the fourteenth century, that the adoption of English as a respectable literary language culminated with Chaucer – and that it could only have happened in London.

There is one last reason why we should be thankful for Chaucer, and it is not just to do with the language he wielded, but the kind of stuff he wrote. With his bawdy, his mockery, his self-mockery, his pricking of hypocrisy and his terrible puns he is the worshipful fader and first foundeur not just of our Englissh, but of something we like to see in our characters.

We love Chaucer and we venerate him for the very good reason that he so obviously loves us. He held up his affectionate and kaleidoscopic mirror to the jumble of London's classes and personalities (and never mind the pilgrimage; *The Canterbury Tales* is an essentially London poem). He holds them so close to us that we can touch their clothes, hear their voice, even listen to the gurgle of their stomachs.

The knight and the miller actually interrupt each other, so closely are they packed together; and as in poetry, so in life. The knight and the miller are still packed together, still interrupting each other, on the everyday pilgrimage that is the number 25 bus.

The rise of English in the age of Chaucer was a function of economics and of politics. The triumph of this once subservient language reflected the confidence and clout of the London merchants who spoke it. One man above all has come to stand for that new class, a man whom Chaucer almost certainly knew very well.

The story of his rise has been handed down and embellished, from generation to generation, to become the programmatic story of London as a city of opportunity.

Richard Whittington

Not only the world's first great banker, but a man who set high standards for philanthropy

Now when I was a nipper we didn't learn our military history from 'Mediaeval Total War'. We didn't sit like lidless lizards in front of video war games like 'Call of Duty – black ops.'

We had a perfectly splendid and fully illustrated magazine for the mildly swotty prepubescent called *Look and Learn*, and I was a devout subscriber. Sometime in the late 1960s *Look and Learn* first published a picture of the climactic moment in the life of Sir Richard Whittington.

It was a banquet that he gave, as Mayor of London, in honour of the King of England – and what a hell of a party it must have been. It would be fair to say that in recent years not every Guildhall banquet has turned out to be a roistering beanfeast of national jubilation.

I once hired a white tie in order to hear a speech by Gordon Brown. On another grim occasion, we all had to go and suck up to President Putin in the hope that he would let BP have some oil contracts. Recent festivities at this historic national venue include the Ofsted Conference, the Royal Life Saving Society Awards and the Leading Hotels of the World Showcase. But in 1415 the Guildhall was still under construction.

With its impressive frontage and its soaring limestone vaulting, it had the air of a Flemish *maison de ville*, which was not surprising, since it was built with the proceeds of the cloth trade with Flanders. The building reflected the prosperity and growing ambition of the Londoners, and tonight they had reason for euphoria.

It was called Agincourt, perhaps the most sensational victory over the French in the whole of English history. Outnumbered at least four to one, the young King Henry V had led English bowmen in a massacre of the enemy elite. The flower of French chivalry lay pincushioned in the mud of Picardy. They lost three dukes, eight counts, a viscount and archbishop. The way was clear for England to renew its claim to the French throne – and now was the moment for Mayor Whittington to lead the rejoicing, on behalf of the City of London.

It was also the moment for this wily and brilliant merchant to demonstrate, before the monarch himself, the central role that he – Whittington – had played in the triumph. The Mayor laid on a fantastic binge. The wenches were as comely and fragrant as any in late medieval London. The minstrels twanged from the gallery. No doubt there were jugglers, strongmen and tumbling dwarves, expertly miming the defeat of the French (and unconsciously reviving the ancient traditions of the building. Beneath the feasters' stamping feet, lost and silent in the foundations, were the ruins of the Roman amphitheatre).

The dishes were rare and costly. The wine ran in conduits. The fire was fed with sandalwood and other aromatic fuel. The twenty-eight-year-old King was amazed.

'Even the fires are filled with perfume!' he cried.

'If your majesty forbids me not,' Sir Richard Whittington is supposed to have said, 'I will make the fire even more fragrant.'

As the King acquiesced, the Mayor drew forth a bundle of bonds – pieces of paper recording the debts owed by the King – and threw them on the flames. 'Thus do I acquit your majesty of a debt of £60,000.'

It is hard to compute £60,000 in today's money, but it must run into tens of millions of pounds. To absolve the king of debts on that scale was not just an act of stunning generosity, it was an act of state. Imagine if the Gnomes of Zurich had gone to Harold Wilson and told him that his country's debts were forgiven. Suppose the bond markets were to hold a sumptuous dinner party for George Osborne, and one of the bankers rose drunkenly at the end to proclaim that the deficit would no longer have to fall on the shoulders of the UK taxpayer but that they would absorb it themselves.

You'd think the world had gone mad; and as it happens there isn't much evidence that this scene took place at all, let alone as depicted in the pages of *Look and Learn*. On the night in question, it looks as though the King was in France, rather than the Guildhall. But the basic truth is indisputable: that Dick Whittington helped bankroll England's military machine at the critical moment in the Hundred Years War; that he lent large and crucial sums to three successive monarchs; and that he absolved Henry V of his debts, as he absolved many others.

You think you know the story of Dick Whittington? Think again. That tale you see at Christmas at the Horsham Salvation Army Hall, starring TV's Jason Donovan as Dick and Anne Widdecombe as his furry feline friend – that pantomime is in one sense an egregious piece of tabloid misreporting. But it is also a powerful lesson in how a top financier can sanitise his reputation and win the undying affection of the public.

The real Dick Whittington was not born poor. There is no evidence that he tied his possessions in a handkerchief suspended from a stick. He did not 'turn again' at Highgate Hill, at the sound of Bow Bells. He was not Mayor of London thrice but four times. He did not have a cat.

Between 1400 and 1423 there were only two years in which he did not make loans to the crown. In that sense, he was of serious importance in economic history. It was fully sixty years later that the Monte di Pieta in Perugia first made its loans to the poor, in exchange for knives or caps or other pawned items. Before the Fuggers of Augsburg, before the Medicis of Florence, there was Dick Whittington, merchant and banker in all but name. Like Chaucer, whom he certainly knew, Dick Whittington was so politically agile as to occupy London's two worlds – the City and the court at Westminster – and he made so much money from the proximity of the one to the other that his personal endowments are still paying out to the needy today.

Whittington was born between 1354 and 1358 in Gloucestershire, and his parents were not peasants but the lord and lady of the manor of Pauntley, with their own coat of arms. It is true that Sir William Whittington had been 'outlawed' for the offence of marrying the daughter of Sir Thomas Berkeley without royal consent (you needed the King's consent to marry the daughter of a courtier, on the theory that he ought to have first dibs). But the Whittingtons were not despoiled of their manor; indeed, they continued to lord it over Pauntley for the next two hundred years, and their descendants can be found to this day in the village of Hamswill.

Richard Whittington's only problem was that he was the youngest of three brothers, and with no chance of inheriting, his options were (a) hang around Gloucestershire hoping to meet a nice rich girl; (b) study for the law at the Inns of Court; (c) enter the Church; (d) enrol for military service with a baron or (e) become an apprentice and enter a trade. We do not know exactly why he chose to become an apprentice, but in his mid to late teens he did indeed make the four- or five-day hike to London, entering at Newgate in about 1371. As we have just seen, London was a city pullulating with money and vice.

The last big plague scare had been a couple of years ago, in 1369, and there was a frenzied feeling to the earthly pleasures of the crowd. We have a letter from the Archbishop of Canterbury (the po-faced fellow who tried to persecute Chaucer) complaining that at this time Londoners were no longer observing Sunday as a day of rest. As Whittington wandered in search of his lodgings he might have seen bears being baited, thieves or card sharps in the pillory, mendicants displaying their fascinating skin diseases and waving their mutilated stumps with Pythoneseque enthusiasm.

He might have been caught up in one of any number of Saint's day parades and processions with all the attendant drunkenness, vomiting and sin. Wide-eyed though he was, young Dick passed these temptations by. His mother had a contact, a mercer by name of Sir Hugh or possibly Sir John or even Sir Ivo FitzWarren, whose family has come over with the Conqueror; and Dick kept right on to his house and the prospect of a job.

To be an apprentice was a serious business. You were required to attend Mass and absorb the sermon, and you had to turn out for archery practice at Smithfield. You might be born of good family, but your existence was Spartan. A junior apprentice might sleep in the loft, and a senior apprentice would have to make do with a bale of hay in the house. You wore a flat, round cap and a very short haircut, with a coarse long coat, and you walked in front of your master or mistress at night with a lantern or with a long club about your neck. In Tudor times, the apprentices were to become a major political force, famed for rioting and thuggery. But as an apprentice mercer, young Dick was already a cut above, and he took to his duties with great conscientiousness.

A mercer is a trader in cloth and apparel of all kinds. It was an age when people were not only getting richer, but wanted to differentiate themselves by the luxury of their gear; and so the rag trade was where the money was. Dick would have learned how to comb fleeces, how to pack bales of cloth, how to distinguish guild marks, how to fold and wrap delicate fabrics; how to rub them between thumb and forefinger, declare that they were the nicest pieces of schmutter he had ever seen and that their price was therefore substantially more than their cost.

King and court were now spending more and more time at Westminster, and the tradesmen made money from the eternal pomposity of officialdom. Skinners supplied the rabbit skin fur for their collars; drapers supplied the heavy fabrics; mercers like Whittington provided just about everything: linen, velvets, taffetas, damask, silks, ribbons. Cloth of gold? Suits you, sir! The royal purchasing agency was called The Great Wardrobe, and if the Great Wardrobe called on your shop, you were blessed with custom from the whole court.

Whittington worked in the mercers' quarter, around Bow Church in Cheapside, and he worked hard, from early in the morning till 8 pm, when the church bells sounded the end of the working day. His name first crops up in the records in 1379, when he had probably just completed his seven-year apprenticeship, and he makes his first loan to the state – five marks to the city authorities.

We glimpse him again nine years later, when he has shinned up the greasy pole to become one of eight common councilmen for Coleman Street Ward. In 1390 he gives £10 – a lot of money, as much as the Mayor would be expected to give – for the defence of the city. By 1393, by which time he must be in his mid- to late thirties, he has attained the rank of alderman. He became sheriff in 1394.

His rise is unremarkable – neither especially quick nor slow – but by now he has enough dosh to be ranked with the great moneymen of the age, men like Brembre or William Walworth. The decisive moment comes in 1397, as the reign of Richard II is moving fitfully to its close.

You will remember that the King was ill-disposed towards the City, for its role in the attempted coup against him by the 'Lords Appellant'; and you will remember that Richard had attacked the City's democratic institutions, by appointing his own Warden. On the death of the Mayor, Adam Bamme, he decided arbitrarily to make Richard Whittington Mayor of London. He was a man, said the King, 'in whose fidelity and circumspection we repose full confidence.' But Dick Whittington knew it was no good appearing to be the glove puppet of the King. He needed the support of his peers. There would have to be an election. So for £10,000 payable to His Majesty he arranged for the City to buy back the ancient freedom of self-government conferred by the Conqueror, and on 13 October 1397 he was duly elected Mayor, with the approbation not just of the King but of the City merchants as well.

Two years later came the coup. Henry Bolingbroke took over, Richard starved to death in captivity and a new dynasty was born. And yet Whittington sailed on regardless; indeed the new king Henry IV agreed that he should be paid a debt of £1000 still owed to him by Richard II. It is a comment on Whittington's chameleon skills that one king should pay him the debts incurred by another. Dick Whittington had the guile and the tact to be in with everyone.

He sold goods worth £2000 to Robert de Vere, the notorious favourite and supposed lover of Richard II. Remember that crackling and burning of expensive drapery in the London house of John of Gaunt, during the Peasants' Revolt? Whittington supplied the replacement soft furnishings. When Blanche and Philippa, daughters of Henry IV, were looking for wedding silks, team Whittington was there with the tape measure. It is tempting to imagine that his calm and expertise gave him a hold over the women of the household, who must surely have been involved in these decisions of colour and taste. The reality, however, is that London's champion mercer had an even more powerful means of binding himself to his royal clients. Between 1392 and 1394 he sold goods worth £3,500 to the household of Richard II, and he was far too smart just to pocket the proceeds. He loaned it back to the cash-hungry monarchs of England.

From 1388 onwards he made no fewer than sixty loans to the crown, with the biggest going to Henry IV and Henry V – and he did it even though usury was illegal.

England was then a good Catholic country, obedient to the teachings of the Bible. 'Usury of any thing that is lent is unclean,' says Deuteronomy, and Ambrose of Milan had raged in the fifth century against the very concept of lending money at interest. 'Thou collectest wealth from the misery of all, and callest this industry and diligence, when it is but cunning shrewdness and an adroit trick of the trade!' said Ambrose, and he no doubt speaks for many who have coped for years with the charges imposed by British banks. In 1139 the second Lateran Council concluded that usury was theft, and indeed it was banned for everyone except Jews; and Jews were able to continue to lend money at interest only because a careful reading of Deuteronomy showed that it was forbidden to charge interest 'to thy brother', which was taken to mean other Jewish people. Lending to gentiles was fine.

It must be said that the Jews suffered terribly for performing this function, which is now recognised everywhere (except possibly Tehran) as vital for an expanding capitalist economy. The story of mediaeval English persecution of the Jews is so hideous that we are sometimes in danger of airbrushing it from the curriculum: the massacres in London and York in 1189–1190; the behaviour of Simon de Montfort in expelling the Jews from Leicester. There were hundreds of other disgraceful episodes. In 1290 Edward I expelled Jews from the kingdom altogether, and the chief moneylenders of the English economy did not return until the age of Oliver Cromwell.

There was a gap in the market, and Whittington filled it with chutzpah. He didn't take interest for his loans, dear me no, nothing so vile as interest. He merely ensured that he was exempt from various dues and taxes that would otherwise go to the Royal Household. Now given that the wool trade dominated the economy, it is not surprising that the most lucrative permanent source of royal revenue was 'wool subsidy' – a tax payable to the King on exports of wool and cloth to the Continent. In exchange for his loans, Whittington obtained letters patent from the King exempting him from wool subsidy; and if he didn't pay wool subsidy, he could export the stuff more cheaply than anybody else; and then he would make even more money, and lend even more to the King, and win himself ever bigger tax exemptions and an ever bigger share of the market.

By 1404 he was exporting wool from both London and Chichester, and in 1407 he had a monopoly of wool exports from Chichester, sending out six shiploads of wool to Calais and a total of 250 sacks. And by adroitly manipulating his position as one of the big lenders to the Crown, he was able to further his own commercial interests. At one stage he followed in the footsteps of Chaucer by becoming the 'collector of the wool custom and subsidy in London'. It is a transparent conflict of interest. It is like asking the Chief Executive of Goldman Sachs to serve simultaneously as head of the Financial Services Authority. He could grant himself a licence to export wool without paying customs duty.

Whittington became rich by the most tremendous dodge. He concealed, or dressed up, the interest that he received on his loans. And yet he was so venerated by the twin poles of London's power – court and City – that he was not only knighted by Henry V, but asked to sit in judgment on usury trials in 1421; as though he was not himself committing usury by another name.

The world of royal finance was strewn with hair-trigger mines. It required genius to negotiate and we must conclude that Dick Whittington was a financier of genius, because throughout his life he retained that essential element of trust. Already in 1382 he was the kind of man who could be given pearls and jewels and other goods to hold, worth a total of £600, without, apparently, being asked for any security in return.

Such was his prestige that he was elected Mayor again in 1406 and again in 1419 (the fourth time, if you include his initial appointment by Richard II), and he died in 1423 with a knighthood and just about the most perfect reputation of any businessman before or since. He was a banker, a usurer in all but name, and yet his life is portrayed every year as a rags-to-riches story of triumph against the odds.

The simple reason for his modern halo is that Dick Whittington gave, and he gave on a scale that is completely alien to modern British culture – though not, perhaps, to modern America.

By the time he died there was scarcely an aspect of London life that had not felt his beneficence. He adorned and improved the Guildhall. He supervised the expenditure to complete Westminster Abbey. He was so appalled by the conditions in Newgate jail, where prisoners were dropping like flies to prison fever, that he opened a separate prison for debtors at Ludgate. He created a ward for unmarried mothers at St Thomas' Hospital, and drainage systems for Billingsgate and Cripplegate.

He rebuilt his own parish church, St Michael Paternoster Royal, and he was so tender-hearted as to provide accommodation for his own apprentices in his own house and to pass a law, as Mayor, forbidding the washing of animal skins in the Thames in cold, wet weather – because so many apprentices were being forced to do it, and were catching their death of cold. He caused the building of one of the first public drinking fountains in London – possibly the very first; and he created a public toilet, possibly the first since Roman times, in the parish of St Martin Vintry. It was not a particularly complicated or sanitary affair, since it was flushed by the Thames at high tide; but it constitutes a vague mediaeval stab in the direction of hygiene, and was known long after as

'Whittington's longhouse'. Even when he died, the cascade of money did not die, and its trickle can still be seen today. Whittington had married Alice, daughter of Sir Hugh or Sir John (or even Sir Ivo) Fitzwarren, but they do not appear to have had any children; and he left £7000 in his will, which has been used over the generations to fund the kind of project that would normally be left to the state. Whittington money repaired St Bartholomew's Hospital. His legacy created a trust, still administered by the Mercers' company, that distributes money to 300 poor people a year, and to this day – six hundred years later – Dick Whittington continues to provide almshouses for those who have fallen on hard times.

In the village of Felbridge, near East Grinstead, there are fifty-six flats available for single women or married couples on low incomes. Go on the website and you will see that they appear to be delightful places, set in rose-filled gardens. There are studios, one-bed and two-bed apartments available for the over sixties who find themselves in straitened circumstances. No pets are accepted, it says; which of course reminds me – why did the fictional Whittington acquire a cat, when there is no trace of his feline friend in the historical record?

Some say it was to do with a print of Whittington, in which his hand was resting on a skull until that image was thought too morbid and the skull was replaced with a cat. Some say it is an echo of a tenth-century tale from Arabia, all about a poor boy whose only possession was a mouse-killing cat and who went on to become one of the great men of the kingdom. But surely the answer is obvious.

The reason Dick Whittington was equipped by posterity with a cat was that it made him appear yet kinder, and gentler and more humane. It was in keeping with his character as it had become understood by the London public. He may have been poor, but like so many poor people he was not too poor to look after a cat; and because the English are particularly fond of animals the cat became a shorthand for the extreme generosity of Whittington's soul.

In that sense, the myth hints at a poetic truth. London needed Whittington's capitalist drive and entrepreneurial spirit. Successive kings needed him to help fund their ventures. Agincourt, that totemic victory over the French, exalted by Shakespeare as a critical moment in the maturing of English confidence, was partly funded by Whittington. He was a major player, economically and politically; but it is his philanthropy that has gilded his reputation.

He deserves that reputation, and the more we delve into the truth behind the legend, the more respectful we become. In 1569, Richard Grafton's *Chronicle* concludes an account of his bequests and euergetism with the exhortation, 'Look on thys, ye aldermen, for it is a glorious glasse'. In the same spirit we can say today, 'Look on Dick Whittington, ye bankers and plutocrats of London, for he is a glorious example.'

Here, for the sake of comparison, is the standard fable of Dick Whittington.

Long, long ago there lived a poor boy called Dick Whittington. He had no mother and no father, and often nothing to eat. One day he heard of the great city of London, where, said everyone, even the streets were paved with gold. Dick decided to go to London to seek his fortune.

London was a big and busy city, full of people both rich and poor. But Dick could not find any streets that were paved with gold. Tired, cold and hungry he fell asleep on the steps of a great house. This house belonged to Mr Fitzwarren, a rich merchant, who was also a good and generous man. He took Dick into his house, and gave him work as a scullery boy.

Dick had a little room of his own where he could have been very happy if it had not been for the rats. They would run all over him as he lay on his bed at night and would not let him sleep. One day Dick earned a penny shining shoes for a gentleman, and with it he bought a cat. After that Dick's life became easier, the cat frightened away all the rats, and Dick could sleep in peace at night.

One day Mr Fitzwarren called all the servants of the house together. One of his ships was leaving for a far-off land with goods to trade. Mr Fitzwarren asked his servants to send something of their own in the ship if they so desired, something which could perhaps be traded for a bit of gold or money. Dick had only his cat to send – which he did with a sad heart.

> Dick continued to work as a scullery boy for Mr Fitzwarren, who was very kind to him. So was everyone else except the cook, who made Dick's life so miserable that one day Dick decided to run away. He had reached almost the end of the city when he heard the Bow Bells ring out. 'Turn again Whittington, thrice Lord Mayor of London' chimed the bells. Dick was astonished, but he did as the bells said and went back to Mr Fitzwarren.
>
> When he returned he found that Mr Fitzwarren's ship had returned, and that his cat had been sold for a great fortune to the King of Barbary whose palace had been overrun with mice. Dick had become a rich man.
>
> He soon learned the business from Mr Fitzwarren, married his daughter Alice, and in time became the Lord Mayor of London three times, just as the bells had said.

There is one final achievement of Dick Whittington that we should mention. It was thanks to one of his bequests that in 1423 there opened London's first public library.

It was located next to the Guildhall, and the idea was that citizens should be able to get hold of books that might otherwise have been reserved for the clergy or the aristocracy. By 1476 that library was filling up with books printed by William Caxton on his wonderful new machine, and then by works from the press of Wynkyn de Worde.

By the time Wynkyn died in 1535 he had published eight hundred books – and that explosion in the availability of the printed word, for loan as well for sale, had incalculable consequences for the intellectual and religious life of London. It was the beginning of a mass market for literature of all kinds.

In the following year King Henry VIII dissolved the monasteries, in one of the greatest pro-business moves of any government in history. Suddenly ecclesiastical land and property became available to the aspirant merchant classes. Fine property was up for grabs – cheap.

The guilds moved in, the Leathersellers taking over a nunnery, for instance, and the Butchers taking over a parsonage. Soon the great Elizabethan trading companies were being founded, beginning in 1555 with the Muscovy company. They were joint-stock ventures financed by London's expert bankers.

In spite of repeated outbreaks of the plague, the population soared, overtaking Venice, and by 1580 it was not far behind Paris. The city burst out of its ancient boundaries in sprawling Tudor ribbon developments.

In the East end there was a mixture of housing and small industrial concerns: bell-founding, glass-making, ivory and horn-working, followed by silk-weaving and paper-making. In the West end, rich men started to build posh houses. With thousands of immigrants arriving from poorer areas of the country, London started to account for an ever larger share of English trade and of the English population.

With an increasingly literate and prosperous bourgeoisie, there was a market for entertainment, from someone who could not only come up with a good story, but who could subtly and not-so-subtly glorify the culture and achievement of Elizabethan England. Whittington not only paid for Agincourt; he helped to subsidise a London literary culture that would eventually produce that battle's supreme artistic commemoration.

THE FLUSH TOILET

You think the flush toilet was invented by Thomas Crapper, don't you? Think again, my friends.

If you go to the Gladstone Pottery Museum in Stoke on Trent, you can see a replica of a most intriguing and visionary device that was first designed to accommodate the perched buttocks of the Virgin Queen. Only two of these fascinating devices were ever made – and one of them was in London.

It was installed in the Queen's now-demolished palace at Richmond in about 1596, and was the invention of Sir John Harington, her godson and one of her most wayward courtiers.

'Big Jack' Harington was a slightly louche and pretentious courtier, who got into trouble by translating lewd verses from Italian and circulating them among the ladies of the court.

He was banished on several occasions. One evening he was languishing in Wiltshire, in the company of Shakespeare's patron, the Earl of Southampton, and the conversation became scatological.

Inspired by the technical problems they had discussed, he wrote a lavatorial treatise called 'The Metamorphosis of Ajax' – Ajax being a pun on 'a jakes', then a common word for a toilet. He sent his efforts, complete with blueprint, to the Queen.

As he made clear, his mission in designing a new bog was social and political – to win back the Queen's favour and to 'give occasion to have me thought and talked of.' He succeeded.

The Queen was said to be pleased with his efforts, and the contraption was installed.

The replica at Stoke is based on his own instructions, and it consists of a rectangular wooden bench with a circular hole – a concept familiar at least since Roman times. The revolution is in the big square cistern to the rear and an oval lead pan below the bench, lined with pitch and filled to about six inches with water. The oval pan sloped downwards towards a plug, to which was attached a long rod with a key handle at the end. When you wanted to empty the pan, you pulled the key handle, and the contents of the pan would empty down the privy shaft.

You then re-closed the plug at the end of the pan, and replenished the pan with water by lifting another rod-plug in the cistern.

Brilliant!

Apart from having two handles, the Harington flush toilet was like a modern toilet in overall concept, and a considerable advance on Whittington's Longhouse.

Alas, it did not catch on.

Though Harington's invention found favour with the Queen (who was fastidious about her personal hygiene, and 'always had a bath once a month, even when she didn't need one'), it was another two hundred years before anything similar appeared for the general market.

What this premature breakthrough perhaps shows is the growing post-Reformation interest in cleanliness, and the lengths to which London courtiers would go to please their monarch.

Some wrote her epic poems, some sonnets. Some brought her new crops from new continents. Some performed before her in companies of players, and some designed new toilets for her in the hope of restoring themselves in her eyes.

It is in honour of John Harington (or so it is sometimes said) that Americans refer to the modern flush toilet as the 'John'.

William Shakespeare

And how London pioneered the modern theatre

Shortly before they opened the reconstructed Globe Theatre in Southwark in 1997, I went down there to interview Zoe Wanamaker, the Harry Potter star of the tip-tilted nose, whose late father Sam had been the visionary responsible for making it all happen.

I wasn't quite sure what to expect, and it may be that I hadn't prepared the interview with my normal attention to detail. But when Zoe and I walked into the middle of that wooden O, and we stood in what was intended to be the auditorium, I confess I was a bit taken aback.

'You mean there aren't any seats?' I said to Zoe.

'That's right,' she said.

'And you seriously expect people to come and stand here for hours on end and listen to Shakespeare?'

'Of course they will,' she said, with the exuberance of an American; and though I was too polite to say so at the time, my first thought was, you have got to be kidding. When you look at the Elizabethan theatre experience, it seems incredible that they put up with it.

They had to leave the limits of the city for the 'liberties', the lawless stews on the perimeter where the theatres were allowed, places like

Southwark, with a reputation for whores and bear-baiting and thievery of all kinds. They had to hold their noses as they went past the industries that were forbidden within the city walls: the fullers with their naturally procured ammonia; the gluemakers boiling up bones into a fog of smell. And if that wasn't enough to knock you out, there were the tanners who liked to make their hides supple by steeping them – there is no easy way of putting this – in vats of stewed dog turd. They then went into a theatre that had no roof, so they ran the risk of being drenched or squinting at the sun.

There was no system of heating or cooling the building. The whole place was at constant risk of catching fire, or just falling over, like the theatre that collapsed in St John Street, killing thirty or forty people and 'two good, handsome whores.' There were pickpockets everywhere, and women constantly at risk of having their plackets groped. There were no toilets, and some playgoers relieved themselves helplessly on the backs of the legs in front of them, so that the ground beneath was a mulch of spilt beer and oyster shells and less wholesome substances.

As for the crowd themselves – well, there has been much debate, but the overwhelming opinion is that, in large part, they really were the London mob. As the indignant Privy Council put it in 1597, they were vagrant persons, masterless men, thieves, horse-stealers, whoremongerers, coney-catchers, contrivers of treason and other idle and dangerous persons. When they put back their warty heads and opened their carious mouths to laugh or shout as one, the actors on stage would be bathed in what the playwright Thomas Dekker called 'the breath of the great beast'. They were the 'penny stinkards', he said. They didn't get much of a spectacle for their penny.

There were no curtains. There was not much scenery. The costumes were eccentrically cobbled together from the hand-me-downs of rich men. The lighting was amateurish and the special effects revolved around the blood or organs of sheep. There weren't any pretty actresses to ogle because the female parts were all played by men, for some English reason that did not prove compelling in other parts of Europe.

The whole thing might go on for three or four hours, followed by a 'jig', a bizarre Elizabethan dance, rather like the satyr play that followed ancient Greek tragedies, but a bit mystifying to us. If you paid a shilling, I suppose you might sit on cushions in the Lords' room; if you paid sixpence there was the relative comfort of the gentlemen's room, but the overwhelming majority were prepared to pay good money – enough to buy a loaf of bread weighing a pound – to stand in conditions of acute discomfort.

No modern English audience would put up with it in a football stadium, let alone a theatre. And yet the Elizabethans loved it, and they came week in week out, in huge numbers. On any given day – assuming they hadn't been closed for plague – you could expect to find two plays being staged in theatres that held between two and three thousand spectators each. So over one week, assuming five days of performances, about fifteen thousand Londoners paid to see a play. That makes sixty thousand a month – in a city with a population of two hundred thousand!

More than a third of London's adult population saw a play every month. These people were theatre junkies. Hundreds if not thousands of plays were produced to feed their habit, and of the pitiful few we have left about a quarter were by one man. By common consent there was one individual who supremely vindicated the hardship of that Elizabethan crowd. With words that were sometimes strange and new, but almost always captivating, William Shakespeare made their discomfort bearable.

He sweetened and transformed the atmosphere of the Globe. He opened windows for the audience into lives and worlds they had never dreamed of. He turned those blank boards into the camp-fire before Agincourt, the Nile-side death scene of Cleopatra, a spooky Scottish castle, the dark and misty battlements of Elsinore and the backlit balcony in Verona where a beautiful young girl (played, ahem, by a boy) appeared to her forbidden lover.

His dramas went global with astonishing speed, disseminated across the high seas by an increasingly adventurous and confident English merchant fleet. In 1607, when the author still had nine years to live, *Hamlet* and *Richard II* were performed on board a ship off Sierra Leone. In 1608 the melancholy Dane was introduced to an audience in what is now the Yemen. By 1609 the ghost of Hamlet's father first turned up on makeshift battlements somewhere in Indonesia, and by 1626 the people of Dresden were hearing the Prince trying to make his mind up about suicide – in German.

The performance was delivered by a group of Germans who called themselves 'the English comedians', in deference to the acknowledged origins of the art form. The point is that England – or more specifically London – was responsible for the export of the commercial theatre, and no other city was.

In the seventy years from the 1576 opening of James Burbage's first theatre to the abominable closure of the theatres by the Puritans, there was a boom unlike anything that has been seen before or since. That concept of the commercial, competitive theatre – you make them laugh, you make them cry, and mainly you make them pay – is after all the direct progenitor of the movies, the greatest popular art form of our times, and it started in London.

Yes, Spain had great theatre, but the Sigla del Oro came after the Elizabethan epoch, and the plays were more limited in their palette, concerned mainly with the strains of an agrarian and feudal society. Certainly, there were theatres in Venice, but, again, they came a little later and they were on nothing like the scale of the London industry. France was to produce the gigantic figures of Corneille, Molière, Racine, but they did their stuff a generation if not a century later.

It was Shakespeare who was the presiding divinity of a specifically London genre. His cult is global in a way that no other writer can match. There are seven thousand works devoted to him in the Library of Congress, and there are regular Shakespeare festivals in Germany, Greece, Spain, Belgium, Turkey, Poland, Korea, Brazil and Mexico. He has been translated into ninety languages. Chinese professors consecrate their lives to his work. An online game based on *Romeo and Juliet* currently attracts 22 million players. There is a tribe in north east India, called the Mizo, who regularly stage *Hamlet* and claim the Danish prince as one of their own.

I will never forget going to Brezhnev's Moscow, in 1980, and watching hundreds of wrapped-up Russians stream into some dim and grimy theatre, to hear an English actor recite a string of Shakespeare speeches including, of course, Hamlet's meditation on whether or not to top himself or rise up against his predicament.

After the performance the put-upon comrades went out silently into the night, except for one gaunt fellow in a flat cap, who spotted the knot of English schoolboys and glared: 'To be or not to be – that is the question!' He tapped his copy of the *Complete Works* and fired my Cold War adolescent imagination. Was he sympathising with the Prince, locked in the claustrophobic hypocrisy of Elsinore? Was he trying to get us a message, that there was something rotten in the state of Russia? Was he a Shakespeare-toting Sakharov?

Or was he (of course he was) just pleased to be able to quote a smattering of Shakespeare? Whatever he meant, my sixteen-year-old soul was proud that he was quoting our guy.

Shakespeare is the greatest hero and ambassador the English language has ever known. He is our single biggest cultural contribution to the world, our riposte to Beethoven and Michelangelo – and a pretty effective response he is, too. He is our greatest quarry of words and characters and predicaments. He is the one author we can truly call universal. He is our Homer.

We know more about Shakespeare than we know about any other Elizabethan dramatist – and yet we know next to nothing. Every fact or factoid is a frail peg from which is suspended a vast duffel coat sodden with conjecture, pockets stuffed with surmise.

We know that he was born on or around St George's Day 1564, and that his father, John Shakespeare, was a local worthy who made his money as a glover or whittawer – a worker of white leather. Shakespeare is supposed to have attended the abattoir in his youth, and some authorities detect in his work a special understanding of slaughtering, butchery and gore. Shakespeare senior was a Rotarian sort of fellow, rising from the rank of ale-taster to sheriff of Stratford-upon-Avon – effectively the mayor of the town.

John Shakespeare wasn't perhaps an entirely spotless character – he was fined in 1522 for keeping an unauthorised dung heap, and in later years he was convicted of usury, a very serious offence. But he had enough money to give William an excellent education (or so we think) at the local grammar school, where the young man probably left knowing at least as much Latin as a modern university graduate in classics (which isn't saying much). We know that in 1582 William Shakespeare married Anne Hathaway at the very young age of eighteen.

Since she was twenty-six, and since they had a daughter Susanna six months later, we can probably conclude that it was the usual thing. We know that two years later they had twins, Judith and a boy, Hamnet, who died in infancy. We know that he pitched up in London sometime between 1585 and 1592, when he is first identified as a published playwright, but on all the key questions we haven't a clue. We don't know why this son of a glover become an actor and playwright. We don't know why he went to London. We have nothing to go on but rumour. He may have been prosecuted for poaching deer at Charlecote in Oxfordshire; he may have been a secret recusant who sought employment with a Catholic family in Lancashire; he may have been a mercenary in Flanders or a traveller in Italy, or he may have sailed the Spanish Main with Drake. We have no real evidence for any of these more or less improbable hypotheses.

For one reason or another – perhaps because he simply needed to provide for his family, and it was the best and most enjoyable way he could make money – he arrived in London. In some ways it was still recognisably the same place that had been discovered by Dick Whittington. The old St Paul's was still standing, though its spire had been hit by lightning and had been removed. The Guildhall and the Royal Exchange were reportedly looking splendid, and there were now one hundred and twenty churches. The potato was beginning to be eaten, with a few reservations from those who thought it was a fad and unlikely to catch on.

Anyone who has been to see a city in the modern Middle East or India will understand what was happening to Elizabethan London. It was starting to surge with unplanned development, unsanitary prefabricated tenements shoved up any old how and in defiance of the authorities. The population of London doubled between 1560 and 1600, and this once-peripheral Roman colony was now far bigger than the mother city on the Tiber. There were more people in London than there were in any other European city except possibly Paris and Naples, and the place was growing all the time. It was the greatest trading centre in Europe, and not just because of the sheepback and broadcloth that had been exported since the Middle Ages. London was now the entrepôt, the place where merchants from Spain and Italy came to find furs from the Baltic and salted fish from Newfoundland, and with the growth of trade there grew the first solid middle class in Europe.

It was estimated that 10 per cent of the population was eligible for poor relief, and 25 per cent was rich enough to contribute to the royal subsidies (or taxes), but as one observer put it, 'the greatest part are neither too rich nor too poor, but do live in the mediocritie'. What did they want, those people who lived in the mediocritie? They wanted what we members of the mediocritie have always wanted.

They wanted booze. Between 1563 and 1620 wine imports from France and Spain rose five times.

They wanted sex. About 40 per cent of the men who lived in the Clink area of Southwark were watermen who made a living from ferrying punters across to the prostitutes.

And they wanted fun. After the bleaching solemnity of the Reformation, the smashing of stained glass windows, they wanted colour and spectacle and the collective release of emotion. Of course there were shows, barbaric scenes in which bears were attacked by dogs, or sometimes an impresario would tickle the fancy of the crowd by tying a chimpanzee to the back of a horse and setting the dogs on both of them. But bears were expensive, and it is natural for human beings to wish to see themselves, to hold a mirror up to their own lives, and so for some time there had been skits and scenes played by touring companies in the balconied courtyards of inns. Eventually it dawned on the impresarios that there could be serious money in such shows, and in 1576 a player named James Burbage made the breakthrough.

Why not create a permanent dedicated space – as they had in ancient Athens – but run on purely commercial lines? Soon theatres were springing up around the perimeter of the city, English theatres, that looked more like the yard of a pub than Epidaurus; and to understand the emergence of William Shakespeare at the end of the sixteenth century it is vital to grasp that these were rival commercial ventures staffed by rival companies.

A man like Philip Henslowe, who owned the Rose and Fortune theatres, would pay his authors between £3 and £5 for a play, and he would make it back in one night – if he had the right play. So suddenly there was a financial incentive not just to write, but to compete to be the best; and if you were a man like Henslowe or Burbage you wanted those bums on the seats in your theatre, and you were prepared to pay the talent for the right stuff.

Shakespeare was just one of a coterie of at least fifteen middle class males who were all toiling at the same craft, each vying to be more esteemed, more praised, and therefore more recompensed, than the rest. There were George Chapman, Henry Chettle, John Day, Thomas Dekker, Michael Drayton, Richard Hathaway, William Haughton, Thomas Heywood, Ben Jonson, Christopher Marlowe, John Marston, Anthony Munday, Henry Porter, Robert Wilson and William Shakespeare. They stole ideas from each other, they inspired each other, they pushed each other to new heights of exertion. It is that sense of rivalry among a defined group of talented people – that is the way to produce genius. Think of Los Alamos. Think of Bletchley. There was jealousy of all kinds.

Richard Burbage famously fixed an assignation with a female fan at the stage door, and went to change from his clothes, only to find that Shakespeare himself had got there first – with the quip that 'William the Conqueror came before Richard'. Sometimes there was physical violence. Marlowe killed a man, and was killed himself in a mysterious pub brawl in Deptford. Ben Jonson killed a rising star named Gabriel Spencer in a duel, and only escaped the gallows by reading the 'neck verse', a mediaeval loophole whereby the literate were allowed to cheat execution by reading the bible in Latin. He had T for Tyburn branded on his thumb, meaning that he would be hanged there for his next offence.

In an atmosphere of such extreme competition it was natural that actors and playwrights would devise a system for pooling risk and sharing responsibility, so they created companies directly analogous to the commercial companies that were being formed to spread the risk of sending boats round the world. After the 1555 Muscovy company came the Turkey company in 1581, the Venice Company in 1583, the East India Company in 1600 and the Virginia company in 1609. Like the commercial companies, the companies of players engaged in takeovers, head-hunting, poaching and the eternal battle for market share.

Think how often Shakespeare describes an event in commercial terms, or as a maritime venture. As Iago says to Cassio, when it becomes clear that Othello has had it away with Desdemona. 'Faith, he tonight hath boarded a land carrack (a kind of boat). If it prove lawful prize, he's made forever.' Or as Brutus says to Cassius in *Julius Caesar*, when he wants him to come in on the assassination, 'we must take the current where it serves, or lose our ventures.'

The Shakespearean theatre was the product of the entrepreneurial maritime culture of the age, and it has been estimated that a 'sharer' or partner in the King's Men – as Shakespeare was – would take a dividend of between £100 and £150 a year, which was not to be sneezed at. London was the high seas, the wooden frames of the theatres were the boats, and the booty was the theatre-going public. And how did each company hope to hoist the maximum number of punters aboard? By studying their tastes and giving them what they wanted.

The audience wanted romance, and sexual excitement, and 'honey-tongued' Shakespeare was famously good at that. Young men were said to plunder *Romeo and Juliet* for chat-up lines. They liked a good laugh, which is why Shakespeare is so stuffed with puns and comic interludes, some of which have aged better than others. They wanted to be wrung out with emotion. They wanted to gasp.

They wanted to be shocked at the implications of an idea and its relevance to the politics of the time. Shakespearean theatre drew strength from both of the power centres of London: the money of the City and the politics of Westminster. It was the City merchants who generated the cash to pay for the leisure hours that Londoners spent at the shows, and it was the merchants who provided the model for the entrepreneurial joint-stock theatre company.

It was the politics of the Metropolis, and the intrigues of the court, that gave the plays that extra topicality, the gasp-factor that requires us to understand the background. Queen Elizabeth had seen off the Armada in 1588; she had executed Mary Queen of Scots and many others. Her secret service was ruthless and her spies were everywhere. But she was a childless woman of late middle years, and the question of succession was agonising.

The Spanish could always try again. There were constant rumours that they had already landed at the Isle of Wight. People wondered how this poor weak woman could survive in the face of the bullying charisma of the noblemen who surrounded her, and in particular her 'favourite', the ambitious, unruly, good-looking, square-bearded, sonnet-writing Earl of Essex.

As James Shapiro has shown in his wonderful *1599*, Shakespeare's plays are not deracinated masterpieces bequeathed to the human race by some garret-bound egghead with a bad haircut. For an Elizabethan audience, they must have derived their energy and their resonance from the events of the time. Shakespeare's dramas are tapping the underlying pool of unspoken – and often unspeakable – anxiety about the stability of the state. So many of his plays are about succession, and kingship, and the perils of subverting the natural order of things – *Hamlet*, *Macbeth*, *Julius Caesar*, *Henry II*, *Henry IV*, *King Lear*, and so on. Probably a quarter of his plays develop this theme, one way or another.

So when an Elizabethan audience saw the conspirators draw their daggers on Caesar, they would have known of the chilling events that had taken place at court. As Shapiro relates: one day Elizabeth was having a row with Essex, and as usual Essex was pushing his luck, reckoning that the old girl still fancied him. He turned his back on her, an unforgivable insult to the monarch, and Elizabeth slapped him. At which point Essex moved to draw his sword on her! Unthinkable. You could not report it or talk about it, but you could show an event from history that was almost like it.

Julius Caesar, the text, was effectively banned; you could not buy a physical copy of the play for twenty-four years after Shakespeare's death. You had to watch the play, and when you watched the story of the tyrannicide you watched with eyes peeled for references to the anxieties of the day.

Think of the moment when Brutus describes the effeminacy of the dictator. Caesar pathetically fails to swim the Tiber, and when he succumbs to fever he cries 'Give me some drink, Titinius, as a sick girl. Ye gods, it doth amaze me. A man of such a feeble temper should, Get the start of the majestic world, And bear the palm alone.' That is just the kind of criticism that one can imagine falling from the lips of some sexist and discontented earl; and the mutterers had support from some of the lower orders.

One Mary Bunton of Hucking was overheard to say 'I care not a turd for the Queen or her precepts.' She was put in the stocks with a paper on her head, detailing her offence, and whipped. How many other Mary Buntons were there, and would they back Essex when he mounted his inevitable rebellion?

Elizabeth took a risk in sending Essex at the head of an army to Ireland, to suppress a revolt, and there was great nervousness about what he would do on his return. The troubles in Ireland reminded everyone of another monarch who had been (a) childless, (b) disliked by the merchants for overtaxing them, (c) who had bogged up Ireland – and who was then (d) deposed by a charismatic earl.

It was the Queen herself who gloomily made the comparison: 'Know you not that I am Richard II?'

When Essex did return from Ireland, at the head of his unsuccessful army, he again behaved contumaciously. He rushed into the Queen's very bedchamber and caught the ageing woman without her make-up and her hair all over the place. As the ladies of the bedchamber scattered in panic, he advanced on the Queen of England.

He kissed her hands, he kissed her neck, and generally made nice in the most gushing way, and there was not a lot that Elizabeth could do about it at the time – though afterwards she simply froze him out. Shortly thereafter Essex decided there was nothing for it. On the eve of the revolt he asked the Chamberlain's Men – who then included William Shakespeare – to perform a play.

And what did he asked them to perform? *Richard II.*

For God's sake let us sit upon the ground,

(says the King, before he is sent away by his usurper to starve to death in a castle),

And tell sad stories of the death of kings;
How some have been deposed, some slain in war …

The story of the deposition of Richard II may or may not be sad. But it was dynamite.

Like *Julius Caesar* it was never printed in Shakespeare's lifetime, and 1,500 copies of a history of the life of the usurper Henry IV were seized and burned by the Bishop of London. We don't know how Shakespeare and Co felt to be asked to perform this seditious theme; we don't know the response of the audience. The following day Essex and his supporters left his house on the Strand and marched through Ludgate to the City, calling on Londoners to join them as they went. The citizens, on the other hand, looked out of their houses and shops and decided that it was a risky proposition. Essex realised his revolt was over, decided to have lunch, and waited to be arrested.

A few days later the repentant earl had his head chopped off in the Tower of London. The queen herself went into a decline, sitting in the dark and moping about the treachery of her favourite. It wasn't long before she was dead, and James I was on the throne – the outcome that everyone had been hoping for. The established order prevailed. As Germaine Greer has pointed out, Shakespeare constantly subverts that order for dramatic effect.

He was the first dramatist to write a play with a black man as the hero, and inferiors – children, servants, fools, vagabonds – are constantly instructing their betters. He shows us a vast pageant of regime change and revolution; and yet the overwhelming message of the Shakespearean sermon is in favour of the status quo. Primogeniture. Orderly inheritance. Dynastic succession – all the proper rewards of good kingship.

Claudius the usurper is punished, and so is Gertrude, and though the election eventually lights on Fortinbras, not Hamlet, we have been laboriously told at the beginning that Fortinbras also has a reasonable claim to Denmark. Caesar's conspirators get their comeuppance, Lear's daughters and their loathsome husbands are all deservedly slaughtered for their ill treatment of an aged ruler (one of the reasons that tragedy remains so huge in Asia), and things don't go at all well for Macbeth. Throughout the comedies, all manner of confusion and gender-swapping and mistaken identity is resolved with Mozartian harmony and multiple weddings. Things turn out all right in the end, and if a new king ends up on the throne he has seized, it will almost certainly mean that he was a better king than the last one.

What was behind this pro-establishment streak in Shakespeare? Was it nervousness, perhaps, of the censors? It was that interplay between the text and real political events that gave the plays their electric tension, that drew the crowds, and that sometimes provoked the fury of the authorities. Ben Jonson was imprisoned and almost had his nose and ears cut off for making what were thought to be anti-Scottish cracks, round about the accession of James I. Thomas Kyd was broken by torture on the rack, and Marlowe's death has often been ascribed to the secret service.

In 1597, two years before the first performance of *Julius Caesar*, the Privy Council actually requested that London's theatres be shut down, claiming that they contained nothing but 'profane fables, lascivious matters, cozening devices and scurrilous behaviours'. When Shakespeare's company, the Chamberlain's Men, performed *Richard II* for Essex, on the eve of his hopeless rebellion, they were brought in for questioning and were thought lucky to get away with it.

In all the circumstances, you might suppose, it was simply prudence that drove Shakespeare to give his plays their essentially pro-monarchy, pro-establishment veneer. Yes? Conceivably.

But it is surely more likely and more satisfying that his dramatic world view reflected what he really felt about the world, and what he felt his audience wanted from him. This was a time of uncertainty about England's global prestige. Ten years after the triumph over the Armada there was still paranoia about a Spanish invasion.

In 1598, a merchant reported back angrily from Brussels where he had seen a dumb show enacted. Instead of Gloriana Imperatrix, Elizabeth of England was portrayed as a fawning, flattering woman who attempts to eavesdrop on conversations between France and Spain, tugging at the sleeve of the King of France, with the audience laughing at the conceit. It was a long time since England had been kicked out of France, and even longer since Dick Whittington had given the King his banquet for Agincourt.

So Shakespeare gave us a certain idea of England, as a place apart, a precious stone set in a silver sea, and in *Henry V* he harks back to that triumph in one of the most rip-roaringly jingoistic plays ever produced. What a glorious thing it was, said Thomas Nashe, to have Henry V represented on stage, leading the French king prisoner and forcing both him and the dauphin to swear fealty. That was the stuff to give the troops.

If the Spanish tried to invade again, they would find a nation prepared to defeat overwhelmingly more numerous foes – just as the English had done at Agincourt. 'We few, we happy few! We band of brothers!' says the king on the eve of battle, setting up an English idea of the heroic ratio – few against many – that was to serve England well through the Napoleonic period and into the Second World War.

And in so far as it was also a time of anxiety about the monarchy, and fear of what might happen on the death of the Virgin Queen, Shakespeare naturally played with those fears, to stimulate the interest of the audience; but he always gave them reassurance in the final act.

Perhaps it has something to do not just with politics, or the demands of the audience, but the fundamental character of the man. We know so little about his family life – how he felt about the death of his son Hamnet, how much time he spent back in Stratford, what were his relations like with his wife and Susanna and Judith, his daughters. We don't know whether he was indeed a hoarder of malt, or what affliction brought his life to an end at the age of fifty-two.

We will never finally pin down the identity of the 'Dark Lady' of the sonnets, any more than we can say for certain what he meant by leaving Anne Hathaway his 'second-best bed.'

But we do know one revealing thing: that he went to a surprising amount of trouble to get a coat of arms, going back a second time to the rather reluctant College of Heralds, and using some ingenuity to claim kin with the Arden family, who were thought to be posher than the Shakespeares.

In other words he was not only the greatest writer in the English language, he was also a little bit of a snob. He was a bohemian actor-playwright who must have consorted with all manner of drunks and desperadoes and fallen women, and yet he ended up with the second-largest house in Stratford, with five gables, ten fireplaces and a frontage of over sixty feet. In May 1602 he paid the vast sum of £320 for one hundred and seven acres in Old Town in Stratford, as well as a cottage in Chapel Lane, and in 1605 he paid £440 for a share in the tithes of Stratford, worth £60 per year and about one-fifth of the total value.

He died a rich man, by the standards of the time; his life was a triumph of entrepreneurship, and he wanted the coat of arms to prove it. His works were taken around the world in the boats of the Elizabethan merchant adventurers, and they helped to create an ideology of Englishness that was to last for centuries: self-deprecating, sceptical of constitutional change, fond of the monarchy and the countryside and capable of drinking any other nation under the table.

The Shakespearean inflorescence coincided with the beginning of the Empire, and for a nation that came to think of itself as uniquely blessed he acquired the status – which he has not lost – of the world's top author. He coined more than 2500 words, and to prove his ubiquity in our speech and thought, I leave you with this tribute by Bernard Levin. Try reading it aloud.

> If you cannot understand my argument, and declare 'It's Greek to me', you are quoting Shakespeare; if you claim to be more sinned against than sinning, you are quoting Shakespeare; if you recall your salad days, you are quoting Shakespeare; if you act more in sorrow than in anger, if your wish is father to the thought, if your lost property has vanished into thin air, you are quoting Shakespeare; if you have ever refused to budge an inch or suffered from green-eyed jealousy, if you have played fast and loose, if you have been tongue-tied, a tower of strength, hoodwinked or in a pickle, if you have knitted your brows, made a virtue of necessity, insisted on fair play … it is all one to me, for you are quoting Shakespeare.

Yes, you are quoting Shakespeare and you are certainly not quoting Francis Bacon. It has always seemed odd to me that people claimed Bacon as the author of Shakespeare.

To be sure, he was a distinguished man and a great scientist, who died of a chill after trying to stuff a chicken with snow. But there is no evidence whatever that he wrote Shakespeare's plays, and in any case Shakespeare is remarkably light on science, or 'philosophy', as it was called.

As Hamlet says dismissively to his fellow Wittenberg student, as they scout around for the ghost: 'There are more things in heaven and earth, Horatio, than are dreamt of in your philosophy.'

Shakespeare famously introduced an anachronistic clock into Julius Caesar's Rome; and yet his audience had no watches, they had no real understanding of the function of the heart or the lungs, they didn't have a clue why an apple fell from a tree towards the centre of the Earth and they found it hard to find a route across the oceans without a grasp of longitude.

When they walked home over London Bridge after a three-hour Shakespearean performance in the early years of the seventeenth century, they saw a world that was technologically almost identical to the world of King John four hundred years earlier. Certainly, fashions had changed, and people wore ruffs and boasted codpieces, and smoked New World tobacco in pipes, but the houses on either side were still heated by coal or wood, and the privies emptied noisomely down the backs into the river, and the wherries below were still powered by nothing but muscle, and the grisly heads were still there on their spikes.

A Dutchman called Peter Morris had installed a water pump on the bridge, using paddles to take up water from the stream – but it was nothing that would have surprised Al-Jazari, who installed a similar device in Damascus in the twelfth century. The houses, the streets, the sanitation, the transport systems – all were still essentially mediaeval in design.

But as London's merchants became more adventurous and competitive, they needed ever better technology. Time is money, and so they needed timepieces more efficient than primitive rope-based escapements. They needed better muskets to fire at the recalcitrant natives; they needed better compasses in order to prevent their ships from foundering.

'Knowledge is power', said Bacon, and pressed for a Ministry of Science. He may not have written Shakespeare, but by the time he died in 1621 his enthusiasm and drive had paved the way for the scientific revolution of the seventeenth century.

It was that scientific revolution that led in turn to the industrial revolution that catapulted England ahead of her rivals and turned London into an imperial cosmopolis.

And that scientific revolution was powered by exactly the same engine as the Shakespearean theatre – the frantic desire for praise, recognition and money among a small group of highly competitive Londoners.

Like the emergence of Marlowe and Shakespeare, it was a scrabble for prestige that was to produce towering talents – and one of the very greatest was almost forgotten.

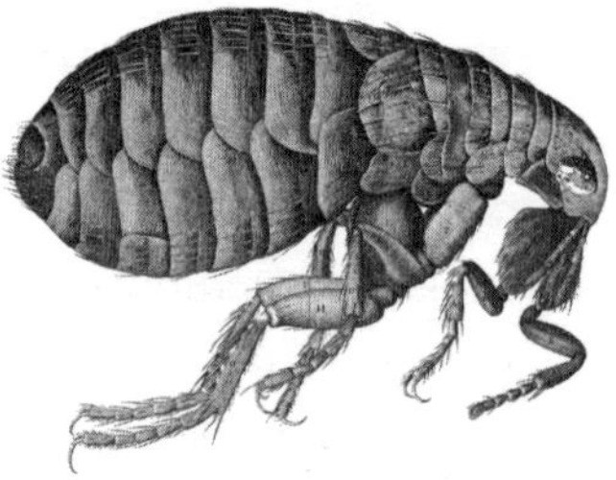

Robert Hooke

The greatest inventor you've never heard of

By Wednesday 5 September 1666 it was over. The fire was out, as if the gods had eaten their fill of destruction. Medieval London was no more. After 1,600 years London had finally discovered an enemy more potent than the Normans, the Danes, the Saxons – a man who was single-handedly responsible for burning down more buildings and destroying more livelihoods than Boudica herself.

He was Mr Thomas Farryner, the baker of Pudding Lane, who forgot his tray of buns. But for sheer boneheaded incompetence I am afraid he is beaten by Sir Thomas Bloodworth, the Lord Mayor.

By the standards of the time the blaze at Pudding Lane was still unremarkable, on the Sunday morning, when this municipal mugwump arrived at the scene. He found an argument taking place.

The constables wanted to stop the spread of the fire by the usual means – hauling down the adjacent buildings with fire hooks. The tenants protested. Since the owners of the houses could not be found, Sir Thomas Bloodworth decided that it was all too complicated. He told the constables to keep going with their water buckets.

'Pish', he said, turning on his heel, 'a woman could piss it out.' As the fire spread over the next two days, it was as if the citizens went into a trance of despair. The fire has been compared to an animal, leaping across the street from one wooden gable to the next; hiding under the thatch before exploding into view, ambushing the firefighters from behind.

Tuesday 4 September was perhaps the worst of all, as the blaze finally reached the thousands of books and manuscripts that had been stored for safekeeping in the cellar of St Paul's. The stones of the dilapidated medieval structure shot up like cannon balls and the lead from the roof ran like water in the streets.

The following morning Samuel Pepys ascended the spire of All Hallows Barking, by the Tower, and looked amid tears at the desolation. London had lost 87 churches and 13,200 houses, the homes of 70,000 people. The Royal Exchange, the shops of Cheapside – all had been incinerated, and the damage has been estimated in today's money at billions of pounds. Modern historians refuse to believe the official death toll – eight – and suggest that hundreds if not thousands of nameless paupers were carbonised in the fireball. As Pepys looked at the curling wisps of smoke, he could see people scrabbling pathetically for their cremated possessions. Huge encampments of refugees had been created at Moorfields and Islington, and angry mobs were roaming the remaining streets in search of the French and the Flemings and other foreigners who (as ever) were blamed for the fire.

It was a commercial disaster for the City – and also a political one. During the recent civil war, the big merchants had been republican in their sympathies. Thanks partly to the invertebrate behaviour of Bloodworth, their pretensions to autonomy had been humbled. It was King Charles II who had finally given the decisive order to pull down the buildings and create the necessary firewalls. It was his younger brother the Duke of York – the future James II – who masterminded the fightback.

Now the pre-eminence – and the very existence – of the City was under threat. Unless the merchants acted fast, there was a risk that investment might never return to the ancient site in the Roman walls. Businesses would migrate to the west and north, and wealth and power would be concentrated near the royal court at Westminster. They needed a man with a plan, and they needed him fast.

To see what they eventually came up with I recommend that you go to a little cobbled square just by London Bridge, called Fish Street Hill. Thousands of Londoners stride past it every morning, in their great trans-river tramp, with hardly a glance at what was once intended to be among the most conspicuous objects in the City. It is the Monument, still the single biggest stone pillar ever constructed, a preposterous Portland periscope.

It is 202 feet high because it is 202 feet from Pudding Lane and the seat of the fire. At the back of the pedestal is a giant square relief in which a bare-breasted woman representing London (and with the full-lipped features, they say, of Nell Gwynn) looks with doting eyes at her saviour, Charles II, whose dopy expression and pencil moustache makes him look a bit like troubled fashion designer John Galliano. It is altogether beautiful in design and concept, surmounted by a gleaming bronze bloom of flame, and well worth climbing.

At the top of its three hundred and eleven black marble steps I puff to the railings and look out, like Pepys, at the panorama of London. There is Canary Wharf, sitting pale in the haze; St Paul's; the towers of the City. If I look down I can see the funny tram tracks of the window cleaning devices on the office roofs.

I look straight down on to a desk in a bank a hundred feet below, where a man is slowly shuffling paper. The buses crawl up King William Street. There are only a few other tourists, including a man who hasn't been in London for ten years.

'What's that?' he asks, pointing at the Heron Tower. 'And what's that?' He indicates Norman Foster's cross-hatched ellipsoid, a building now so famous that it is used as a shorthand for the City.

'That's the Gherkin,' I say.

'Oh, that's the Gherkin,' he exclaims – as if there were any other building on the horizon that looked remotely like a gherkin.

If Pepys were up here with us, I imagine he would be not so much amazed as shocked to see how the spires of lovely seventeenth-century churches have been engulfed in a tidal wave of concrete and glass. And yet there is still something about this view that he would have recognised.

In the weeks after the fire there was a competition to redesign the City. John Evelyn, the diarist, proposed a splendidly classical matrix of boulevards and piazzas. Sir Christopher Wren did the same. A man called Valentine Knight produced a scheme so revolutionary that he was arrested. It rapidly became clear that none of these plans would work. Their shops and houses may have burned to the ground, but Londoners still held title to the smouldering sites. They wouldn't give them up.

In the end the harmonious neo-classical schemes were junked in favour of the ancient pattern. One man more than any other was to fix that pattern on the ground, and to measure out the plots of the new-built London. For the rest of the century he was to be a familiar figure, striding around the ruins with his 'waywiser', his own invention for measuring distances.

He designed or otherwise had a hand in fifty-one new or rebuilt churches. Indeed, he did the first sketch and proposal for the very monument on which I am standing. He was not Christopher Wren.

He was Robert Hooke, and in the phrase of London's leading modern historian Stephen Inwood, he was the forgotten genius of the seventeenth century – and I hope all Hooke fans will turn next to Inwood's remarkable biography. When Hooke died in 1703 he was alone and wretched and covered with lice, with a reputation as a sexually peculiar old miser. A view had gained ground among his contemporaries that he was querulous, boastful and an inveterate nicker of other people's ideas. It was not a fair verdict.

He was in fact one of the most astonishingly inventive minds of his or any age. He was almost Da Vinci like in his range of interests, from painting and architecture to a Daedalic array of scientific innovations and theories. He looked up; through large telescopes that stuck from his roof that enabled him to be the first man to see the spot on Jupiter, and the first to calculate the revolutions of Mars.

He looked down; through microscopic lenses of all kinds. Hooke was the first to squint at semen and notice the funny tadpoles within. He was the first to cut open a section of cork with a sharp penknife, place it under a microscope, and identify the little boxes that made up the tissue. He called them 'cells', the name they have borne ever since.

He not only designed the Monument and assorted churches, but a range of beautiful country houses. He is credited with the invention of the sash window. The air pump and the air gun emerged from his teeming brain, as well as Hooke's Law of Springs (strain is equal to stress), a principle of physics that is no less important for sounding a bit dull.

It was true that he came up with all manner of devices that he did not quite bring to perfection. There was the whalebone crossbow for killing whales, the self-replenishing lamp for seeing in the dark, the universal algebraic language, the semaphore using four-foot letters. He designed a bizarre batsuit for allowing a human being to fly, as well as thirty other flying contraptions, none of which got airborne. But his insights were often far ahead of his time.

Long before the invention of the stethoscope he said that it was more sensible to listen to the chest of a patient than to follow the normal practice and taste his urine. He looked at fossil shells and worked out that the biblical account of Creation could not be the whole story. He was the first to give a scientific lecture on the effects of cannabis and to propose that degrees of brightness should be measured in candlepower.

He deduced that there was an element in the air that allowed fire to burn and he even had a claim – a fateful one, as it turned out – to have hit on the principles of gravity before Isaac Newton. He has more entries than any other scientist in an authoritative encyclopaedia of the instruments of science – and yet until lately his career and achievements had been almost totally eclipsed by others. He is an illustration of the need to have good PR, and I hope to give him some now.

Robert Hooke was born in Freshwater on the Isle of Wight on 16 July 1635, the son of an impecunious vicar. His father hoped he would study for the cloth, but young Hooke claimed a headache. He preferred to imitate local craftsmen, making wooden watches and floating model boats on the River Yar. His father died when he was thirteen, and by today's standards he then did something outlandish: he walked to London, carrying his entire inheritance of £100 in his pocket.

He arrived at a monster of a City, a place of 400,000 people – as big as the next fifty towns of England put together. As he proceeded through the sprawl of Southwark and over London Bridge, the boy would have seen at least some novelties unknown to Shakespeare. The fruits of trade were starting to appear – I mean literally fruits: bananas and pineapples from the tropics. Toothbrushes (invented in China in 1498) were at last making an impact on English dentition. The fork was becoming much more commonplace.

The London Bridge water pump had been augmented by a network of elm wood tubes – though nothing the Romans would have found especially impressive. People were carried around in sedan chairs or even hackney carriages, and fashionable women wore funny black patches on their faces, in the shape of stars or crescent moons, though they did not, on the whole, wear knickers. Men increasingly wore wigs. London was acquiring the social and cultural division that has lasted to this day, between an affluent and politically powerful West end, and an East end full of relative poverty. The first great squares had been laid out at Covent Garden and Lincoln's Inn Fields. But there was one respect in which the London of Robert Hooke's arrival was very like the London of William Shakespeare and even Dick Whittington: it was still a city of awful plagues, and at its heart was a network of higgledy piggledy streets and overhanging wooden houses. It was one great firetrap.

Showing considerable gumption, Hooke took himself to the house of the portrait painter Peter Lely – the man who painted Cromwell, 'warts and all.' He might have been apprenticed to the artist, since he had flair for drawing, but paint, like religion, gave him a headache. He headed next for Westminster School, where he presented his cash to the great Dr Busby and asked for an education.

Busby specialised in what we would now call flagellation. His results were remarkable. Contemporaries of Hooke included John Locke and John Dryden, and in a short space of time the adolescent had mastered the organ, the first six books of Euclid and become proficient in Latin and Greek while dabbling in Hebrew and other Eastern languages. He was also starting to look a bit odd. He was said to be 'very mechanical' at Westminster, and he later claimed that he spent so much time on the Turn-Lath that he twisted his back.

His condition has been subsequently diagnosed as Scheuermann's kyphosis, which involves the development of wedge-shaped spaces between the vertebrae. Whatever the cause of his malformation, he was generally agreed to be a sorry sight, with pointy features and bulging eyes in an overlarge head. Up to Christ Church, Oxford, went this strange hunched spermatozoon, and there he fell in with a group of scientists – or 'philosophers' as they called themselves – though even our modern term science is too narrow to capture their range of interests and enthusiasms.

It was an age of post-Copernican confidence in reason, and man's ability to disprove the judgment of the ancients. Galileo had pointed his optic tube at the heavens and the geocentric view of the universe was no more. Aristotle had been dethroned. A school of English science had been born – an empirical school in which you tested things in practice and then tried to deduce a theory.

Not for them the approach of René Descartes and the French, which was – and to some extent still is – to establish whether something could work in theory before establishing whether it was any good in practice. Hooke was recruited by his fellow student Robert Boyle, Old Etonian son of the Earl of Cork – the author of Boyle's Law. Boyle noticed his mechanical gifts and set him to work on a vacuum pump. Also at Christ Church was Christopher Wren, with whom Hooke forged a working relationship that was to last decades and was to lead to at least a thousand meetings, walks and conversations between the two men, and untold riches for London. Boyle and Wren were among a widening circle of scientists and dilettanti that Hooke frequented on his return to the capital.

They debated everything from magnetism to human flight to the circulation of the blood. They bodged and fiddled and speculated, with beautiful devices of polished brass and wood. By the time of the Restoration in 1660 they needed more cash for their operations, and they were hopeful that King Charles II would live up to his reputation as a supporter of their inquiries. The Royal Society was formed. Since the King's subsidy was in fact rather disappointing, and since it was necessary to fund the Society through the subscriptions of its members, it consisted largely of periwigged toffs who could afford to pay. That was why it was so necessary to leaven this membership with genuine scientific talent.

Hooke was the ideal man to serve as their professional scientist, and in 1662 he was made curator of experiments. He was commissioned to give a series of lectures for a fixed stipend and to lead the quest for knowledge. He would delight the society by blowing up glass balls. He would do his best to oblige their barmy desire to grow moss on a dead man's skull or make a coach that ran on legs instead of wheels. He demonstrated the world's first pressure cooker, turning a cow – horns, hooves and all – into a kind of gelatinous paste that his fellow members claimed to find delicious.

It must be admitted that half the time Hooke and Co did not know what they were doing, but then nobody had tried their experiments before. So much of the world was a mystery.

They were puzzled by the act of breathing, and wanted to establish what the point of it was. Years ago Harvey had said it was to animate the blood, but it was not clear what that might mean. Hooke led a horrific experiment in which he cut open the thoracic cavity of a living dog and everyone craned round to try to work out the relation between the lungs and the heart. It was still not obvious. He vowed not to repeat the experiment, because of the torture of the poor hound. But only a few years later the Royal Society were at it again. Their curiosity was insatiable.

Did the air animate the frame, with the motion of the lungs somehow physically driving things along? Or was there perhaps something in the air that entered the bloodstream? Another dog was found (the first having expired) and Hooke punctured a hole in its pleural membrane, to which he fixed a tube and some bellows. By keeping the beast's lungs continuously filled with air he was able to establish the motion of the lungs was not indispensable to life.

The dog's eyes remained bright. He even wagged his tail. Aha, said Hooke and the Royal Society as the loyal dog breathed his last. There must be something in the air. But what?

Hooke was not afraid to experiment on himself, and at one stage he sealed himself in a case and made that case airtight by surrounding it by a separate container, with water in the gap. He then commanded the air to be pumped from around him, and only gave up when his ears began to pop. He self-medicated with a bewildering range of substances, and recorded his potations in his diary. He took sal ammoniae (ammonium chloride) and woke 'strangely refresht'. 'This is a great discovery in Physick. I hope that this will dissolve the viscous slime that hath so much tormented me in my stomach and gutts.'

Having drunk a strong cup of Turkish coffee he would try to counteract the caffeine with laudanum or syrup of poppies; or perhaps, to wake himself up again, he would shove some nutmeg or ginger or tobacco up his nostrils. One week he would have a daily dose of iron and mercury – these days regarded as more or less fatal – the next week he would sustain himself entirely with boiled milk. On one occasion he decided to drink two quarts of 'Dulwich water' from a source in south London, and found that it went down well. He later discovered that 'many have died of Fluxes and some of Spotted Feaver upon drinking Dulwich water', but one imagines that by this stage Hooke had an iron constitution.

I mean that literally: he would drink wine mixed with steel filings – to what medical end we are not told – and wake up with his head 'benumm'd'. His body could cope with almost anything. He took infusions of 'crocus metal' – probably oxysulphide of antimony – and vomited repeatedly the following day. He then moved on to stale Chester beer and then went to bed after a libation of spirit of urine and laudanum mixed with milk.

Then he switched to something called 'conserves' and 'flowers of sulphur' which he seemed to think worked all right on day one, though by the following day it had caused such bad and bloody dysentery that 'he swooned and was badly griped'. He was continually putting honey or bitter almond oil in his ear or taking enemas or being bled of seven ounces of blood. He was a walking testament to human resilience. Others were less fortunate.

When his friend John Wilkins, Bishop of Chester, fell ill with kidney stones, the prescription was four red-hot oyster shells in a quart of cider, and blistering with cantharides or Spanish fly. Wilkins died. Hooke was no less peculiar in what would now be called his private life. He does not seem to have been especially attractive to women, and though he had mistresses (several pairs of bras were found among his effects when he died) they were generally servants, or close relatives who were in some way dependent on him for shelter and income.

He would make a pass by 'wrastling' with them and he recorded his orgasms in his diary thus:)-(. So a typical entry might be the vigorous session he recorded with his servant Nell Young on 28 October 1672. 'Played with Nell.)-(. Hurt small of back.'

He was a Professor Branestawm, a man obsessed with Heath Robinson gadgets and breakthroughs, and yet with nothing like the tranquil obliviousness of Branestawm. Hooke was deeply conscious of his reputation, and vulnerable to mockery. On 25 May 1676 he was having coffee with some chums when he heard of a new play, called *The Virtuoso* by Thomas Shadwell. Restoration comedy was now in full swing. The barbarism of the Puritans was long forgotten. Hooke went to see what it was all about.

It was, I am afraid, all about him. It was a no-holds-barred parody of the Royal Society, their delectable disputations and crackpot experiments. In scene one the main character, Sir Nicholas Gimcrack, is discovered lying on a table in his laboratory, with a thread between his teeth, the other end of which is tied to the belly of a frog. He informs the audience that he is simultaneously learning to swim and to fly.

Everything seemed to be a reference to Hooke. Gimcrack is a man who spent thousands of pounds on microscopes to look at eels in vinegar, mites in cheese and the blue of plums. He uses absurd scientific terms, saying 'it comes first to fluidity, then to orbiculation, then fixation, so to angulization, then crystallization, from thence to germination or ebullition, then vegetation, then plantanimation, perfect animation, sensation, local motion and the like'. Everyone knew that this was lifted more or less directly – like all the best parodies – from Hooke's ground-breaking work *Micrographia*, his beautifully drawn account of the fleas and lice and nettle stings he could see with his microscope.

Shadwell then went on to make fun of Hooke's wacko transfusions, as Gimcrack and his sidekick, Sir Formal Trifle, describe how they have transferred blood between dogs and even put sheep's blood into a madman. This last was taken direct from life.

Hooke and his colleagues had tried in vain to get the physicians at the Bethlem to let them experiment on their patients, and they had at last persuaded a mentally unsound divinity graduate called Arthur Coga to be given a transfusion of lamb's blood and a fee of one pound for his pains. He seems to have survived this lunacy, and the Hooke character Gimcrack boasts of the success of the operation. He ceased to be mad and became wholly ovine, he tells the audience. He sprouted wool all over. 'I shall shortly have a flock of 'em. I'll make all my own clothes of 'em.'

The idiotic Gimcrack is then seen reading the Geneva Bible by the light of a rotting leg of pork, making a tarantula dance to music and watching military campaigns take place on the surface of the moon. All these activities were references to Hooke's notions or experiments, and yet the point and message of the play was the most stinging thing of all. As the comedy moves to its climax, Gimcrack's house is besieged by a mob of ribbon weavers complaining that he had invented a machine that would put them out of work. Hooke/Gimcrack comes out to appease them.

'Hear me, gentlemen,' he says. 'I never invented an engine in my life. As God shall save me, you do me wrong. I never invented so much as an engine to pare cream cheese with. We virtuosos never find out anything of use. 'Tis not our way.'

Sitting in the audience, Hooke burned with indignation. His life and work were being held up to the most withering satire. People were holding their sides with laughter. 'Damned dogs,' he wrote in his diary. *Vindica me Deus* – may God avenge me. 'People almost pointed.'

As a criticism of Hooke, the notion of uselessness was especially unfair. So much of what he did was practical; so many of his experiments were sheer economic logic. England for most of his life had been engaged in a struggle with Holland for maritime supremacy, and London was the centre of an expanding commercial empire. The tonnage of shipping in England's foreign trade rose 60 per cent between 1630 and 1660, and a further 80 per cent between 1660 and 1688. In other words, the number of ships in England's merchant fleet more than doubled in Hooke's lifetime.

It was crucial for all those captains to have an idea of where they were, to avoid being shipwrecked and to avoid being beaten by the Dutch. That is why Hooke worked so hard on all manner of aids to navigation. There were his quadrants and sextants, minutely engineered with their little brass screws and their markings so fine as to be invisible to the naked eye; these were to be used for gauging one's position against the stars. There was a shipboard windmill that he hoped (vainly) might be handy for turning a capstan and shifting a boat off the shallows. He invented a depth sounder and a wheel barometer.

He even tried his hand at diving equipment and personally pioneered the idea that it might be possible to breathe underwater with a sponge soaked in salad oil pressed to your mouth. It was not a success. His next solution was a series of inverted buckets full of trapped air, which was little better. He threw himself like a ravenous squirrel at the toughest nut of all – the secret of longitude.

It wasn't that he particularly wanted to tell the time that he worked so hard on the spring-regulated watch – a new concept to replace the primitive escapements that had existed since the Middle Ages. It was because he believed a mariner would have a much better chance of working out his longitude if he had an accurate record of the time at dawn and sunset.

As for his terrestrial projects, it wasn't for the sheer intellectual pleasure of it that he formulated Hooke's catenary law of arches – viz that an arch should exhibit the same curve as an inverted hanging chain. He came up with the theory because he built a hell of a lot of arches, and he needed them to last. He produced his work on road engineering because people genuinely couldn't make up their minds.

Was it more efficient to have a smooth journey on a soft road or a bumpy journey on a hard road? Hard and bumpy was best, said Hooke, and the thinner the wheels of your carriage the better. Across a vast front Robert Hooke advanced human understanding, sometimes by small steps, sometimes by leaps, and his satisfaction was the esteem of his peers.

To understand the scientific revolution of the seventeenth century, you have to peer into the coffee shops that had sprung up in his lifetime, and which had become a characteristic institution of the city. They had begun in 1652 with Pasqua Rosee's Head, opened in St Michael's Alley off Cornhill by a Turkish immigrant called Pasqua Rosee. The coffee shops sold the exotic provender that English merchantmen were locating with ever increasing navigational accuracy in the waters of the Indies and the Americas.

There was Arabian coffee, West Indian sugar, Virginia tobacco, China tea and South American cocoa. By the time Hooke died in 1703 there were five hundred of the places. Hooke's favourites were Garraways or Jonathan's or Man's, but he spread his favours widely. He loved coffee houses because they were places you could show off. They were marts of ideas. His diary records that he would go to Man's and chew the fat with Christopher Wren or John Aubrey, and in one coffee-slurping session they would cover the scotoscope for seeing in the dark, the refraction of light, the anatomy of the helical muscle of the gut and the way cliff pigeons love salt. He and Wren then had a more detailed discussion of Hooke's plans for a flying chariot with horses.

The coffee shop was a place you might go to tell your friends about a new technique of glassmaking or how to make phosphorus. If you were lucky, a chap in a coffee shop might let fall some priceless piece of information, such as 'quicklime, white of eggs, blood or slime of snails makes a cement for water pipes as hard as stone'; and sometimes Hooke would share some tip of his own: such as his discovery that if you cut off the top of your thumb you could cure it in four days with Balsamum Peruvianum.

Very often the assembly of philosophers and virtuosi would be so carried away that they would conduct experiments on the spot. Hooke twice climbed to the ceiling of Garraway's to prove that the Earth was rotating in a certain direction. A dropped ball would fall slightly to the south east of the place where you would expect it to land if it fell in a straight line, he claimed; not because the ball had swerved but because the Earth had moved while it was in flight.

On at least one occasion the experiment seemed to work. The ball landed to the south east of true. Great was his rejoicing. It was a heady atmosphere, fed by the new drugs of nicotine and caffeine and cocoa, and the competition for acclaim was intense. In due time the London coffee shops were to become places where people traded stocks and shares or bought insurance. Lloyds of London was born in a coffee shop. From the very beginning they were places where reputations rose and fell as if on a bourse.

You could figuratively buy Hookes or sell Boyles or Newtons, depending on how the philosophers were doing with their experiments. The coffee shops became such hotbeds of gossip and rumour that at one stage in 1675 the King attempted to have them shut down. 'In such houses divers false malitious and scandalous reports are devised and spread abroad, to the defamation of His Majesty's government and the disturbance of the peace and quiet of the realm,' it was proclaimed – though later the King was talked out of so unpopular a measure.

Hooke often recorded how he was received by his fellow coffee-drinkers, on one occasion noting dolefully that they drank everyone's health but his own. This was the environment in which his ego was either pumped or deflated, and as he encountered other scientists and their achievements he engaged in the feuding that was to cost him so dear.

His problem was that he experimented in so many fields that he was always jealous of any advance that he had missed. He rowed terribly with the great Dutch scientist Christiaan Huygens over who had been the first to invent the spring-regulated watch. To make matters worse he accused the poor Secretary of the Royal Society, an excellent man called Henry Oldenburg, of passing his breakthroughs over to the foreigner.

Hooke's conceit was often to announce, on hearing of some development, that he had come up with the idea years ago, and he would offer to prove it at the next meeting. So he would go off and rootle around in his papers, and sometimes he did indeed find some kind of apparent confirmation. When he formulated his famous law of springs, he was so excited that he wrote it down in code, so that no one who swiped his diary should be able to work it out. He wrote 'ceiinosssttuu', which is an anagram of '*ut tensio sic vis*.'

He was once in a coffee shop imparting the secret of flight to his friend Edmund Wild when three strangers walked in. Hooke clammed up, and Wild – along with the rest of the world – was to remain in the dark.

He fell out badly with John Flamsteed, the future Astronomer Royal, who as a young man wrote to Hooke asking for advice on an optical problem. Sensing an attempt to steal his ideas, Hooke refused, and Flamsteed wrote plaintively: 'He affirms to know several secrets of the meliorating and improving of optics, of which we have yet had no treatise ... Why burns this lamp in secret?' Hooke called him a 'conceited coxcomb'.

The feud with Flamsteed blew up at Garraways in 1681 when they were having a discussion about lenses. Tell you what, Flamsteed, said Hooke 'somewhat captiously' – laying a trap for his opponent – if you have a lens with a flat side and a convex side, which side should you point at the heavens? Poor Flamsteed was caught off guard. He panicked. Er, it doesn't much matter, he said, but on the whole the flat side should point at the sky.

Ha! Hooke pounced and launched a verbal battery designed to show that it had to be curvy side up. 'He bore down on me with words enough and persuaded the company that I was ignorant in these things which he only understood not I', protested the astronomer.

Hooke caused great international offence by writing an essay attacking the Polish astronomer Johann Hevelius, and accusing him of using primitive and out of date technology. I, Hooke, he proclaimed, am in the process of constructing a sensational new quadrant for the study of the heavens, a machine far better than anything made by Hevelius.

It was indeed a marvel, full of novelties such as a water level for exact perpendicular and a clockwork mechanism for diurnal rotation. But it didn't really work, and some of its refinements took centuries to be perfected in the hands of others. Hevelius wrote bitterly against those who sought to destroy his good name and reputation, and who seemed to despise everything they did. Where was the evidence, he demanded, that Hooke could produce the goods himself? And a lot of people thought there was something in what Hevelius said.

When Hooke was not claiming that he had pre-invented just about everything, he was stealthily trying to borrow the ideas of others. Gottfried Wilhelm Leibniz arrived in London with his calculating machine. Hooke prowled behind it, removed the back plate and – much to the consternation of Leibniz – produced his own mechanical calculator.

This machine worked well and was favourably reviewed until someone pointed out that it was no quicker than pen and paper. Never mind! said Hooke, in typical style. 'I have an instrument now making, which will perform the same effects with the German, which will not have a tenth part of the number of parts …' and so on. The machine did not materialise, but Leibniz was appalled at his conduct, and wrote in strong terms to the Royal Society.

Hooke was a scrapper and a controversialist, a man who despite his undoubted achievements was acquiring a reputation as a braggart. And yet all of these rows and feuds might have been forgotten had he not picked a fight with the intellectual Goliath of his age.

It was Hooke's curse to fall out catastrophically with the man whose insight and genius were to dominate our understanding of the physical world for the next two hundred and fifty years. By the winter of 1683–4, Hooke's mind was roaming over all sorts of things. The Polish Jan

Sobieski had just saved Christendom by fending off the Turks at the gates of Vienna, so he was reminding the Royal Society of the possibilities of warning against invasions with hilltop semaphores and telescopes.

It was also the coldest winter in memory, and Londoners had the first Frost Fair for one hundred and twenty years. The Thames froze solid for seven weeks, and there were shops and booths set out in formal streets on the ice. Londoners entertained themselves with horse and coach races. There was bear- and bull-baiting and there were plays and brothels, and in the words of John Evelyn it was altogether a Bacchanalian triumph.

Hooke made himself useful, meanwhile, by working out the durability of the ice on which they frolicked. He took a bar three and a half inches thick and four inches wide and fifteen inches long, and determined that it would not break until it was asked to take a weight of 350 pounds. He also verified, by means of an especially complicated experiment, that a block of ice weighed seven-eighths as much as water of equivalent volume, and that one-eighth of the bulk of an iceberg would therefore appear above the surface of the sea: another helpful thing for sailors to know.

It was in this busy January 1684 that he was having a conversation with Sir Christopher Wren and Edmond Halley, and Hooke boasted that he had cracked the inverse square law. OK, said Wren, who was by now President of the Royal Society. I'll give you two months to bring me a proof and you can have a prize of forty shillings. Peasy, said Hooke, with typical self-assurance. I've had it taped for ages. I am just waiting for others to try and fail for a good long time, so they will really appreciate my efforts when I make them public.

Wren raised an eyebrow. Oh yeah? he said, or words to that effect. You betcha, said Hooke, and went off, alas, to do something completely different.

The inverse square law is one of the building blocks of the universe. It states that the gravitational attraction between two bodies is the inverse square of the distance between them. So if the distance between body x and body y is ten, then the gravitational attraction between them is 1/100. Hooke had in fact speculated about gravity in some of his lectures, and he had written to Isaac Newton in 1679 suggesting that the inverse square law might apply. The idea was not original to him – a Frenchman called Bullialdus seems to have been first in 1645 – and he certainly had not offered a mathematical proof. But that letter and his sense of unacknowledged priority were to become a source of poisonous rancour.

After Wren had issued his challenge to Hooke, Edmond Halley went off and repeated the conversation to Newton, who had been made Lucasian professor of Mathematics at Cambridge at the age of twenty-nine, and it was the pale, mystic and flowing-haired Newton who now decided to apply himself seriously to the problem.

Hooke continued with his kaleidoscopic curriculum. One day he was developing strange boingy-boingy shoes that he claimed could propel him twelve feet upwards and twenty feet forwards – though we have no eyewitness accounts of an egg-headed man bouncing down the street, and we may assume that this was one of his inventions that was still being perfected.

He continued to give his Gresham lectures, sometimes very sparsely attended – a solitary fat man or a group of schoolboys picking their noses. Sometimes he would go and sit in the lectures given by his enemy Flamsteed, gazing so balefully that Flamsteed accused him of driving the rest of the audience away.

He had learned Dutch so that he could read the works of the great microscopist Leeuwenhoek, and now he tried to learn Chinese. But the proof of the inverse square law he did not attempt.

It was Newton who buried himself for two years in his room, and who thought deeply about the way the heavens and the Earth were put together. In April 1686 he published his findings. Amid the happy fossickings of the Royal Society into their favourite topics – pressure-cooked chocolate, monstrous infants, giant intestinal worms – Newton's *Philosophiae Naturalis Principia Mathematica* arrived like a bombshell.

On 28 April 1686 Sir John Hoskins chaired a meeting at which he declared that Newton's work was 'so much more to be prized, for that it was both Invented and perfected at the same time'. Hooke was enraged. He was convinced that Newton had filched the idea from him, and made the point volubly at the coffee house after the meeting.

'Hooke made a great stir, pretending Newton had it all from him, and desiring they would see he had justice done him,' said an eyewitness. News of Hooke's behaviour reached Newton, and Newton was frankly even more outraged than Hooke. It was one thing to posit the inverse square law of gravity – an intuitive conclusion from the obvious fact that gravity was a notably weak force. It was a quite different thing to be able to sit down and do the original mathematics.

As he heard more and more of Hooke's obstreperousness, Newton's fury grew. Hooke pretended that he could not be bothered with the drudgery of dry calculations and observations, whereas the reality was that he simply wasn't capable of it, raged Newton. 'For tis plain by his words that he knew not how to go about it.' It was a cruel remark, but probably true, and Hooke was deeply stung.

To the end of his days he continued to fume. In 1690 we find him referring to the inverse square law as 'the theory I had the happiness to invent'; or to 'the proprietys of gravity which I myself first discovered and showed to this society many years since ... Of late Mr Newton has done me the favour to print and publish as his own invention.'

Instead of doing him justice, Hooke said, Newton had made a pretence of falling out with him and being offended. It was all to no avail. The argument was lost. Indeed, the argument was probably lost that first evening in the coffee house, when Hooke protested his primacy. He had boasted too often, he had claimed credit too freely.

Whatever insights he may have had into gravity, he lost sympathy by his peevishness. Newton struck his name out of the third book of *Principia Mathematica*, and in later texts he was downgraded from Clarissimus Hookius (most distinguished Hooke) to plain Hookius.

The feud only ended with Hooke's death in 1703. The way was open for Newton to be made President of the Royal Society, a post he occupied for twenty-four years. There are those who think the all-powerful Newton now engaged in an eradication of the memory of the man who had so irritated him. They blame Newton for the fact that we do not have a single demonstrable likeness of Robert Hooke. Whether or not Isaac Newton actively conspired to burn paintings of his critic – and it seems unlikely – Hooke has come down to us as an archetypal sore loser, an also-ran, a hunched and bitter Salieri unable to reconcile himself to the incandescent Mozartian genius of Newton.

In reality, you might argue, it was Newton who was the loner, the recluse, the weirdo who dabbled in black magic. It is Hooke who emerges from Inwood's study as an engaging and basically clubbable man. Yes, his domestic and sexual relations were peculiar, and given that for many years his mistress was his niece Grace, he was lucky to live under the Restoration rather than under the Puritans. But there is a kind of odd sweetness to his nature.

He had a free-spirited housekeeper called Martha, and sometimes he would take refuge from her impudence with his former housekeeper and mistress Nell Young. It is perhaps a measure of his generosity that he remained on good terms with Nell, even though she ran off and slept with a younger man shortly after Hooke injured his back in the course of)-(. Sometimes he would go off and have 'much discourse' and tea and cake, though not)-(with a Mrs Moore.

He would dine with Pepys, who rated him so highly that he said 'he is the most, and promises the least, of any man in the world that I ever saw.' It was a measure of his indefatigable love of science that he continued to give his lectures when no one much could be bothered to come.

He was a gregarious soul, who was endlessly going for walks with his friends, or just hanging out in coffee houses with Francis Lodwick or 'Lod', John Hoskins or 'Hosk', Richard Waller or 'Wall', Edmond Halley or 'Hall', Alexander Pitfield or 'Pif' and Mr Currer or 'Cur'. He wasn't always that obsessive about his reputation, in that he happily let Wren and others take the credit for buildings that he had played a major role in designing or constructing. His range of accomplishments was vast.

Together with his favourite watchmaker Nicholas Tompion, he effectively launched the London clock and watch industry in Clerkenwell. He seems to have been very near to formulating a theory of evolution, saying that there had obviously been species in the past that no longer existed, and that 'it seems very absurd to conclude that from the beginning things have been in the state we now find them.'

He asked himself whether Ireland and America might not have been formerly joined, whether the bottom of the sea might have been dry land, and what is dry land might have been the sea. He was on to something big, and he knew it.

He was a scientific optimist, who wanted people to 'throw off that lazy and pernicious principle, to know as much as their fathers, grandfathers or great-grandfathers did.' At one stage of their long feud, Newton wrote him what was meant to be a conciliatory letter, in which he made the famous remark that 'if I have seen further, it is because I have been standing on the shoulders of giants.' He is not generally thought to have been referring to Hooke. But if he wasn't, he should have been. Robert Hooke had many triumphs, but made two big mistakes.

Like so many British scientists who have followed him, he failed to draw the full commercial and practical conclusions of his breakthroughs. And he allowed the first draft of his story to be written by those who wanted to put him down.

* * *

If you had ascended to the top of the dome of St Paul's in 1700, shortly before Hooke died, you would have looked out over a city that was still breathtakingly rural.

Hyde Park and St James's Park were surrounded by farmland or open fields. Inigo Jones's Covent Garden piazza was part of an island of development; but north of Holborn and west of Charing Cross there was a sea of green. Down Fleet Street and the Strand you could see gardens with rose bushes and lavender. Orchards peeped from behind the city taverns, while Hampstead and Highgate were distant hilltop hamlets. From your eyrie you would have heard the lowing of cattle being herded to market and the hissing of geese as they chased a lady's sedan chair. You could see boys fishing or swimming in the river by what was still – incredibly – the only bridge across the Thames.

London Bridge looked increasingly tatty. The Tudor Nonsuch House was in a state of decay, and other shops and houses had been lost to fire, giving a gap-toothed and tumbledown impression. From the top of St Paul's you could see that London was still essentially a collection of mediaeval villages – one hundred and fifty of them – each of them centred on its own church, inn or marketplace. Every village had its mixture of classes: posh houses and little rows of cottages; and people of all backgrounds would meet in the same churches and hostelries, and cheer the same kind of mediaeval processions that Dick Whittington had come upon when he arrived in London.

What you would not have spotted, hundreds of feet up, was the impact of the technical changes proceeding from the brains of men like Robert Hooke: hundreds of inventions that were cumulatively to transform agriculture, manufacturing and trade of all kinds. You would not have guessed, as you listened to the distant bleating and shouting of London, that this was a society on the verge of making the terrifying leap from agrarian to industrial. And yet the world's first steam-powered pump had just been built in 1698, in London, by Thomas Savery; and though it was a pretty inefficient contraption it led directly to James Watt's device of 1776. Jethro Tull was about to produce his revolutionary seed drill of 1701. The furnaces of Coalbrookdale would be alight by 1709.

And so if you had gone up to look from that dome of St Paul's, one hundred years later, you would have found the city changed out of all recognition. As your eye swept the horizon you would have found it hard to tell where the city ended. People had switched from burning wood to Newcastle coal, and the air was thick with brown smoke. You could see the noble squares that had been laid out after the Treaty of Utrecht in 1713 – Grosvenor Square and Mayfair. You could see the masterpieces of Georgian architecture that succeeding generations have tried to emulate: Berkeley Square, Cavendish Square, Portland Place, Fitzroy Square. You could see that the bridge had been rebuilt, with every shop and house knocked down, and the mediaeval arches completely reclad in stone. Now there was also Westminster Bridge, opened in 1750, with tiny black figures scurrying across, and Blackfriars bridge, opened in 1769. As your eye swept from east to west you could see the growing gulf in reputation between the two sides of London: fancy houses in the west, with rows of plane trees and chestnuts in the squares; appalling tenements in the east.

Stretching as far as you could see were ribbons of houses, bounded by brick kilns and gravel workings and rubbish pits burning with Phlegethontean fire. You could see the sweatshops and factories and mills and shipyards where Londoners now worked, men and women, pitifully old and monstrously young, in often degrading conditions. Stables and cowsheds had become dormitories for labourers who had migrated from the countryside, in flight from the enclosures. The roofs of their dwellings fell on their heads; their wages failed to keep pace with the price of bread; they were continually vulnerable to technical advances – the spinning jenny, Arkwright's rollers – that devalued their labour, and yet they had no union to represent them. Their lives were short, their diseases exotic. They were as numerous as locusts and as poor as rats, as one observer put it.

The technological advances of Hooke and others had exalted the importance of machines; and since machines were expensive, society became ever more divided – between those who toiled at the looms, and those who owned or financed the means of production. As the capitalist and industrial revolution took place, London and England became vastly richer in per capita output; and yet some became much richer than others, and many lived in squalor. As London grew, the lives of Londoners became more unequal. There were, as ever, two responses to this problem.

There was the conservative view, that inequality was an unavoidable part of the human condition, and perhaps even divinely ordained; and then there were radicals, people who put themselves at the head of movements for change, who campaigned for the emancipation of the poor. Two of the very greatest eighteenth-century Londoners can be broadly said to embody these divergent views of the world. There was Samuel Johnson, who has a claim to be called the father of compassionate Conservatism; and then there was his foe John Wilkes, the London demagogue and radical he despised and railed against, and with whom he was eventually reconciled.

THE KING JAMES BIBLE

'In the beginning God created the heavens and the earth,' says Genesis 1.1, and there are large numbers of Americans – perhaps millions – who believe that to be literally true. They hold that the world was created in 4004 BC, and that God fashioned every creature that walks or crawls on the face of the earth, and that He plonked them there in their current form. They therefore dispute the most important theory of the last two years (evolution; formulated by Charles Darwin in London), and they hold their beliefs with rock-like certainty thanks to the power and persuasiveness of a single book.

When the pioneers lurched in their wagons across the prairies, shooting Indians and buffalo, they did so armed with the same book that British missionaries took to India and China and Africa. It was a London book – or at least the London version of an ancient book. The story of the King James Bible or the Authorised Version begins in 1604, shortly after the accession of the stuttering and sexually ambiguous Scottish monarch.

The Church of England was still new, and plagued with factions of all kinds. So in a stroke of genius he brought the clerics together for a conference at Hampton Court, and though they bickered about this or that point of doctrine, they agreed on one thing: that it was time to produce a single and authenticated version of the word of the Lord. Six companies or committees of scholars were formed, in London, Oxford and Cambridge, with forty-seven translators altogether, almost all of them members of the clergy.

The leader of the London operation – charged with rendering Genesis to Kings II – was Lancelot Andrewes, and if there is one man who can be said to have been in overall control of the mission, it was Andrewes. He was a bishop, scholar, and preacher of famous sermons, a man of such naturally poetic diction that TS Eliot ripped him off without acknowledgment in 'the Journey of the Magi' ('A cold coming we had of it ...').

The work of translation went on for years, and though the scholars were disrupted and dismayed by the Gunpowder Plot of 1605, James urged them on in the name of religious harmony. In 1609 the Revising Committee met in Stationer's Hall, in Ave Maria Lane in London, and as

David Crystal has pointed out, the Bible was written in a London dialect that had been moving towards standardisation since Caxton's day.

All sorts of criticisms have been made of the King James version. Many of the most familiar quotations are in fact from William Tyndale's 1534 edition: let there be light, the truth shall make you free, let my people go, am I my brother's keeper?, the powers that be, the signs of the times, blessed are the peacemakers ... Even for 1609, it was written in archaic-sounding language. People had by then stopped saying 'verily' and 'it came to pass' and they said 'you' instead of 'thee' or 'thou' and 'appears' instead of 'appeareth'.

Hebrew experts said it had failed to capture the original, with fourteen different Hebrew words all being rendered in English as 'prince'. One learned Hebraist said he 'would rather be torn in pieces by wild horses than that this abominable translation should ever be foisted on the English people'. Even though the government proclaimed that this was the only edition appointed to be read in churches, it took some time for the text to become truly agreed. One unfortunate printing of 1631 left the word 'not' out of the commandment – 'Thou shalt not commit adultery'.

But it was the King James Bible that took hold in men's hearts, perhaps because of an inspired feature of the revising process. It was agreed that a selection from each company should edit the other company's work. This was done by reading out the entire text for a revising panel to review.

So the work was written to be spoken aloud, and the words gained their matchless euphony. 'It lives in the ear,' said F.W. Faber, 'like music that can never be forgotten'.

The King James Bible has contributed 257 idioms to the language, more than any other work. Tony Blair and George W Bush allegedly studied it together. So they knew what it meant to have 'feet of clay' or to 'reap the whirlwind'.

Samuel Johnson

He gave the world compassionate conservatism

Say the words Samuel Johnson's London and we conjure an image of England's first great age of liberty, and enlightenment, and all-round fun.

When we close our eyes and think of the eighteenth century, we see coffee houses, and 3-am revels, and women talking back for the first time in history, and rakes lolling against the bared bosoms of fan-waving beldames, and all around a ferment of science and medicine and literacy and burgeoning democracy.

So it is a shock to come across an episode that reminds you how much society has changed in a few hundred years and how the British state, in that supposedly enviable period, could do things to its citizens that we find barbaric today.

Such as the punishment proposed for a peculiar clergyman named William Dodd. At the age of forty-eight he had become one of the most popular preachers in London. His sermons were so packed with nobs and ladies of fashion that queues formed outside the church, and he was so moving on the subject of prostitution that his audience, some of them prostitutes personally rescued by Dodd – would sob and wail as he spoke. He had a long perfumed robe of silk, and a diamond ring, and he threw swish parties at a country house adorned with paintings by Titian, Rembrandt and Rubens, and in due course he naturally fell into debt.

He decided to borrow from the Earl of Chesterfield, one of his former pupils, a man who had been very generous in the past. Except that on this occasion Dodd decided to save time by not telling the Earl, forging his signature on a bond for £4,200, and vaguely assuming that Chesterfield, if he discovered the theft, would allow him to pay it back over time. Alas, the Earl had failed to see the funny side.

On 26 May 1777 Dodd was sentenced to be hanged to death. In his agony, Dodd knew that his only hope was to appeal to the mercy of the authorities – ultimately, in those days, the King. And he knew that there was only one man who had the clout, the literary gifts, the force of argument and the sheer moral prestige to make that appeal. In his hour of peril, Dodd reached for a sixty-eight-year-old lexicographer, poet, biographer and all-round genius, a man accepted throughout the kingdom as England's principal man of letters, the sole author of the first dictionary of the language and therefore the supreme admiral of the all-conquering fleet of English words that has sailed into every port and up every creek and inlet in the world. That man was Samuel Johnson.

It is easy to forget how huge a celebrity he was, and by the standards of modern celebrity he looked pretty peculiar. He had a proud Roman conk and prominent lips, and a small ill-fitting wig perched on top of his head. He had scars from infantile scrofula and an operation on the lymph glands in his neck, and he had lost the use of one eye, and when he walked it was with a lurching spasm as though he were in fetters, and he blurted and twitched and dribbled so compulsively that he was turned down for several early teaching jobs on the grounds that he would scare the pupils.

He ate with fierce concentration, veins bulging and a sheen of sweat appearing on his brow; and yet he had such natural charisma that women sought the right to sit near him at tea, and men of power would attend his shambolic morning levee in the hope that some pearl would fall from those flobbery lips.

This reverence can seem puzzling. Who reads *Rasselas*, his allegorical yarn about a prince of Abyssinia? He wrote one play, a tragedy called *Irene*, in which the heroine was garrotted on stage in the final act, provoking such howls of merriment that it folded after nine days. TS Eliot argued that he should be ranked among the major English poets, and yet there cannot be an A-level student who studies 'London' or 'The Vanity of Human Wishes'. His essays were hailed as masterpieces then and ever since, and yet they are exactly the kind of volumes that council libraries are selling off for 10p or sending to landfill. As for his poems in Latin and Greek, I expect their audience in modern literary London is exactly nil.

In so far as he is remembered, it is as the great harrumphing voice of political incorrectness, a literary John Bull, whose views would today be considered outré to the point of unacceptability. On a casual reading he seems to be a sexist, xenophobic, monarchy-loving, free-market defender of the inevitability, indeed the desirability, of human inequality. It is hard to see how any modern Fleet Street editor would dare employ him.

He was willing to love all mankind, he declared, except an American. 'Sir, they are a race of convicts, and ought to be thankful for anything we allow them short of hanging.' Ireland was worth seeing, but not worth going to see. The French were dirty, blowing into the spouts of teapots to make them pour properly.

As for the Scots, they were mainly liars who had no cabbage until Cromwell introduced it, and they subsisted on horse-food, and the finest sight a Scottish person could see was the high road leading to England. He thought the decline in the use of the cane would harm educational attainment, since what boys gained at one end they lost at the other.

His views on women were so outrageously chauvinist that no one, even on the *Sun*, even on the *Daily Telegraph*, would dream of printing them. 'Wise women don't trouble themselves about the infidelity of their husbands,' he decreed, though when he heard that Lady Diana Beauclerk was giving her husband the run-around he adopted a shameless double standard. 'The woman's a whore, and there's an end on it.'

It wasn't just that Samuel Johnson was opposed to women having jobs. He thought it was a bit off for them even to paint or draw. 'Public practice of any art, and staring in men's faces, is very indelicate in a female,' he said; and as for a woman preaching, it 'was like a dog walking on its hind legs. It is not done well, but you are surprised to find it done at all.'

I tried this gag on a fifteen-year-old daughter. She was notably underwhelmed.

And yet Johnson was so venerated in his lifetime that George III paid him a stipend of £300 a year just to exist. Tourists would come in search of a glimpse of his residence at Johnson Court off Fleet Street, like rubbernecking fans amid the mansions of Beverly Hills. When he died Edmund Burke was among his pallbearers; he was buried at Westminster Abbey, with a cenotaph at St Paul's and another memorial at Lichfield Cathedral and across the land there were assorted sermons on this doleful event in the life of the nation.

His conversational squibs, his sallies, his ruminations were each deemed so individually precious that they were noted down by the Scottish lawyer and patron saint of journalism, James Boswell, and consecrated in a 1,400-page biography which is itself one of the landmarks of our literature.

How did Johnson become so famous that Boswell thought it worth scurrying after him, notebook in hand, to record his slightest grunt? It is a story of struggle, failure, depression and a neurotic compulsion to achieve.

Samuel Johnson was born in Lichfield, Staffordshire on 18 September 1709, and he sometimes liked to imply that his background was very humble indeed. 'I have great merit in being jealous for subordination and for the honour of birth,' he bragged, 'for I can hardly tell who was my grandfather.'

This was going it a bit. Johnson's father Michael was actually Sheriff of Lichfield, and his mother was dimly connected to various members of the gentry. It was certainly true that Michael, already fifty-two when Samuel was born, was not the most dynamic of booksellers, and all his life Johnson dreaded his father's ineffectual bumbling and 'bustle', which he defined as 'getting on horseback on ship'.

Encouraged by the elderly antiquarian, Johnson the schoolboy showed much verbal promise, punching out poems in Latin and English on subjects ranging from daffodils to the battle between the Pygmies and the Cranes. At the age of nineteen he went to Pembroke College, Oxford, and it was here that he sustained his first major reverse. Johnson the elder fell into debt, and Samuel became so poor that he faced the humiliation of not being able to complete his studies. When a fellow-student noticed his toes poking through his shoes, and kindly left a new pair outside his room, Johnson threw them away in a rage.

After four terms he was forced to quit Pembroke, leaving his books ignominiously at Oxford, and for years he went into a depression. Teaching jobs came and went until Johnson had reached the age of twenty-five without a single consummated love affair. At which point he married a merchant's widow called Elizabeth Porter.

The relationship has filled scholars with a prurient psychological rapture. It was one of the accidents of Johnson's childhood that his mother gave him immediately to a wet nurse, whose milk was sadly infected with the tuberculosis that scarred his face. What did it mean to the young man that his bride was fully twenty years older than him? Was it important that she was described as 'very fat with a bosom of more than ordinary protuberance?' Why did he call her 'Tetty' or 'Tetsy'? You don't have to be Sigmund Freud to have a stab at that one.

Johnson and Tetty set up a school together near Birmingham, and among the pupils was the young David Garrick, who would later regale fashionable London dinner parties with affectionate but hilarious through-the-keyhole accounts of their conjugal relations. Despite the loyalty of a small band of pupils, the school eventually began to fail. Johnson was seized with dread that he would not be able to provide for Tetty, to whom he showed a deep devotion both in life and death. In 1737 a poverty-stricken Johnson, together with his brightest pupil David Garrick, began their famous 120-mile march to London.

In fact, they didn't walk all the way, but rode and tied with a single horse – one of them riding ahead on the horse, and then tying it to a tree or post for the other to pick up. When they came to London, they came to a place of between 650,000 and 700,000 souls and perhaps already the most populous city on Earth. It was a place of shattering poverty and dung in the streets, where the rural poor were being sucked in to feed London's hunger for labour, where neighbours were already unknown to each other. But it was also a place of exciting disputation, where blasts and counter-blasts were constantly being loaded into the metaphorical blunderbusses of literary men; and Johnson knew that London was the place where at last he could make his name.

'Why, sir,' he later said, 'you will find no man at all intellectual who is willing to leave London. No, sir, when a man is tired of London he is tired of life, for there is in London all that life can afford.' Having been pretty apathetic on the subject of God, Johnson was becoming devoutly religious, and all his life his character has a curious self-mortifying quality.

Like many creative people, his temperament involved indolence and footling around, sometimes assisted by alcohol, followed by a crescendo of guilt, followed by a frenzy of productivity. London provided all a man could need to spur him to action. There was the simple need for money, and to keep his wife; and as he pointed out with his characteristic bluff Johnsonian pseudo-philistinism, 'No man but a blockhead ever wrote except for money.'

There was the need to prove himself. He was an Oxford dropout, a failed teacher, and a provincial. He said 'woonce' instead of once, and 'shuperior' instead of superior, and David Garrick, who rapidly attained fame as an actor and producer, used to take him off by squeezing a lemon into a punchbowl, with uncouth gesticulations, looking around the company and calling out, 'Who's for poonsh?'

Although Johnson was a dogged defender of the class system, he could be sensitive to slights. Even when he was famous, there was a nasty moment when a society hostess failed to introduce either Johnson or Sir

Joshua Reynolds to two posh ladies, the Duchess of Argyle and Lady Fitzroy; and after the two men, leaders of the great professions of letters and painting, had been waiting in the corner in embarrassed silence, Johnson called out in a loud voice, 'I wonder which of us two could get most money by his trade in one week, were we to work hard at it from morning to night?'

Even though he believed ideologically in the necessity of rank, we can detect a buried indignation that people could out-gun him by birth and not talent; and that aggression was part of his success. It was an age when men judged each other not just by money or other worldly measures, but by the swiftness and smartness of their conversation. Long before *Have I Got News For You*, or *Never Mind the Buzzcocks*, or *QI*, or any of such banter-based programmes, the British were interested in wit and repartee, and Samuel Johnson was the champ.

He was the king of the tart rejoinder, the master of the scorching put-down, and he didn't mind who knew it. Oliver Goldsmith, he would declare, was good on paper but hopeless viva voce. Charles James Fox was hooked on the easy applause of the Commons, but never went *mano a mano* with the master. Edmund Burke, now – Burke was a different matter. The author of *Reflections on the Revolution in France* is rated one of the great orators of history, and when he was ill an enfeebled Johnson admitted: 'That fellow Burke calls forth all my powers. Were I to see Burke now, it would kill me.'

And yet on his day it was Johnson who had the edge, not least because of the sheer physical energy of his performance. He was not only large and shambling, and therefore intimidating, unlike other literary types, he was easily provoked into exuberant displays of strength, if not downright violence. He had been taught to box in Lichfield by his uncle Andrew, and was said to be terrifyingly good. When a man took his seat at the theatre, and refused to move, Johnson picked him up, chair and all, and threw him into the orchestra pit. When he went to a fireworks display and the fireworks failed, he started a mini-riot. Told of a particularly dangerous whirlpool in the Isis near Oxford, he tore off his clothes and dived in.

He once challenged a smaller friend to a footrace, and when they reached a tree he snatched him up, popped him on a low-hanging branch and continued the race. On another occasion he was walking down the street with his characteristic roll of the head and convulsive starts when he came up behind a porter carrying a heavy load. For no reason at all, Johnson knocked the load off the porter's back and, amid general bewilderment, continued on his way.

He was what they would now call 'up for it'. One morning at 3 am two young men of fashion, Bennet Langton and Topham Beauclerk, decided to roust Johnson from his lair, a few years after Tetty had died. He appeared in a nightcap, armed with a poker, and said, 'What, is it you, you dogs? I'll have a frisk with you!'

In a jiffy he was down in his clothes, and they were out to a tavern to see in the dawn over a drink of Bishop, a favourite of Johnson's made of sugar, wine and oranges; and in a state of deep refreshment they rolled into Covent Garden where he insisted on trying to help the irritated fruit and veg sellers to set up their stalls. Then they went out for a row on the Thames, and Johnson was still calling for more entertainment when the younger men decided to pack it in. He was then pushing fifty, and a shining example to us all.

It was that inexhaustible spirit that made him so hard to beat in debate, as someone observed: 'Sir, there is no arguing with Johnson, for when the pistol misses fire, he knocks you down with the butt end of it'; or as Boswell put it after Johnson observed complacently that he had 'had a good talk', 'Yes, sir, you tossed and gored several persons'.

He was fired by a simple Homeric desire to achieve praise and renown, and it was no accident that *The Iliad* was his favourite work of literature, and that he often quoted the advice of Glaucus to Diomedes, that he should αἰὲν ἀριστεύειν καὶ ὑπείροχον ἔμμεναι ἄλλων – always be the best and have the upper hand over the others.

So it was useful that he was, additionally, a genius. Of that there can be no serious doubt.

He had an astonishing ability to use the simplest Anglo-Saxon words to get to the heart of human motive, and to mint observations that were both fresh and true, and which endure in their hundreds today. He could be extremely funny, though sometimes you perhaps had to be back there in the eighteenth century to appreciate the full richness of the gag.

He was once being conveyed on the Thames, where it was the custom for sailors to hail each other with what Boswell calls 'coarse raillery'. Johnson took some incoming salvo, and unleashed this sensational retort: 'Sir, your wife, under pretence of keeping a bawdy-house, is a receiver of stolen goods.' Long before Edward Lear produced his famous surrealist recipe for Gosky Patties, Johnson said that 'cucumbers should be well sliced and then dressed with pepper and vinegar and then thrown out as good for nothing.'

When a young man lamented that he had lost his Greek, Johnson replied, 'I believe it happened at the same time, sir, that I lost all my large estate in Yorkshire.' And when a magistrate was droning on about how he had sent four convicts to a penal colony in Australia, Johnson said he wished he could be the fifth. He was, in other words, not only funny but also rude, and that helps to explain his popularity then and since.

In a nation addicted to evasion and embarrassment, we treasure people who are rude, because we assume (rather primitively) that they are more likely to tell the truth. Johnson was once disparaging the works of Laurence Sterne when a Miss Monckton said that well, actually, she thought they were really rather good.

'That is because, dearest, you're a dunce,' he said.

People are 'blockheads' or 'dogs', and when he was asked who was the greater poet, Derrick or Smart, he said, 'Sir, there is no settling the point of precedency between a louse and flea.' For all their famous hypocrisy, the British also love a person who seems honest about his pleasures, however vulgar. Johnson once said, 'If I had no duties and no reference to futurity, I would spend my life driving briskly in a post-chaise with a pretty woman', and there he articulates the eternal dream of the British male. Is that not the manifesto of Jeremy Clarkson, and all the millions who follow him? We think of him as a scholar, as 'Dr' Johnson, a man who spent his hours peering at ancient texts; and yet he also devoured romantic novels; he disliked the honorific 'Dr', and was one of the greatest students of human nature – one of the greatest moralists – of his or any age.

Long before Jeremy Paxman or any other anthropologist of the English psyche, he spotted our strange standoffishness. If a Frenchman bumps into another Frenchman, or if a German comes across another German in a foreign country, they will fall into easy conversation. Show an Englishman into a room with the other Englishman, says Johnson, and one will sit on a chair and the other one will stand by the window, and each will go to some lengths to pretend the other does not exist.

He noticed the frailties of his fellow journalists and writers, how everyone claims to have some high motive for their work. Pshaw, said Johnson: there was one reason why writers were writers, and that was the pleasure that goes with repetition of their own names; and he paints a ludicrous picture of the author stealing round the coffee houses, 'like a monarch in disguise', and cocking a pathetic ear to hear what the world is making of his latest effort – when the crushing reality is that no one is even talking about the thing.

Time after time you come across a dictum of Johnson, and you find yourself nodding and saying, yes, that's us, that's the human race:

> 'Almost every man has some real or imagined connection to a celebrated character.'
>
> 'Nothing is more hopeless than a scheme for merriment.'
>
> 'The safe and general antidote against sorrow is employment.'
>
> 'The cure for the greater part of human miseries is not radical, but palliative.'
>
> 'Every animal revenges his pains on those who happen to be near.'

And there are many more.

Even if his tragedy, *Irene*, became an accidental comedy; even if his poetry is not much on the syllabus, his couplets have a weight that is entirely Johnsonian. 'Here falling houses thunder on your head', he writes in his satirical poem on London, 'And here a female atheist talks you dead'.

It is a lapidary style in the sense that it is as economical as a Latin inscription. He not only wrote the famous epitaph to Oliver Goldsmith that you can see in Poets' Corner – '*Olivarii Goldsmith, Poetae Physici Historici, qui nullum fere scribendi genus non tetigit, nullum quod tetigit non ornavit*', (Oliver Goldsmith, poet, philosopher, historian, by whom scarecly any style of writing was left untouched, and no one touched unadorned) – but of all the lines in Goldsmith's plays the most famous was actually contributed by Johnson: 'How small of all that human hearts endure, That part which laws or kings can cause or cure.'

There is a lot of thought in that couplet. Many journalists have been paid many thousands of pounds to say the same thing at considerably greater length. But by the time Dodd the dodgy clergyman came to appeal to Johnson, his prestige and his moral authority derived from one superhuman literary effort.

It took forty Frenchmen fifty-five years to produce a dictionary of French. It took the Accademia della Crusca twenty years to produce a dictionary of Italian. It took Johnson nine years to produce his dictionary, and he personally wrote forty thousand entries. There is a mistaken view these days that Johnson played it for laffs, mainly because of a handful of chucklesome entries.

Oats are defined as 'a grain which in England are generally given to horses, but which in Scotland supports the people'. A patron is a 'wretch who supports with insolence, and is paid with flattery'. A lexicographer is a 'harmless drudge'. There is the fabulously brain-stretching definition of a 'network' as 'anything reticulated or decussated at equal distances with interstices between the intersections'.

Challenged by a woman to explain why he had wrongly defined the pastern as the knee of a horse, he said, 'Ignorance, madam, pure ignorance'. And yet any suggestion of bluff British anti-intellectualism, or amateurism, is entirely illusory.

Johnson's dictionary was a breakthrough. Noah Webster may have sniped at his predecessor, but he took over thousands of entries; and when the Victorians began their great oeuvre in 1888, they called it the 'New English Dictionary', and it was new in the sense that it was the first to presume to move out of the shadow of Johnson.

It is an immense thing to be the definer of not just any old language, but the language of what was then the greatest country on Earth. It is above all an act of fantastic self-assertion, to freeze the great torrent of words as they change and glide through history and say: That's it. That's what they all mean, and they mean it because I, Johnson, say so.

Small wonder, then, that Dodd turned to him as the man to save his bacon.

The fun-loving cleric was no mean author himself, with fifty-five titles under his belt, including a charming volume on Shakespeare. But to compare him to Johnson, the Prospero of language, was to compare a popgun to a dreadnought. The interesting question, really, is why did Johnson agree to help? You may wonder why he turned his vast guns to the aid of this perfumed chancer.

Whatever Dodd's charms, he was an obvious rogue. It was only three years earlier that he had been involved in a stunning case of bribery, when he offered £3,000 to Lady Apsley, wife of the Lord Chancellor, if she would help wangle him into the lucrative living of St George's Church in Hanover Square. You have to remember that these were still the days when being the vicar of such a place was a cushy number, and well worth some greasing of palms.

The chicanery was detected. The letter was traced to Dodd's wife, a buxom former servant girl. The King was shown the appalling document, and was so outraged at the insult to his Lord Chancellor and therefore to the crown itself that he sacked Dodd from the list of royal chaplains.

As London was convulsed by the scandal, Dodd's persona was satirised on the stage of the Haymarket as 'Dr Simony', a man reviving the ancient sin of trading in holy offices. Dodd wrote a letter to the papers, pathetically claiming that one day he would be able to explain it all –

and then fled to Switzerland to escape the gossip. News reached London of his escapades; he was seen at the Paris races in a Phaethon and dressed as a French fop, and when he returned to London, and preached his last sermon on 2 February 1777 (before a large and still adoring congregation), he was surely a notorious figure.

When Johnson received Dodd's appeal for help, he must have known the detail of his final crime; how he went to an innocent broker with the forged bond, and how he persuaded him to cash it on the pretext that Lord Chesterfield had reasons, ahem, for not wanting to do it in person, and how he had scooted away with the then huge sum of £4,200.

Johnson had only met Dodd once, many years before, and when the letter reached him at his rooms in Bolt Court, it is said that he was 'much agitated'.

He walked up and down his chamber reading it, and then declared, 'I will do what I can.' He certainly did. Johnson made extraordinary exertions on behalf of this conniving cleric, many of them in secret.

We need to understand that he was very far from being the straightforwardly reactionary conservative of caricature. He was more complicated, more compassionate, and stricken with a sense of duty.

Johnson's analysis of society seems weird to us today, because we accept from childhood the idea of equality. We accept, or at least we assert, that the perfect state of humanity is one of equal brotherhood and sisterhood, and that in an ideal world we would all treat each other and respect each other as equals. Johnson doubted that this was realistic. It just wasn't how people worked, he said.

'No two people can be half an hour together, but one shall acquire an evident superiority over the other.' Even today, we might reluctantly agree that there is a grain of truth in that. But Johnson went further, and beyond the bounds of modern political discourse, in saying that equality was not only unrealistic, but undesirable. He was once attacked by a female journalist called Mrs Macaulay, a lady of strident Whiggish views. Remember the lines from 'London', about the female atheist who talks you dead? That was her. She was London's leading Guardianista, the Polly Toynbee of her day. Mrs Macaulay says everyone would be much better off if we all had the same size plots of land, and no one could domineer over anyone else. Nonsense, says Johnson, mankind is happier in 'a state of inequality and subordination'. If everyone was equal, he says, the human race would never get anywhere. There would be no intellectual improvement, because all intellectual improvement arises from leisure, and you can't have leisure – vital gentlemanly time needed to think – unless some people work for other people. When Johnson sees a beggar in the street, he feels compassion, all right. But he is not exactly consumed with outrage at the disparity between the lot of the beggar and his own. Oh no.

According to Johnson, beggars are not only inevitable but indispensable. 'It is better that some should be unhappy than that none should be happy, which would be the case in a general state of equality,' he says. Inequality turns out to be essential to almost every human institution.

It is the only way to get things done. You need hierarchy, he says, with a chap at the top, and people set under him. Otherwise the whole thing seizes up. 'Though many men are nominally entrusted with the administration of hospitals and other public institutions, almost all the good is done by one man, by whom the rest are driven on; owing to confidence in him and indolence in them.'

And do you know what, he says, the human race actually rather likes it that way. 'There is a reciprocal pleasure in governing and being governed', he says. Well, one can see why the governors might get a kick out of lording it over everyone else, but what exactly does he mean by this 'pleasure in being governed'?

Is he saying that we are all masochists, yearning to be bossed around? It turns out that the pleasure in being governed is pure self-interested common sense. 'Men will submit to any rule by which they may be exempted from the tyranny of caprice and chance. They are glad to supply by external authority their own want of constancy and resolution, and court the government of others, when long experience has convinced them of their own inability to govern themselves.' We are starting to see a more generous interpretation of his feeling. He doesn't propound inequality out of snobbery or lust for hierarchy. He believes it is for the benefit and protection of the little guy. And that was the point of the eighteenth century Toryism of which Johnson was the great exponent.

Never in Johnson's lifetime were the Tories the majority party. They were the underdogs. They stood up for small shopkeepers and the monarchy, while the Whigs were the party of big business and 'progress'.

There is an embarrassing scene when Johnson goes to see the King, and comes out saying what a damn fine gentleman he is, never mind what anyone says. But Tories didn't reverence the King out of some atavistic juju, but because he was thought of as the protector of the people. You needed the King there as an ultimate bulwark against the advance of the rich and the powerful. 'I fly from petty tyrants to the throne', says Johnson, the man whose parents submitted their child to be touched by the monarch, in the deluded hope that he would be cured of scrofula.

If we look at his economic thinking, it is on the face of it pretty Tebbit-esque. He attacks the raising of wages for day-labourers, on the grounds that it will only make them idle, and 'idleness is a very bad thing for human nature'. He applauds luxury – luxury in food, luxury in buildings – and makes the classic conservative argument for the trickle-down effect. 'A man gives half a guinea for a dish of green peas. How much gardening does this occasion?' Think of all the labour required to get those green peas to market, says Johnson. Think of the jobs. And isn't it much better, he goes on, to spend that half guinea on green peas, and keep people in work, than just hand the money over to some poor person so that he may afford a meal? That way, you help the 'industrious poor, whom it is better to support than the idle poor'. Listen, he says: suppose we were to revive the ancient luxury dish of peacocks' brains? People would protest that it was a sign of luxurious decadence. But think of all the peacock carcases that we could give to the poor!

Now some of this makes Johnson sound like one of those 1980s yuppie monsters, boasting how the consumption of champagne was economically essential and riffling his banknotes under the nose of a beggar. In fact, he was the very opposite of hard-hearted. He was personally hopeless with money, on one occasion hiding five guineas and then losing it. He was arrested for debt, and yet – in the words of his friend Hester Thrale – 'he loved the poor more than I saw anyone else do'.

He was so generous that on many evenings he gave away all his silver between his home and the Mitre tavern, where he dined. His letters are full of intercessions on behalf of the unfortunate, such as a palsied painter he helped to find a place in hospital. He looked after his nearest and dearest with affection and devotion.

Among the creatures of his strange menagerie at Bolt Court was an old blind poetess called Mrs Williams, whose table manners were said to be revolting, and yet Johnson would take her with him across fashionable London. Then most famously there was Frank Barber, his black manservant, on whose behalf Johnson's labours were extraordinary. He got him out of the navy. He attended to his education, and treated him as his ward, and Frank Barber was the principal beneficiary of Johnson's will.

It was an instinctive humanistic anti-racism that made him lift his glass at a gathering of Oxford men and stun the company by saying, 'Here's to the next insurrection of the negroes in the West Indies.' It was Boswell the Whig who produced the weaselly arguments in favour of slavery. It was Johnson, the Tory supporter of the underdog, who saw its evil, and the hypocrisy of the Whigs.

'How is it that we hear the loudest yelps for liberty among the drivers of the negroes?' he asked. 'It is impossible not to conceive that men in their original state were equal,' he went on, and no, there is no confusion in his thought.

Johnson believed that subordination and inequality were inevitable and in some sense desirable; and yet there is no inconsistency in thinking that all human beings are equal in dignity. If further proof were needed of the gentleness of his nature, I offer the occasion when he was staying at a house in Wales, and the gardener caught a hare among the potato plants, and brought it in to be cooked for dinner.

Johnson asked to hold it for a moment, then shoved the terrified creature through an open window and shouted at it to flee. Or I might cite his treatment of his cat Hodge, whose oysters he would personally go out and buy. Beneath the veneer of blustering intellectual intolerance, he was, in fact, a terrific old softie.

So as he paced up and down his room, and wondered whether and how to help the cheque-forging parson, we can imagine that he was motivated by straightforward compassion – a compassion perhaps intensified by a couple of episodes in Johnson's own past. The life of William Dodd was at stake because he had clashed with the Earl of Chesterfield, his former pupil who had dobbed him in and refused to indulge his crime. And this Earl of Chesterfield was the son of that famous Earl of Chesterfield with whom Johnson had engaged – a quarter of a century earlier – in one of the most spectacular spats of English literary history.

When a cash-strapped Johnson was looking for patrons to help finance his dictionary, he approached Lord Chesterfield, a famous diplomat, politician, man of letters and super-suave theorist of etiquette. After some slight encouragement, Johnson turned up chez Chesterfield, but was for some reason kept waiting in an outer room, and after a long interval left empty-handed and in a thoroughly bad mood.

Seven years later the dictionary was complete. Johnson's opus was beginning to command public attention – at which point the languid Earl of Chesterfield penned some pieces saying how frightfully good he thought it was.

Johnson immediately fired off a letter, which contains some of the most magnificent put-downs in literature. 'Is not a patron, my lord, one who looks with unconcern on a man struggling for life in the water, and when he has reached ground, encumbers him with help? The notice which you have been pleased to take of my labours, had it been early, had been kind; but it has been delayed till I am indifferent, and cannot enjoy it; till I am solitary, and cannot impart it; till I am known, and do not want it.'

Chesterfield was in fact quite tickled to be so rebuked, and kept the letter on a table for visitors to read; but we can imagine that Johnson's sympathies were engaged by the very thought that another man called

Chesterfield – the son of his old foe – was about to play a part in bringing poor Dodd to the gallows.

And then there is one other memory that the case of Dodd may have stirred. Almost forty years earlier, Johnson's younger brother Nathaniel had died in sad circumstances in Somerset, after falling into debt. There is a suggestion of suicide, and of forgery; and who knows, perhaps it was the thought of his young brother's despair that helped to decide Johnson in favour of action. He turned his pen to the aid of Dodd, and with a zeal that was almost obsessive.

Whatever the task he was set, his conscience would thrash and goad him until it was complete. This was a man who had to touch the posts he passed in a certain order, who had to enter rooms in a certain way, and whose inner demons compelled him to collect the peel of every orange he ate. Woe betide him if there was a task he had failed to complete, because his conscience would be on at him – clicking its tongue and tapping its foot – until the job was finally done. If you want a single episode that sums up the guilty compulsions of Samuel Johnson, think of how he had once failed as a young man to go to Uttoxeter to do an errand for his father, and how fifty years later he went to expiate the omission, and stood bare-headed in the rain before the spot where his father had had his stall.

Here are some of the things he churned out – anonymously – on behalf of a man he scarcely knew. He wrote a speech to the Recorder of London, to be read out on the occasion of Dodd's sentence to death at the Old Bailey.

He wrote a 'convict's address to his unhappy brethren', a sermon given by Dodd to his fellow inmates at Newgate jail.

He wrote a letter for Dodd to the Lord Chancellor, and one to Lord Mansfield; a petition from Dr Dodd to the King; a petition from Mrs Dodd to the Queen; he wrote several long articles in the newspapers pointing out that a petition had been presented to His Majesty, signed by twenty thousand, calling for Dodd's release.

He wrote a petition in the name of the City of London, and he also wrote a document called Dr Dodd's last solemn declaration.

It was all terrific Johnsonian stuff. It was also useless.

The King was implacable. Pardon was refused. Amid enormous crowds Dodd was conveyed in a mourning cart to Tyburn, bound in halters, praying and weeping as he passed a street where he once lived in such style.

As he ascended the scaffold, an official called Mr Villette was handed the last solemn declaration (secretly written by Johnson) so that he could read it to the baying multitudes.

It was full of orotund protestations of faith, and repentance for the delusion of show and the delights of voluptuousness and his general failure to crack down on spending. Vanity and pleasure had required expense disproportionate to his income, and distress, importunate distress, had urged him to temporary fraud. The gist of it was that he was a good Christian, even though he had behaved very badly. It was also, alas, quite a long document, and the official decided that the crowd would become impatient. So they decided to save it for another time, and they got on with hanging William Dodd.

The cart pulled away from the gibbet, and down he dropped. As if that were not indignity enough, he was whisked off, while his body was still warm, by the ghastly body snatchers who then haunted the Golgotha of Tyburn Tree. They took him off to the famous surgeon John Hunter, who tried to pump the air back into his lungs with a pair of bellows.

That, too, was no use. Dodd was as dead as a dodo. All Johnson's exertions had been in vain. As he wrote in protest, under his own name, to the Secretary for War, it was the first time in history that a clergyman had suffered public execution for immorality.

It is an episode that shows many of Johnson's best qualities: his compassion, his energy, his phenomenal literary fertility. In his willingness to write anonymously, it shows the spirit of charity and obsessive sense of obligation that was so strong in his make-up.

And yet when Dodd was interred, and the controversy was over, the greatest and most competitive spirit of eighteenth-century England could not quite resist the chance for glory, the serotonin boost of praise and esteem that had driven him all his life.

When a Mr Seward challenged Johnson, and said that the 'convict's address to his unhappy brethren' could not possibly be by Dodd, and that Johnson must have had a hand in it, Johnson did not admit it, but then nor could he bring himself to deny it.

So he came up with one of his most famous gags.

'Depend upon it, sir,' he said, 'when a man knows he is to be hanged in a fortnight, it concentrates the mind wonderfully.'

* * *

Incurable show-off he may have been, but I hope I have convinced the reader that Samuel Johnson was a gentle and kind man. He rooted for Dodd. He felt the hardship of the poor. 'Slow rises worth, by poverty depressed', he said in his early satirical poem, 'London'.

He was a compassionate conservative, in today's language; and yet there is little doubt that he was a conservative – one of the principal fathers of a political philosophy (if that is not too big a word) that holds that there is a hidden wisdom in old ways of doing things, and that you monkey with the established order at your peril.

He opposed the American colonists in their war of independence. They were seditious renegades, he said, and wrote a pamphlet called 'Taxation No Tyranny' in which he urged that they should cough up whatever the government of George III demanded. And he deeply disapproved of anyone who whipped up the mob to insurrection. 'He is no lover of his country that unnecessarily disturbs its peace,' he said. Which was not entirely the view of eighteenth-century London's greatest radical.

THE BOW STREET RUNNERS

There cannot be many cities in the world where tourists are invited to buy a copy of a policeman's helmet as a souvenir of their trip. There they are in the kiosks, along with little red telephone boxes, Routemaster buses and pairs of pants saying 'I (heart) London'.

This tells you something important about the way the city is policed, that the wearers of these characterful blue bonnets are not to be equated with any sinister apparition of state control. They are not there to be directed by interior ministers to break down your door in the night. They are not securitate. They are not even gendarmes or carabinieri.

They are meant to be part of the street scene: unarmed, friendly, and willing to tell you the time. In the much-quoted phrase of the founder of the Metropolitan Police Force, Sir Robert Peel, 'the police are the public and the public are the police'. Which means they are not remote from us, they are part of us. British policing is 'by consent'.

This may seem a fine distinction, between British and other 'papers-please' styles of policing, but it is important. Such has been Londoners' historic insistence on the liberty of the individual that for many years there was serious and principled resistance to having a police force at all.

There were constables, like the dim-witted Dogberry in Shakespeare's *Much Ado*, with his malapropish use of official-sounding language. There were watchmen paid by the guilds; and as London swelled in the early eighteenth century, and as the slums and the rookeries became havens for thieves, there were people who were paid by magistrates to catch the criminals.

The trouble with this system of rewards was that the thief-catchers actually had a motive to encourage theft. The most mind-boggling of these characters was Jonathan Wild (1682–1725). He posed as the 'Thief-taker general of Great Britain and Ireland', and persuaded the authorities that he was a kind of Batman of law enforcement – while simultaneously organising bands of thieves to take property of all kinds.

These stolen goods would then be 'found' and Wild would claim his reward, which would be shared with his gang. If any of the thieves wanted to rat, or stop thieving, Wild would denounce them and have them sent to the gallows. To the poor duped public Wild was Robocop, a hero. When in

1720 the Privy Council consulted him on how to control crime, he replied rather brilliantly that more lavish rewards were needed.

In the end the fraud was exposed and Wild was hung; and yet still Londoners were reluctant to see a state-backed police force. It was tyrannical, people said. It was foreign. By the end of the eighteenth century the city was relying on the Bow Street Runners, 'a set of brave fellows, always ready to set out to any part of the town or kingdom at a quarter of an hour's notice'. They were able to patrol the streets and make arrests on the authority of the magistrates at Bow Street; and yet because they were also paid by results they suffered from the same temptations as the thief-catchers. They eventually became involved in massive scams to share rewards between criminals and fences.

By the early ninteenth century the pressure was growing, in some quarters, for a professional force. In 1811 the public was outraged by the failure of the authorities to do anything about some grisly murders in east London. John William Ward, a future foreign secretary, brushed aside the outcry. 'I should rather half a dozen people's throats should be cut in Ratcliff Highway, every three or four years, than be subject to domiciliary visits, spies and all the rest of Fouché's contrivances', he said, referring to the blood-crazed behaviour of Joseph Fouché, Napoleon's minister of police.

The pressure grew in the disturbances following the 1821 death of Queen Caroline (a kind of Lady Di figure, who provoked angry and extravagant mourning), though in 1823 *The Times* was sticking to the line that a centralised police force was 'an engine invented by despotism'. Finally in 1829 Peel got his Bill through parliament and a professional force was born.

In deference to public anxiety about the new state-authorised officers, Peel did his best to ensure the civilian nature of the force. He dressed the men in top hats with blue swallow-tail coats and armed them only with a truncheon (or a cutlass on dangerous beats). Though Londoners at first booed the policemen, they became an immense success, championed by Dickens and others. There were spectacular falls in crime in the second half of the ninteenth century, and it stayed low until the 1960s.

Londoners had got their first demonstration that policing worked. If there was a cost to liberty, it didn't seem very high – and they decided it was worth paying.

no. 45

John Wilkes

The Father of Liberty

It was the February of 1768. England was still in the grip of the mini-Ice Age, the Thames had frozen over again, and it was hellish cold in Westminster. A door opened one morning in a street not far from Dean's Yard, in a handsome town house that once stood on a spot now occupied by a government ministry – these days the department of education and 'skills'. A pair of bright eyes looked out.

To call them ill-matched was too kind. They had a lascivious nose-goggling squint, of a kind that these days would be corrected at birth. Beneath the eyes was a mouth with hardly any teeth, and a chin that jutted more than any decent chin should. The whole face was the stuff of children's nightmares; and yet as the owner of these features sniffed the air, he had not only an odd charm, he exuded confidence.

He was forty-one, and had the satisfaction of having just returned after four years of not-very-punishing continental exile to the city he loved and where he had made his name. There was a glint in that squinting eye, of a man who was agog to discover what it was – as he put it – that the womb of fate was big with. He shoved down his hat and tightened his coat about his tall lean frame, and remembered that if anyone stopped him he was supposed to call himself 'Mr Osborn'.

Seldom can there have been a feebler alias. That cross-eyed squint and jutting jaw had already been satirised in one of William Hogarth's most famous cartoons, an image that had been run off in its thousands for the enjoyment of friend and foe alike. He was known to the King of England as 'that Devil', the most turbulent of all his subjects, and was conceived by some of the monarch's most strait-laced ministers as the biggest threat to the peaceful government of the country.

He was a human wedge, a jemmy inserted into the weakest points of the constitution, to be driven deeper and deeper by the forces of popular indignation until it seemed the whole edifice might crash. He had scandalised the House of Lords by his co-authorship of one of the most obscene (or most puerile) poems ever written. He had duelled with one peer over a point of honour, and still bore a vivid scar in his groin sustained in another duel with a fellow MP – an episode that some scholars now believe was a stealthy attempt by the Establishment to bump him off.

His lower abdomen had sufficiently recovered for him to keep up his romantic strike rate. Though his heart had just been broken by an eighteen-year-old Italian of internationally celebrated charms, he had consoled himself in Paris with at least two well-born mistresses, neither of whom seems to have resented the other. He was a considerable scholar of Latin and Greek, who had already bested Dr Johnson in lexicography, who had lately dined with Boswell, had helped David Hume with his English usage, and who had laughed with Voltaire at the superstitious terrors that still enslaved much of the human race.

As he stepped out into Marsham Street that February morning, his position in history was already secure. He was a household name, who had been at the centre of legal proceedings that upheld the liberty of the individual and limited the power of the state. He was already so popular that when he had first stuck his toe back onto English soil, a year earlier, the church bells were rung in his honour and crowds formed outside the house where he was staying.

His name was John Wilkes, and he walked with a spring in his step because he had an idea what he was going to do next. He was flat broke – he was more than broke; his debts were immense. He was an outlaw, liable to arrest at any time and to fresh deportation. But something told him that he had enough wind in his sails to try it on again. He was going to stick two fingers up to the King and the King's toadies.

He was going to do the thing they dreaded: to stand again for the parliament that had expelled him. In so doing he was going to vindicate an important principle of democracy.

I have a terrible feeling that as a fifteen-year-old I wrote a pompous essay on Wilkes, in the course of studying for history O-Level. Thankfully the document has been lost, but the gist was that Wilkes was a berk, a second-rate chancer, an opportunist, an unprincipled demagogue who floated like a glittering bubble on a wave of popular sentiment that he did not really share. It may be that in some places that is still the conventional opinion.

If so, it is wrong. It is not just that I have come to admire Wilkes for his courage and his dynamism and his boundless animal spirits. Any sober assessment of his work confirms that he really was as his adoring crowds saw him – the father of civil liberty. He not only secured the right of newspapers to report the proceedings of the House of Commons, he was the first man to stand up in Parliament and urge explicitly that all adult males – rich or poor – should be allowed to vote.

His campaigns were fervently supported by Americans, as they chafed under the misguided governments of George III. There is a Wilkes County in North Carolina, where the principal township is still Wilkesboro, home to a noted chicken-packing plant and a country music festival. When in 1969 the first black Congressman, Adam Clayton Powell, was excluded from the House of Representatives, it was to the case of John Wilkes that Justice Earl Warren famously alluded, in quashing that exclusion, in overturning the House's wrong and partially racially motivated decision, and in ruling that it was the sovereign right of the people and of the people alone to elect their representatives.

Wilkes has a good claim to the paternity of key democratic freedoms not just in Britain but in America, too, and that is a pretty big claim to make about anyone.

John Wilkes was born in 1725 or 1726, and his life spanned most of the rest of the eighteenth century. It was an era of explosive growth in the power and wealth of London. By the time he was born, Hawksmoor's churches were already up, and the squares of Mayfair were being laid out. The Bank of England and the Stock Exchange had been founded in the last thirty years. Thanks to the 1713 Treaty of Utrecht, Britain was acquiring new colonies in the Americas and elsewhere, and money was pouring into the pockets of merchants of all kinds. There was money from simple trade – importing sugar from the West Indies, say, and then refining it in the docks of London. But more lucrative still were all the associated services that made this commerce possible: the bankers who financed the building of ships and the stocking of plantations, the insurers who took a punt on whether or not the ships would sink or the crops would spoil, the brokers who dealt in shares in the joint-stock operations.

All these people brought money to London, and the needs of the growing mercantile bourgeoisie drove the flywheel of industry, promoting services and manufacturing of all kinds. Wilkes was born in St John's Square, Clerkenwell, now the scene of architect's studios and fancy restaurants specialising in parts of animals not normally eaten by people.

Clerkenwell was where Nicholas Tompion had done his experiments with springs and watches, to the orders of Robert Hooke; and now it was a European centre of watch and clock-making. Their wives wanted to show off their jewellery and their tableware, and Clerkenwell was the place to find your cutlers and your jewellers. Then they needed a safe place to store their trophies, and Clerkenwell locksmiths opened their shops and answered the need.

The Wilkes family themselves were in trade. His mother was a tanning heiress, and his father Israel Wilkes was a distiller. He liked to pretend that he was really a brewer of beer, and that none of his malt mash was associated with the social disaster of gin, whose impact on the working classes is viciously summed up in Hogarth's *Gin Lane* (the one where a terrified baby is seen tumbling into an open sewer from the arms of his insensible mother).

Whether or not Israel Wilkes was guilty of intoxicating the defenceless proletariat with mother's ruin, there was a widening income gap between people such as the Wilkes family – the successful bourgeoisie – and the urban poor. London was unsafe, it was unsanitary, and the proletariat were continually assailed by technological change that threatened to devalue their labour. In 1710, a hundred years before 'Luddism' became a name, the London framework knitters had smashed more than a hundred stocking knitting frames to stop their masters from employing too many apprentices. In 1720 Spitalfields silk weavers attacked and abused women wearing calico – cheerful and cheap printed cotton from India. They tore the clothes from their backs and denounced them as 'calico madams'.

These weavers were not bad people; they were just in despair at being endlessly slapped around the chops by the great invisible hand of Adam Smith. It is one of the most astonishing features of Wilkes' career that he was to become the champion not just of democratic 'reform', in the sense that someone like Edmund Burke understood it – a limited concept that meant extending political participation to a small number of men who were thought able to grasp what was going on and who had the leisure for discussions – he was to be the genuine hero of the poor, with a patent brew of insolence and exuberant jingo. That is a surprising outcome, because his parents were determined that he should be a scholar and a gentleman.

Unlike his siblings, he enjoyed a careful and expensive education. He was sent to tutors in Thame, and thence to Leiden University in Holland – then a more prestigious institution than either Oxford or Cambridge, sunk as they were in torpor and jobbery. At university he learned the habits of debauchery that were to last him a lifetime. It is not that he wasted his time at Leiden. He sharpened his mastery of Latin and French; he loved the classics. He first met some of the intellectuals who were to welcome him during his exile into the circle of the philosophes. But he was a firm believer in what you might call a rounded education. As he later said: 'I was always among women at Leiden. My father gave me as much money as I pleased, so I had three or four whores and got drunk every night. I woke up with a sore head in the morning, and then I read.' For the first time since the fall of the Roman Empire, it was now acceptable to discuss fornication in this way, as the supreme recreation of a civilised society. Wilkes associated sex with intellectual creativity. As he once told Boswell, 'Dissipation and profligacy ... renew the mind. I wrote my best *North Briton* in bed with Betsy Green.'

At the age of only twenty he was back from Leiden and at the urgings of his family he had married a well-off but neurotic woman some ten years older than him, by the name of Mary Mead. It was not a happy union, and in due course the couple separated. But in 1750 they produced a daughter, Polly, who was to inspire in Wilkes an unwavering paternal duty and affection. Even those who disapprove of Wilkes (and there are many) are deeply moved by his devotion to the child, brown-eyed, lively and quick-witted as her father, but cursed with the same prognathous chin. During the summer, the family lived in a property of his wife's at Aylesbury, and here he became a pillar of the community: a feoffee of the Grammar School, a trustee of the local turnpike, a JP. He might have settled down to a life of quiet squirearchy, but he loved London, and he discovered that he was in increasing demand as a wit and a man of fashion.

'It only takes me twenty minutes to talk away my face', he boasted. Sometimes this was reduced to ten minutes. He was elected to the Royal Society in 1749, and to the Beefsteak Club in 1754. In 1755 he was so confident of his position in the world that he launched a sarcastic attack on Dr Johnson himself, on the occasion of the publication of his dictionary.

Johnson had remarked that the letter H hardly ever comes at the beginning of any but the first syllable of a word. Ha! said Wilkes, in a letter to a paper, 'The author of this remark must be a man of quick apprehension and comprehensive genius, but I can never forgive his unhandsome behaviour to the poor knighthood, priesthood and widowhood, nor his inhumanity to all manhood and womanhood ...' and so on. He blasted Johnson with twenty-six examples of H beginning an internal syllable, and the great man was so stung that he amended subsequent editions, pointing out that there were some compound words where you might find an H at the start of an internal syllable.

Like Blockhead, he said. Wilkes was very far from crushed. He went around in 'gay and fantastic dress', accompanied by two dogs called Dido and Pompey. Most famously of all he participated in the idiotic rites of the Medmenham Monks. Think of Silvio Berlusconi's bunga-bunga room, but with an ecclesiastical theme.

The place was a semi-ruined abbey on the lush banks of the Thames near Marlow, and its proprietor, Sir Francis Dashwood, was keen that his fellow monks should exhibit a robust heterosexuality. High-class hookers or adventurous ladies of fashion were invited to dinner, at the end of which they – the women – would choose a partner and repair to the monk's cell. Children born to such unions were called sons and daughters of St Francis.

One evening, when the candles were guttering low, and half the monks were hogwhimpering drunk, and the lurid shadows of their cavortings were flickering on the erotic frescoes on the ceilings, it is almost certain that Wilkes regaled his fellow celebrants with a reading of a poem by a friend of his called Thomas Potter, wayward son of the Archbishop of Canterbury.

It was called 'An Essay on Woman'. Silly tripe though it was, it was to cause him a lot of trouble. Wilkes was engaged in lexical duels with Dr Johnson. He was hobnobbing with earls. He had made it, big time. The next stage, the next fashionable job, was to get into parliament. After one inglorious episode in Berwick, where he made the mistake of failing to bribe the electorate, he was elected MP for Aylesbury as part of the faction of William Pitt the Elder, later to become the Earl of Chatham.

Wilkes did not shine. His teeth were bad; his voice indistinct. But in 1760 his moment came, with a crisis for the Pittites. George II died, and his grandson George III took over.

This was long before his 'madness'. George III was a serious Teutonic sort of fellow who began with his famous guttural announcement: 'I glory in ze name off Briton!' He wanted the best for his country, and he was persuaded that this meant a more active role for the King. The powers of the King of England had been much reduced since the civil war; but there was room for some creative ambiguity. With his residual ability to dissolve parliaments, and to summon and dismiss prime ministers, the monarch could clearly exercise considerable political influence.

George III fat-headedly decided to see what happened if he threw his weight around. He began by advancing the career of his former tutor and father figure, a man who was rumoured to be romancing his mother: Lord Bute (pron. Boot). He used his first King's Speech, on 12 November 1760, to push the Bute agenda and announce that he would seek an end to the Seven Years' War.

Pitt's empire-building wars were popular in the City. They added the big pink patches, in India and Canada, to the *Daily Telegraph* map that used to hang on my wall as a child. They brought wealth to London. And now this Hanoverian monarch and his languid Scottish Old Etonian mother-bonking minister were threatening to call a peace – and all because of the cost; as we would put it these days, the need to make 'cuts' in the defence budget. William Pitt would not hear of it. He left office. His supporters were indignant, and Wilkes found his metier – not as a speaker, but as a writer. Together with a chum and fellow libertine, the poet Charles Churchill, he began to bash the regime in print.

He launched a paper, the *North Briton*, so called because his main target – Bute – was a Scot; and he began a line in frenzied Jock-baiting that has been ever since a dreary staple of London newspapers. All those pieces complaining about the tartan mafia; all that fulminating about the West Lothian question, and the constitutional outrage that English taxpayers are paying for free nursing care and tuition for the indolent Scots – they all have their origins in the journalism of Wilkes. The funny thing was, he actually quite liked the Scots, and in 1758 he had toured the place, announcing that he was never happier than when he was in Scotland. But that is journalism for you.

His stuff caused such offence that for decades to come angry Scots army officers would stop him in the street and challenge him to a duel, and Scottish children would burn effigies of John Wilkes until Victorian times. For people like Wilkes, this was the age of the Enlightenment, when a civilised man was able to follow Voltaire and do and say more or less what he wanted. Many others were still capable of being deeply shocked.

There was poor old Lord Talbot, who had made such a glorious chump of himself during the Coronation of George III. As part of the ceremony, he was meant to ride into Westminster Hall, salute the King and back out again. This was a lot to ask of a horse, but he rehearsed it many times, and thought he had it taped. Alas, on the day itself the beast was alarmed by the noise of the crowd, turned round, lifted its tail and presented its rear end to the King. At which the entire English nobility roared with laughter and burst into applause – not the done thing at a Coronation. Wilkes milked it for all it was worth. The horse was a legendary steed, he wrote in the pages of the *North Briton*. It was like Quixote's Rosinante; it was like one of the wandering planets of Milton, a celestial body. The horse had such marvellous natural style, he said, that it should be awarded a pension by the crown.

These days that would be classed as gentle stuff. Lord Talbot was apoplectic. He demanded to know if Wilkes was the author of the anonymous skit, and he demanded satisfaction. On 5 October 1762 they fought a duel at Bagshot Heath, a sinister place frequented by highwaymen. Wilkes arrived with his second, wearing the red officer's coat of the Bucks Militia. He had a terrible hangover, having been up with the monks of Medmenham until 4 am, and thought the duel was not until the following day. Talbot insisted on fighting that night, and went into a terrible rage. Was Wilkes the author or not? he demanded. Wilkes refused on principle to answer the question, and said that God had given him a firmness of spirit equal to his lordship's.

The truth was that Wilkes was in a dreadful position. His eyesight was wonky, whereas Talbot was an athlete with a good pair of eyes. Worse, if he killed Talbot he would probably be hanged, while Talbot would be sure to win a King's pardon. At 7 pm, with a bright moon, they went into the garden of the Red Lyon coaching inn. They stood back to back. They walked eight yards apart; and on the word they whirled about and fired at the same time.

It says something for eighteenth-century ballistics or for their collective terror that they both missed, but Wilkes had acted with bravery and honour. He walked up to Talbot and said that, yes, he was the author of the offending satire, while Talbot said that he was the noblest fellow God ever made.

In a way, the affair was absurd. Talbot was the victim of a monstrous sense of humour failure, and Wilkes was conscious of the glory he could win by fighting an honourable duel. But there was more to it. Talbot represented the government, and its general indignation at these anonymous attacks. Wilkes was sticking up for the right of journalists to write and publish anonymous attacks without the fear of retribution. Wilkes' reputation soared, and so did his romantic chances.

He wrote to Churchill that 'a sweet girl whom I have sighed for unsuccessfully these four months, now tells me she will entrust her honour to a man who takes so much care of his own. Is that not prettily said? Pray, look out honour in the dictionary, as I have none here, that I may understand the dear creature.'

In a sense it was all a great game to Wilkes. He knew that he was doing it all partly for self-promotion, and like many another polemical hack he knew that he often turned up the volume of his attacks far higher than his victims deserved. When he later met Boswell in Italy, he admitted that he duffed up Johnson for crimes the great man had not actually committed. He treated him 'as an impudent pretender to literature, which I don't think, but 'tis all one. So is my plan.' Political writers were like Zeus at the end of *The Iliad*, he later said, arbitrarily dishing out blessings and curses from the tubs of good and evil.

Sometimes their subjects got a bashing, sometimes a whitewash. Most politicians these days accept that is how journalism works. They develop a thick skin. Not so the ministers of George III. Since Wilkes' admission of authorship to Talbot, other figures were starting to sue; and as the circulation of the *North Briton* grew – to a dizzying high of two thousand! – the controversy grew hotter. Damned by Wilkes as a Scot and a peacemaking toady of the King, Bute found himself hissed and stoned by the mob.

Wilkes was offered all sorts of bribes to shut him up: the governorship of Canada, directorships of the East India Company. He declined. When the Peace of Paris was signed in 1763, he said it was like the 'peace of God, which passeth all understanding'. On 23 April 1763 he published No 45 of the *North Briton*, with page after page of sarcastic attacks on ministers. At one point he denounced the cider tax, a means, he said, by which the homes of free-born Englishmen might be invaded by the authorities on the pretext of looking for illegal hooch. It was unconstitutional to search people's homes to see if they were fermenting apple juice, he said, and he called for resistance. For King George III it was too much.

Though Wilkes was technically loyal to the crown, everyone knew that the attacks on the peace, on Bute and others were effectively attacks on the King. He demanded that Wilkes be arrested. The ministers were nervous. It wasn't that easy to arrest an MP, even when the King was in a rage. There was parliamentary privilege, after all.

Nor were they entirely sure what kind of charges to make against Wilkes. After much faffing about they went for a charge of 'treason', and sent the King's Messengers with a 'general warrant', in which they named the offences but not the culprits. Armed with this extraordinary document the King's Messengers – the nearest thing in those days to police officers – went off to arrest anyone they could find who had anything to do with the *North Briton*.

They entered buildings and ripped papers from the presses. They arrested ink-stained journeymen printers and their servants and apprentices, and rounded many of them up in a pub. Altogether they arrested forty-eight people, not including Wilkes. They found the editor of the *North Briton* in a state of alcoholic elation. He gave them such a lecture on parliamentary privilege that they crept back to their political masters for reassurance.

Yes, said Lords Halifax and Egremont, the secretaries of state: you must arrest Wilkes. Eventually he consented to be taken to their presence – though he insisted on a sedan chair, for a distance of a hundred yards or so, and was followed by a cheering crowd. Wilkes then gave a thoroughly cheeky interview, in which he announced that 'all the quires of paper on your lordships' table shall be as milk-white as at the beginning'. The infuriated ministers sent him to the Tower of London.

By now word was starting to spread. People had become familiar with Wilkes as the scourge of an unpopular government. He was becoming a martyr to liberty. Parades of notables came to see him in the Tower. Ballads were composed in his honour – one of them called 'The Jewel in the Tower', whose theme was that Wilkes was the most precious of all the gemstones in the kingdom, and allegedly written by a noble lady. Within days, a dozen inns bore his crooked visage on their signs, and a great crowd followed him as he was taken from the Tower to Westminster Hall for his hearing. This took place in the south-east corner of that great building, before Lord Justice Pratt, later to become Lord Camden. Pratt became a judicial hero himself.

Publishing a libel was not a breach of the peace, he ruled. Wilkes was protected by parliamentary privilege. He was let off. 'This is not the clamour of the rabble,' the demagogue told the judge, 'but the voice of liberty which must and shall be heard.'

Wilkes was pupating, morphing from a larrikin scribbler and man about town into a radical. Perhaps it was the inheritance of his mother's Puritanism and non-conformism: in the personality of this libertine and show-off there was now emerging a streak of principle and cussedness. Wilkes was becoming consumed with a genuine obsession: to uphold liberty, and above all the freedom of the press.

Furious at his release, the King's ministers leaked what they hoped would be a damaging detail. Among the effects being returned to him by the state was a packet of condoms. Like the rest of his 'private' life, this did him no harm whatever in the eyes of the London public.

Wilkes proceeded to retaliate. He launched legal actions against the secretaries of state. He accused them of trespass and robbery, since in the course of ransacking his house someone appeared to have made off with a silver candlestick.

Nor was he alone in exploiting the case of No 45 to torment the ministry of George III; no fewer than twenty-five journeymen printers and apprentices entered suits against the messengers. For what must have been the first time in British history, working-class men were using the legal system to stick up for liberty and to attack the emanations of the state – the King himself. Wilkes was in the ascendant, and set up a new printing press in Great George Street, from which he peppered the government with squibs, blasts and further editions of the infernal *North Briton*. Then he had a stroke of bad luck.

On the floor of the printing shop one of his men – a printer named Samuel Jennings – spotted an interesting scrap of paper. It seemed to be some sort of filthy poem, with corrections in the hand of Mr Wilkes himself. It wasn't much good as poetry, and plainly intended to be a political satire. One pair of decidedly unheroic couplets read: 'Then, in the scale of various pricks 'tis plain/Godlike erect, Bute stands the foremost man'.

Hmm, said Jennings: that's rum. I'll take that home and read it to my wife. What he had found was a proof sheet of the Potter-Wilkes 'Essay on Woman', which Wilkes had rashly caused to be printed in a limited edition of thirteen copies. We don't know what Mrs Jennings thought of the poem, with all its coy f***s and c***s, but the following day she used it to wrap a pat of butter for her husband's lunch. This repast took place in a pub called the Red Lion, where they obviously didn't mind about customers bringing packed lunches.

Jennings shared his meal of onions, radishes, bread, butter and beer with another printer, called Thomas Farmer. Oho, said Farmer, reading the butter-smeared words that appeared beneath his knife, what's all this about? He took the paper back to his own printing shop, and showed it to the foreman.

The foreman showed it to the owner. The owner was a Scot named Faden. He hated Wilkes. He consulted a dodgy libertine parson called Kidgell, who took it to Lord March, who took it to the secretaries of state. Halifax and Egremont read it with rapture unconfined. They could see it was a load of schoolboy nonsense, but it was surely enough to get their enemy locked up. It was one thing to scribble a smutty and insulting poem – but to have it printed!

That was sedition. That was blasphemy. Wilkes was betrayed by one of his printers, a man called Curry, who was paid for handing over some incriminating proof sheets. Having failed with Lord Justice Pratt, the King and his ministers hatched an audacious and unprecedented plan – to have Wilkes simultaneously put on trial in the House of Commons and the House of Lords. 'The continuation of Wilkes' impudence is amazing,' sniffed the King, 'when his ruin is so near.' The King was personally requesting MPs to try John Wilkes MP for seditious and dangerous libel. It was an abuse of his constitutional position, and it is incredible and pathetic that MPs bowed to this monarchical pressure.

In a debate of stunning pomposity, speaker after speaker stood up to monster Wilkes and No 45. The paper was false, scandalous, seditious, libellous, insolent, and, as someone harrumphed, 'it tended to alienate the affections of the people'. Worst of all for Wilkes was the moment when Pitt staggered to his gouty feet – Pitt, under whose banner Wilkes had fought, Pitt, in whose name he had raved against Bute – and joined the general condemnation of the *North Briton*. Next door in the House of Lords the government sprang what they hoped would be the decisive trap.

Their lordships watched in puzzlement as bony Bishop Warburton rose to say he had been libelled by Wilkes in an obscene poem. Even as he spoke, copies of this text, freshly printed at the orders of ministers, were being passed among the trembling peers. Next up was Lord Sandwich, he who invented the swift lunch composed of a piece of meat between two slices of bread. Sandwich had once been a Hellfire Club chum of Wilkes, but they had fallen out over one of his pranks (thought to have involved the introduction of a baboon kitted out with horns), and now he was full of indignation.

Pandemonium broke out as he began to read: 'Awake, my Fanny, leave all meaner things. This morn shall prove what raptures swiving brings. Let us (since life can little more supply Than just a few good fucks, and then we die), Expatiate ...' etc. etc.

Some peers had to leave the chamber to collect their senses. Others thought it ludicrous that Sandwich should be moralising – as one put it, like the devil preaching against sin; and at first it looked as though neither of these parliamentary trials would be successful. People were appalled at the sneakiness of the government in the whole affair – bribing a man's servant to betray him about a smutty poem, and then, in the very height of absurdity, printing more copies of the poem than Wilkes himself.

Curry was vilified for his treachery, and later committed suicide. One of Wilkes' parliamentary victims demanded satisfaction in a duel, and when he shot Wilkes in the groin there was a general and not baseless suspicion that it was an Establishment assassination attempt. When the public hangman tried to obey the edict of the Commons and burn a copy of No 45, he was interrupted by tumultuous crowds. They seized the paper and beat off constables who tried to interfere. Perhaps sensing the mood of the public, the courts now confounded the government, and ruled that general warrants were illegal.

No longer could the King's Messengers make arbitrary arrests, or arbitrary seizures of private property. The King's public appearances were now met with silence, and when he went to the theatre he was treated to cries of 'Wilkes and Liberty!' But Pitt's U-turn was decisive. On 19 January 1764, Wilkes was expelled from the Commons while he was visiting his daughter in Paris.

In the courts a reluctant jury convicted him of libel for publishing the *North Briton* and 'An Essay on Woman', and since he failed to turn up for the sentencing, he became an outlaw. He could no longer sue. He had no protections under the law. He could be arrested at any time and he could be shot on sight by a sheriff. But what did he care? He was in Paris, with his beloved daughter Polly, and he was lionised. For the intellectuals of pre-revolutionary France, Wilkes was a hero, a man who had stood up to the crown and won. A French king might claim that '*l'état, c'est moi*'. No English king could dream of saying any such thing, not after what Wilkes had done to general warrants. When he wasn't in Paris, he was doing a kind of grand tour. He met Voltaire in Geneva and was entertained by the great scholar Johann Joachim Winckelmann in Rome. At one stage he had dinner with Boswell, who found Wilkes in terrific spirits. Explaining his happiness, he confided: 'Thank heaven for having given me the love of women. To many she gives not the noble passion of lust.'

For much of his exile the chief but by no means the sole object of his lust was an eighteen-year-old 'actress' by name of Gertrude Corradini. The great thing about Gertrude, Wilkes told a friend, was that unlike most English and French women of that epoch she believed in taking her clothes off in bed. She was possessed, he said, of the 'divine gift of lewdness' – the perfect complement, one would have thought, to the 'noble passion of lust'. Alas, Gertrude possessed the divine gift of lewdness in such abundance that when she gave birth, and Wilkes consulted his diary, he worked out that she had been in the company not of himself but of a man who claimed to be her 'uncle'. Wilkes was sad, because he loved Gertrude, but, as we have seen, he was easily consoled. Much more worrying was his financial position.

He was meant to be writing a history of England and editing the poems of Charles Churchill. Like most sensible authors, he had already spent the advance, but nothing much had been written. He had sold his books and his house in Aylesbury. He owed money in France. It was time to go back to London and face the music, and so that cold January of 1768 he was furtively prowling down Marsham Street and pondering his options.

He began by standing for the City of London. Despite the frenzied support of the poorer liverymen – 'my brother joiners, carpenters, soap-boilers, distillers' – he came last. He then astonished everyone by announcing that he would go one bigger.

The great thing about being an MP – as he had demonstrated – was that you had parliamentary privilege, and a protection against being sued for libel; and so now he stood for Middlesex, that small county north of the Thames that has been engulfed by Greater London. The poll was to take place in Brentford, and soon the town was gripped with Wilkite fervour. Whatever Wilkes really stood for, the poor of London felt he was on their side.

The cost of bread was rising. The winter was perishingly cold. Their jobs were precarious. But when Wilkes stood up and began his incantatory shout of 'Independence! – Property! – Liberty!' they were wild with excitement. To an illiterate weaver or sawyer, the concept of Wilkes and Liberty could be simply rendered with a scrawl of a squinting man. Simpler still were the digits 45, the number of his seditious edition of the *North Briton*, which came to be a shorthand for liberty itself.

It became a magic number, scrawled on every door in Brentford. After Wilkes had been elected, mobs several thousand strong marched down the Great West Road to London, stopping every carriage they could find, calling on its occupants to huzzah for Wilkes, and hurling mud and stones at all who refused to join the jubilation. They stopped the coach of the French ambassador, handed him a glass of wine and ordered him to toast 'Wilkes and Liberty!', which he did with good grace, standing on the steps of his carriage. When the Austrian ambassador declined to do likewise, this 'most stately and ceremonious of men' was turned upside down and the numbers four and five painted on the sole of either shoe.

The diplomat stormed into Whitehall the following day, to protest on behalf of his government, and found that ministers could not stop laughing. Not everyone was thrilled by Wilk-ism. He told the story himself of how he had come upon an old lady shaking her head at one of his pub signs as it swayed in the wind. 'He swings everywhere but where he should', she said. Wilkes passed her, turned around and bowed with his usual politeness.

The government was in a blue funk. Wilkes was an outlaw who had been elected to parliament. As Lord Camden wrote to the Prime Minister, there was a real risk that if they arrested and punished him, the fury of the mob would be uncontainable. But what else could the government do? He still faced counts of blasphemy and libel, and he had shamelessly absconded to France rather than face his sentence. He was the publisher of infamous attacks on the King and his ministers.

If they turned a blind eye, then the whole authority of the crown would be held up to ridicule. In the first hearing, on 20 April 1768,

Wilkes was dismissed by Lord Mansfield, who said slightly mysteriously that the wrong type of warrant had been made out for his arrest. In the end it was Wilkes himself who insisted on being delivered into custody and having a trial; because that, he knew, was the best way of testing the matters at issue – the right of free speech and the privileges of an MP – and ensuring the maximum publicity. Being an MP meant you couldn't be sued for libel, and being in prison meant you couldn't be sued for debt: so the best thing of all was to be an MP in prison!

He was being remanded in custody when a crowd of his adoring fans tried, unhelpfully, to intervene. On Westminster Bridge they overpowered his guard and unhitched the horses of the carriage conveying him to the King's Bench Prison. One of them told him: 'I tell you, Master Wilkes, horses often draw asses, but as you are a man, you shall be drawn by men.'

Wilkes whispered to the tipstaves – the guards – that they had better scarper, and that he would see them later on in jail; and in due course, having gratified the mob with the sensation of having released him, he put on a disguise and slipped into the prison. Like Charlie Chaplin in *Modern Times*, he had worked out that prison was the safest, best and cheapest place to be. He had been elected by the people, and martyred by the government. He was a cult hero.

To all Americans who felt bullied and belittled by the King of England, Wilkes was their man. He was discussed and quoted in the *Virginia Gazette* more than any other man, while the men of Boston sent him turtle feasts. In Newcastle in England they had crazy 45-themed banquets, at which 45 gentlemen sat down to lunch at precisely 45 past one, and consumed 45 gills of wine, with 45 new-laid eggs in them, followed at precisely 45 minutes past two by 45 dishes including a 45-pound sirloin of beef, after which there took place a ball with 45 ladies and 45 dances and 45 jellies, and the whole thing being wrapped up with great mirth and festivity at 45 minutes past three. 'In china, in bronze or in marble, he stood upon the chimney pieces of half the houses in the metropolis', it was said. He swung upon the sign-posts of every village.

His number appeared on sleeve buttons and breast buckles, punch-bowls, snuff boxes and mugs. There were wigs with 45 curls, and special bras with 45 pieces; and yet he was cheered just as loudly by people who could afford none of this stuff. When no one else seemed to be speaking up for them or their problems, Wilkes was somehow for them. When robbers and pirates wore Wilkite blue cockades in their hats, it was because he stood not just for free speech and parliamentary privilege, but for anyone who felt an injustice at the hands of the system or the state.

As a man who was technically loyal to the King and to the constitution, Wilkes was a lightning rod, a focus for legitimate protest. He was no revolutionary, but in his jovial and satirical style he chipped away at the renewed pretensions of the monarchy. He was a very English and a very Londonian response to a constitutional problem.

We didn't have a Terror in late eighteenth-century England. We didn't have decapitations of the aristocracy, and instead of Danton and Robespierre we had John Wilkes. But there were moments when it looked ugly.

Wilkes' prison was next to a large open space called St George's Fields, and on 6 May 1768 the crowd had grown so huge and noisy that the government sent in troops. The mob was good humoured at first, and took off the boot of one of the soldiers, burning it as a symbol of Lord Bute. Then they became more insulting; a man was shot by mistake. A full-scale riot broke out, and the troops opened fire over their heads, hitting and killing about half a dozen spectators.

The whole of the city was soon in uproar, said the visiting Benjamin Franklin, 'with mobs patrolling the streets at noonday, some knocking all down that will not roar for Wilkes and Liberty'. Five hundred sawyers tore down a new wind-driven sawmill. The coal-heavers and the Spitalfields weavers rioted, and the sailors stopped the boats from leaving London. George III threatened to abdicate, and Wilkes's popularity soared to the stratosphere.

French intellectuals sent him messages of support; American proto-revolutionaries visited him in prison. The cry of 'Wilkes and Liberty!'

was heard in Boston and the number 45 was inscribed on doors and windows across town. Even in Peking an English sea captain came across a Chinese merchant who showed him a porcelain bust of an Englishman with a squint and a jutting chin.

'He knockifar your king,' said the Chinese merchant. 'Your king fooly king. Do so here [draws hand across throat] cutty head.' I assume that being a Chinese he was urging the King to execute Wilkes, rather than the other way round.

Wilkes wrote articles blaming the government for provoking and planning the St George's Fields massacre. By 1769 Grafton's shell-shocked ministry had taken enough. They moved that Wilkes should be expelled from parliament for his libels, and the motion was carried by 213 to 137. Wilkes was nothing daunted. He immediately stood in a by-election, for the same seat, and on 16 February he was returned unopposed. The Grafton ministry was in a quandary. Wilkes was making the King and his ministers appear wholly absurd, and he was becoming so popular that Benjamin Franklin believed the people would have traded him for the monarch.

Prison was no particular barrier to his way of life. He seems to have left more or less at will to attend election hustings, and among the hampers of food he received from his supporters were a firkin of rock oysters, a Cheshire cheese, a brace of fat ducks, turkeys, geese, fowls and so on. When one of his supporters made the mistake of visiting in the company of his wife, Wilkes spotted her as an ex-girlfriend, passed her a billet-doux, and she was soon visiting regularly and without her husband.

A group of Wilkes-backers was preparing to pay off his debts. The date of his release from prison was approaching. The only option, the Grafton ministry decided, was to expel him from parliament again. This time the shameful lickspittles of the Commons voted that he was 'incapable' of election, and to make matters worse they used military force to impose a stooge candidate – Colonel Henry Luttrell – on the people of Middlesex.

It was an outrageous abrogation of the sovereign right of the people to decide who shall represent them. Plenty of pamphlets and blasts were produced on either side, of which the most famous is Samuel Johnson's 'The False Alarm'. Johnson the Tory argued that the House was right to expel Wilkes, because the House was the only judge of its own rights. Wilkes replied, in 'A letter to Samuel Johnson LLD' that 'the rights of the people are not what the Commons have ceded to them, but what they have reserved to themselves'. For Wilkes the key point was that political power emanated from below, and did not percolate down from above.

In April 1770 Wilkes was released from prison amid national rejoicing. A table 45-feet long was laid in a London street. In Sunderland 45 skyrockets were fired at 45-second intervals and in Greenwich there was a salute by 45 cannon fired in sequence. In Northampton 45 couples did a country dance called the Wilkes wriggle. The affair of the Middlesex election was over for now. Wilkes was no longer an MP; but he had already spotted the first step of the way back. On the very day after his release the officers of the City of London gathered in the Guildhall to make him an alderman of the city.

Wilkes now began the long and distinguished Part Two of his career, in which the libertine demagogue evolved into a highly effective London politician, and eventually Mayor of the City. He was still capable of striking powerful blows for liberty. He prevented the packing of juries, opposed the death penalty and banned the press gang. He was also instrumental in tearing down the ancient barrier between press and public, the prohibition on the reporting of parliamentary proceedings. What with the frenzy surrounding the Middlesex election, the political press had been expanding fast; but ever since Caxton's first press there had been a law against reporting parliament. For the city merchants, this was plainly illiberal. It looked like a royal attempt to prevent them finding out what was being done in their name.

Wilkes, ever the champion of the City radicals, organised a challenge. Various printers started to break the law, and to print verbatim accounts of what had happened. As Wilkes had foreseen, the King's Messengers were sent to arrest the printers, in particular a man called Miller. At which point a constable appeared and arrested the messenger.

This unlucky fellow was taken before the Lord Mayor, one Brass Crosby, a drunken follower of Wilkes, who appeared in his nightshirt and proclaimed that no power on Earth could allow a citizen of the City of London to be seized without the consent of a magistrate. The King was enraged, and called for the Lord Mayor and another alderman to be sent to the Tower. But Wilkes – well, His Majesty had finally learned his lesson.

Chatham reported that 'his majesty will have nothing more to do with that devil Wilkes'. It was another chapter in the central conflict of the capital, between the Cities of London and Westminster, between the desires of the merchants and (in this case) the reactionary wishes of the crown.

Once again Wilkes was able to enlist the support of the mob. They attacked the carriage of Lord North and virtually demolished it around him. Ministers acquiesced in the privilege of the City to read parliamentary reports. Wilkes had helped establish a vital democratic freedom, even if the real parliamentary struggle these days is not to keep their debates secret but to persuade the papers to report them at all.

Wilkes's Mayoralty was a splendid affair, and with the multilingual Polly playing the role of lady mayoress he put on all kinds of balls and parties at the Mansion House. As ever, he ran into debt, and when he ran into debt Wilkes pursued his usual strategy. He ran yet again for parliament and in 1774 he was elected unopposed, serving as an MP and Mayor of London at the same time. Wilkes now gave regular speeches, full of research and a liberal idealism. He denounced rotten boroughs, and argued that greater weight should be given to the large population of London – still a good point today.

In 1776 he became the first parliamentarian that I can discover to call for every man, rich or poor, to be able to vote. 'The meanest mechanic, the poorest peasant and day labourer, has important rights respecting his personal liberty', Wilkes told a snoozing handful of MPs. 'All government is instituted for the good of the mass of people to be governed,' he concluded. 'They are the original fountain of power.' Alas, this noble Bill was tossed out with a desultory voice vote. But Wilkes was years ahead of the French, who instituted universal (male) suffrage only after their Revolution in 1792. He had effectively begun a campaign for the extension of the franchise that was to last until 1928 and the granting of votes for women. He was right about voting, and he was right about America and her struggle for independence. In many ways this was the perfect Wilkesian cause – simultaneously allowing him to stick up for liberty and to bash the government of George III.

Stop calling it a rebellion, he warned MPs in 1775. Unless the government made a better effort to understand American feelings, 'the whole continent will be dismembered from Great Britain, and the wide arch of the raised empire will fall.' His speech was published in the *Boston Gazette*. In April 1775 he obtained the signatures of two thousand of his fellow City radicals, liverymen who cared more about free trade and low tax than 'sovereignty' over America. The capitalists happily signed Wilkes' petition, in which he accused the King of 'trying to establish arbitrary power over America', and to what must have been the mortification of ministers Wilkes exercised his right to present the petition personally to the King.

For the first time the two antagonists were eyeball to eyeball, or as near as Wilkes' ocular peculiarities would allow. The veteran troublemaker bowed low, and with every appearance of deference he handed the insult into the gracious hands.

George III afterwards said that 'he had never seen so well-bred a Lord Mayor' – though he immediately changed the rules so that the scene could not be repeated. By the end of the year, Wilkes was becoming so zealous in his pro-American sympathies that he is suspected of downright treason, and actively abetting a network that was raising cash for American guns.

In November 1777 he denounced the American war as bloody, expensive and futile. 'Men are not converted, sir, by the force of the bayonet at the breast'; and in 1778, by which time things were going pretty badly for the blundering British, he was scathing. 'A series of disgrace and defeats are surely sufficient to convince us of the absolute impossibility of conquering America by force, and I fear the gentle means of persuasion have equally failed.' This was not demagoguery.

As ever in war, the public was starting to rally behind 'our boys', and Wilkes was incurring some unpopularity for his stance. If you want any further evidence of his daring willingness to pursue the logic of liberty, take these remarks in the course of a speech on the relief of Catholics. 'I would not, sir, persecute even the atheist ... I wish to see rising in the neighbourhood of a Christian cathedral, near its gothic towers, the minaret of a Turkish mosque, a Chinese pagoda and a Jewish synagogue, with a temple of the sun ...'

It is here, on the issue of religious tolerance, that we can see what finally mattered to Wilkes. When it came to persecuting the Catholics, he was far more interested in the serious defence of liberty than the acclaim of the mob.

Sir George Savile's Catholic Relief Act was a modest measure designed to give Catholics full rights to buy and inherit land and to join the army. This piece of common sense caused a panic in sectarian Scotland, where stories circulated that the Pope had ordered undercover Catholics to join the army and turn their fire on the Protestants. Riots broke out, and soon the trouble spread to England.

A bonkers MP called Lord George Gordon began to whip up anti-Catholic feeling, gathering a petition of 120,000 signatures for the repeal of Savile's Act – and it is important to note that his sickening proposals were supported by old political chums of Wilkes in the City of London. On 2 June 1780 Gordon led a huge mob, fifty thousand-strong, from St George's Fields to Westminster, and as the debate on his motion was going on he would pop out from parliament to wind up the crowd with reports on those MPs who were opposing their bigotry.

At 11 pm the mob went wild. They broke into the chapel of the Sardinian ambassador, in Duke Street, smashed it up and set it ablaze. The Bavarian embassy received the same treatment. The next day the rioters followed the example of the Peasants' Revolt and stormed Newgate and other prisons with pickaxes and sledgehammers, and soon the jails were burning and tinkling with the noise of felons taking off their fetters.

Parliament evaporated in alarm. The King ordered the army to act, without permission of magistrates, to subdue the mob; and yes, there were some thugs and criminals among them, but on the whole these were the very people who had carried Wilkes aloft during the Middlesex election – labourers, apprentices, journeymen, waiters, domestic servants, craftsmen and small traders. And once again John Wilkes was at the heart of the tumult – on the other side.

A mob was attacking London Bridge, setting it on fire in several places, when a party of soldiers appeared on the scene – headed by Alderman Wilkes MP!

A struggle ensued, in which many of the rioters 'were thrown over into the Thames'. Later that day the crowd turned their attention to the Bank of England, the very symbol of money, power and the capitalist conspiracy, the building that in our own time was daubed and bombarded by the G20 protestors. Where was Wilkes, the firebrand radical? He was leading a detachment of troops, who shot and killed several rioters and drove the rest away.

Wilkes ordered a proper crackdown in his ward of the City. He closed the pubs, he confiscated weapons, he locked up the ringleaders and was generally hailed as Mr Law and Order, the man who had got a grip on the situation. Nathaniel Wraxall said he had offered 'indelible proofs' of his loyalty to the crown. He had certainly damaged his standing as the all-purpose hero of the London mob; for which he deserves even more credit.

We have seen that Wilkes disliked violence – remember his concern for the safety of his guards, when the crowd tried to liberate him on London Bridge. In the case of the Gordon Riots, he disliked the violence, but mainly he abhorred the cause. He was nauseated by the anti-papism of his colleagues, such as Alderman Frederick Bull, and though he was now marked down as a pro-Catholic he frankly didn't care.

Dr Johnson wrote approvingly to Hester Thrale: 'Jack Wilkes headed the party that drove them away. Jack, who was always zealous for order and decency, declared that if he be trusted with power, he will not leave one rioter alive.' Johnson was being ironical. Wilkes had not always been a champion of the cause of order and decency, or not in Johnson's view – and here he was, doing exactly what the doctor would have ordered himself.

Perhaps it is time to accept that there was in fact much in common between these titanic figures of eighteenth-century London. On the face of it, they were polar opposites. Johnson was a Tory, Wilkes a radical. Johnson was a monarchist, Wilkes was relentlessly insubordinate to the very king to whom he formally protested his loyalty.

Johnson was a sexually tormented Christian and possible auto-flagellant; Wilkes was an exuberant libertine. And yet when they met, at one of the great dinner parties of world history, it all went swimmingly.

The venue was the home of Charles Dilly, a publisher, in the Poultry; the date was 15 May 1776, and the idea was Boswell's. He wanted to see what would happen if he plunged the great man into unexpected company. He decided to prepare him a bit. The doctor might not approve of all his dinner companions, he hinted. Humf, said Johnson, it was up to Dilly to invite whomsoever he chose. What if Dilly's radical friends were there? 'Poh.' What if Wilkes were there? 'What is that to me, sir?'

When Johnson and Boswell arrived chez Dilly, it was the first time Wilkes had seen his ideological foe up close. If Wilkes looked odd, Johnson looked bizarre, with his shambling bear-like frame, his scrofulous skin and absurd little wig. At first Johnson's weak eyes were unable to make out the company. 'Who is that gentleman, sir?' Boswell identified Mr Arthur Lee, the American independence campaigner. 'Too, too, too,' muttered Johnson, under his breath, as he often did when disturbed. Then Johnson glimpsed a tall man, fashionably dressed, with a peculiar face. 'And who is that gentleman in lace?' 'Mr Wilkes, sir.' Over to Boswell's *Life*:

> The information confounded him still more; he had some difficulty to restrain himself, and taking up a book, sat upon a window-seat and read … The cheering sound of 'Dinner is on the table', dissolved his reverie, and we all sat down without any symptom of ill humour … Mr Wilkes placed himself next to Dr Johnson, and behaved to him with so much attention and politeness that he gained upon him sensibly. No man eat more heartily than Johnson, or loved better what was nice and delicate. Mr Wilkes was very assiduous in helping him to some fine veal. 'Pray give me leave, Sir: – It is better here – A little of the Brown – Some fat, Sir – A little of the stuffing – Some gravy – Let me have the pleasure of giving you some butter – Allow me to recommend a squeeze of this orange; or the lemon, perhaps, may have more zest.' – 'Sir, Sir, I am obliged to you, Sir,' cried Johnson, bowing and turning his head to him with a look for some time of 'surly virtue', but in a short while, of complacency.

Wilkes carried out many seductions, but the buttering up of Samuel Johnson was perhaps the most accomplished of them all. Way back in 1759, when he was a new MP, Wilkes had attempted to appease Johnson's hostility by doing him a great favour. Frank Barber, Johnson's black manservant, had been press-ganged into the navy. As we have seen, Johnson was devoted to the former slave, and would make him his heir. He was desperate to secure his release, and after various people had tried and failed Wilkes stepped in and had a word with the Admiralty.

Like Johnson, he objected to the racism of slavery (and when he was Lord Mayor he was notably kind to at least one destitute former slave). Barber was returned to Johnson; and yet as far as we know Wilkes received not a word of thanks for his kindness. Now, at dinner almost twenty years later, they were getting on famously.

They seem to have swerved the issue of the hour – America – on which they plainly did not agree, but there were plenty of other safe topics. They talked about Horace and Homer and the Restoration poets, and above all, the two hit it off on the subject of Scotland and its hilarious deficiencies. The boldest thing about *Macbeth* was the bit where

Birnam Wood comes to Dunsinane, Wilkes said. You know why? Because Scotland doesn't have a shrub, let alone a wood. Ha ha ha!

Ho ho ho! rocked the doctor. The following day Johnson wrote to Hester Thrale, brooding on the whirligig of time. 'Breaking jokes with Jack Wilkes upon the Scots. Such, madam, are the vicissitudes of things.'

Johnson and Wilkes met up again for dinner in 1781, and Boswell reported that his friend was 'very glad to meet Wilkes again'. It looks as though Johnson was starting to revise his opinion about the justice of Wilkes' expulsion from parliament, and in 1782 parliament finally agreed.

MPs gave in to the umpteenth motion by Wilkes, and it was one of the great moments of his life to watch the clerks of the House standing at the tables and inking out the offending passage in the *Journals*. In 1784 Johnson died, and in that year the King renounced the royal prerogatives he had first asserted in the ministry of Bute.

Wilkes had achieved his manifesto, and he spent his declining years as a pillar of the Establishment. He still conducted feline prowlings between the houses of his various mistresses and offspring, but he managed also to be an efficient and well-paid chamberlain of the City while producing editions of Catullus (Latin) and Theophrastus (Greek).

His popularity with the London proletariat had certainly waned since the Gordon Riots, and he made no particular effort to sustain it. When an old woman saw him and called out, in a quavering voice, 'Wilkes and Liberty!' he snapped, 'Be quiet, you old fool. That's all over long ago.'

This self-dismissal has led some po-faced historians to conclude that he was somehow not serious, and that the blaspheming womaniser had no real principles. On the contrary, he had spent two decades fighting for liberty. He had secured freedom from arbitrary arrest, the right of voters to decide who shall sit in parliament and the right of the press to report and criticise the doings of the Commons.

He did not initially support the secession of the thirteen colonies, but he inspired Americans with his principles, and by the 1770s he was so disgusted with the North government that he was a de facto American revolutionary. As for his impact on England, it was important that his radicalism was tempered by a basic loyalty to the King, or at least to the system. Wilkes was too well mannered and too ironical to be anything like a revolutionary in the French sense. Of course it helped that we English had chopped our king's head off a century earlier, but the Wilkite reforms surely helped the country to contain the economic distress and social unrest of the late eighteenth century.

They had a more gentle programme, conducted with satirical brilliance by a cross-eyed rogue who cheered them all up. They gained freedoms – business people, the working classes, religious minorities – and it was not long before those freedoms were in striking contrast to the totalitarian nightmare of Revolutionary France. A German called Friedrich Wendeborn came to London at the end of the eighteenth century, and he envied the poorest Londoners for the liberty and independence they possessed. 'A foreigner will at first hardly be pleased with the manner of living in London,' he wrote, 'but if he has sense enough to perceive and value the freedom of thinking and acting which is to be enjoyed in England, he will soon wish to conclude his days here.' That freedom of thinking and acting was partly obtained by John Wilkes.

If you look for St George's Fields today you will find no trace of the prison where he was kept, or the place where thousands of his supporters faced the soldiers of George III. But you can see the nearby obelisk at St George's Circus, erected to Brass Crosby, the drunken night-shirted Lord Mayor who refused to allow City printers to be arrested for reporting parliament.

All around are the estates of modern Lambeth and Southwark; the fashionable restaurants, the Borough Market, the thousands of flats of people whose lives have been invisibly influenced by Wilkes and the London he helped to create: vast, 900,000 or a even a million strong by 1800, ready to be the metropolis of the greatest empire ever seen – but a city whose self-confidence resided in the freedoms enjoyed by rich and poor alike. And yet I doubt there are that many Southwark residents who have a totally clear idea of what took place all those years ago on St George's Fields.

Wilkes enjoyed good health almost to the end of his life, and though his dentition made him sometimes hard to understand, he was always rated excellent company. Towards the end he became rather thin, and by the age of seventy-one he was suffering from marasmus, a disease of malnutrition.

The day after Christmas 1797 he sensed that the end was near, and called for a glass of wine. When Polly had produced one, he toasted 'my beloved and excellent daughter', handed back the glass, and after a short time he died.

* * *

You could argue that Wilkes was not only important in inspiring American revolutionaries. His political successes helped to pave the way for the relative calm and prosperity of nineteenth-century London. From the French revolution of 1789 to the Russian Revolution of 1917, via the series of European revolutions of 1848, almost every other country underwent some violent upheaval, frequently involving the murder or expulsion of their monarchs.

Not so in London, where the Wilkes experience had taught governments to compromise, and to move gradually and piecemeal towards parliamentary reform. So Britain acquired the reputation for political stability that has proved so commercially and financially beneficial to this day.

As London grew richer, the population exploded, from about a million in 1800 to 6.6 million by the end of the century. In 1820 William Cobbett had called the city the 'Great Wen' – a boil or eruption on the face of England; and if you had gone up St Paul's in 1900 you would have seen that the suppurating sore of urbanisation had spread over seventy square miles.

As ever greater numbers arrived from the countryside, they moved into rookeries; they divided old family dwellings into steaming and squalid flats; it became more urgent to find ways of conveying them around the city. London's fourth, fifth and sixth bridges were built in quick succession: Vauxhall in 1816, Waterloo in 1817 and Southwark in 1819.

The old port in the Pool of London became too small, and from 1801 they started to dig the new purpose-built docks: first at London Dock, in Wapping, and then on the Surrey side and at Canary Wharf. In 1831 a new London bridge was opened, just a few yards to the west of the old structure – and the old bridge was finally destroyed.

In 1836 there came the first commuter train, arriving at London Bridge station from Greenwich, and the crowds were indescribable. Horsedrawn omnibuses crept across the new bridge, with men sitting perched on the roofs of the carriages like Indian commuters, their machines trying hopelessly to make way against a tide of wagons and other omnibuses moving in the opposite direction, the drivers whipping their poor blinkered beasts in an ecstasy of frustration, and all vehicles surrounded by a human glue of men in stovepipe hats and bonneted women and urchins trying to pick their pockets.

On one day – 17 March 1859 – the bridge was used by 20,498 vehicles and 107,074 pedestrians. These crowds had arrived at the station thanks to a machine more powerful than human or animal muscle. The steam age had hit London.

Once again the urban poor were afflicted by a new surge of automation. Print workers on *The Times* were thrown out of work by the 1828 invention of the steam cylinder press; sail-makers lost out to the paddle-steamers, and the smog rose over the city. One Londoner recorded this lurch forwards, and a technological revolution was echoed by a revolution in painting style.

'Jack has a great variety of talk, Jack is a scholar, and Jack has the manners of a gentleman.'

Samuel Johnson on John Wilkes, *Correspondence*

THE SUIT

If you go to the UN general assembly and behold the representatives of the nations of the earth, there is one thing about their appearance that strikes me as superficially surprising. Here they are, the legations of 192 countries, each with its own proud history and cultural traditions. And yet hardly any of them are in what you might call the garb of their native land.

There are no sealskins or grass skirts; there are no feathered head-dresses or tattoos or leopardskin accessories or elephant tail fly-whisks or nose-bone decorations. There are hardly any kaftans or djellabas. As far as the eye can see there are men in suits – and where there are women, they are wearing the female equivalent of the suit. And these suits are not red or gold or blue or green or striped candy pink.

They are strictly dark, sub fusc, with notched lapels, light shirt and tie. Every man on the planet who wants to be taken seriously wears a suit, of a kind that was conceived in the Regency period – the early 1800s – by a man called Beau Brummell, or George Bryan Brummell (1778–1840).

On the face of it, there is much to disapprove of in this character. He was a dandy and royal toady who gambled and frittered his money on dissipation and clothes. He claimed that he took five hours to dress and recommended that boots be polished with champagne. When asked how much it would cost to keep a single man in clothes, he replied, 'With tolerable economy I think it might be done for £800'. This was an outrageous thing to say, when the weekly wage of the average Londoner was about £1.

He was a sybarite, a piece of gilded human flotsam, and the model for future layabout Bertie Wooster characters who care too much about clothes and are always flicking invisible specks of dust from their Mechlin sleeves. And yet there are several reasons to think well of Beau Brummell. The first is that he was not so much of a royal suck-up as all that.

There was a famous occasion at a party in 1813 when the Prince of Wales came up to four of these Regency bucks, and acknowledged two of them, Lord Alvanley and Henry Pierrepoint, but 'cut' Brummell and another man called Henry Mildmay. At which Brummell said, 'Alvanley, who's your fat friend?' That was not how royalty expected to be treated. And though he was immensely influential on men's dress, he actually took the fashion in the opposite direction to ostentation and show.

This was the era of the Napoleonic Wars, and Brummell led the reaction against French-style frills. He led the fashionable male Londoner away from colourful frock coats, satins, velvets, buckles. He introduced trousers instead of breeches and stockings and he favoured neck ties over cravats. The overall effect was meant to be more sombre but more elegant. In the words of Byron, Brummell's dress was unremarkable except for 'a certain exquisite propriety'.

In other words, Beau Brummell hugely simplified things for us men. He gave us a global uniform that is always acceptable, so that billions of human beings no longer have to worry what on earth to wear. He also gave London a global reputation for being the hub of male fashion, and to this day Savile Row and Jermyn Street tailoring is a major money-spinner for the UK economy. Suits you, sir! we say as we twang our tape measures, and supply some Middle Eastern despot with fifteen pinstripes and a Harris tweed for the grouse moor. Yes, Beau Brummell deserves his statue.

JMW Turner

The Father of Impressionism

People go to art galleries for all sorts of reasons: to edify their souls, to make assignations, to get out of the rain. But it is not often they are rewarded with a thermonuclear bust-up between two of the world's greatest artists.

The scene was the Royal Academy, then in its former home of Somerset House, in the final bustle of preparations for the summer show of 1831. There was none of the chaste white space of your modern gallery, no learned notes or reverential silence.

From floor to ceiling the walls were crammed with the offerings of the Academicians, each painting shouting to be noticed above its neighbours. To hold the centre space of a wall – that was clearly an accolade. To be excluded was an insult.

Into the principal room of the exhibition stomped a fifty-six-year-old man with a battered stovepipe hat and a shiny black coat. In one hand he held an umbrella-cum-swordstick that he used on his continental travels. He had a powerful conk, a protruding chin, and with an inside leg of only nineteen inches long, he was stumpy even by the standards of the day.

He might have been some Dickensian coachman or innkeeper, except for the pigment lodged beneath his fingernails.

He was Joseph Mallord William Turner, a painter so confident of his genius that he had already proclaimed, 'I am the great lion of the day'. Now the great lion was seeking whom he might devour.

Once again his eye roamed over the Academy walls. There was no getting round it. His vast pink and gold fantasy of imperial Roman decay – *Caligula's Palace and Bridge* – had vanished, to be replaced by some chocolate boxy view of a large grey church. Then Turner's blazing eyes alighted on the culprit – a man who had not only had the gall to remove *Caligula's Palace*, but who had painted the very landscape that now hung in its place.

Turner had known John Constable since at least 1813, when the two men had sat together at dinner. Constable had always been kind to the great lion – in public, at any rate – and praised his 'visionary qualities'. It was only a few years ago that Turner had personally informed the younger man of his election to the Academy (though there is some doubt about which way he actually voted); and now Constable had used his position on the Hanging Committee to perform this monstrous switcheroo. It was, as they say, a hanging offence.

Turner let rip. In the words of one witness, David Roberts RA, Turner 'opened upon him like a ferret'. Constable did his best to clamber back on to the moral high ground. My dear Turner, he protested. He was completely disinterested. He was simply anxious to discharge his sacred duty to hang the Academy's paintings to best advantage. It was all a question of finding the best light, and doing justice to Turner's work, and so on. But no matter how much Constable wriggled and twisted, said David Roberts, Turner kept coming back with his zinger. 'Yess,' he hissed at Constable, 'but why put your own there?'

'It was obvious to all present that Turner detested Constable,' Roberts reported. 'I must say that Constable looked to me, and I believe to everyone, like a detected criminal, and I must add Turner slew him without remorse. But as he had brought it on himself, few if any pitied him.'

Turner was furious for a mixture of reasons. There was certainly an element of chippiness. Constable was the good-looking heir of a well-to-do Suffolk corn merchant, who had privately declared that Turner was 'uncouth', which in those days meant strange, or out of the ordinary. Turner was a defiantly self-made cockney, born above a barber's shop in Maiden Lane, who dropped his aitches all his life.

Constable was a conventionally pious and uxorious fellow, who by that stage was wearing black in memory of his wife. Turner was known to be scornful of the married state, and once exploded, 'I hate all married men!' – a generalisation thought to have been aimed at Constable. 'They never make any sacrifice to the arts,' he went on, 'but are always thinking of their duty to their wives and families or some rubbish of that sort.'

No, Turner and Constable were not cut out to be chums. But what drove Turner wild that day was not just the underhand manner in which Constable had promoted his own painting – but the disagreeable reality that the canvas in question – *Salisbury Cathedral from the Meadows* – was a stunner. As Turners go, *Caligula's Palace* is in the not-half-bad category, but over the last 180 years I am afraid it has been beaten hollow for a place on the biscuit tins by *Salisbury Cathedral*. Turner was a shrewd enough judge of a painting's commercial potential to see that he had been not only cynically bumped by his rival, but bumped in favour of an arguably superior product. He thirsted for revenge, and the next year he got it.

In 1832 Constable exhibited his *Opening of Waterloo Bridge*, a painting to which he attached great importance and on which he laboured, apparently, for ten years. Everyone knew he could do clouds and trees and sky and haywains, and little kids lapping water from the stream, but could he do the grand occasion?

Turner was not only an acknowledged master of the pastoral watercolour, but he had done colossal and portentous canvases of Dido founding Carthage, or Ulysses deriding Polyphemus, or the Battle of Trafalgar. Now it was Constable's turn to compete in that genre, and he was vulnerable.

A great painter once told me that every painting must have a 'hero', a point of light or colour or interest to which the eye is drawn before wandering over the canvas. The trouble with Constable's *Waterloo*

Bridge is that there is certainly a lot going on – crowds of spectators, waving bunting, flashing oars, soldiers in busbies; and yet for all the glints of silver and gold and vermilion and crimson lake there is no focal point. There is no hero.

It is a bit of jumble, and it was hard luck that it was exhibited in a small room, next to a very simple Turner seascape. According to CR Leslie RA, who saw what happened next, Turner's effort was 'a grey picture, beautiful and true, but with no positive colour in any part of it'. As was the custom of the day, Constable was working on his own picture on the very wall of the gallery – titivating the decorations and the flags of the barges with yet more crimson and vermilion, each fleck of colour somehow detracting from the others.

Then Turner came into the room, and stood behind him. He watched as Constable fiddled away. Then he went off to another room where he was touching up another picture, and returned with his palette and brushes. He walked up to his picture and without hesitation he added a daub of red, somewhat bigger than a coin, in the middle of the grey sea. Then he left.

Leslie entered the room just as Turner was walking out, and he saw immediately how 'the intensity of the red lead, made more vivid by the coolness of his picture, caused even the vermilion and lake (crimson) of Constable to look weak'. Constable turned to him and spoke in tones of despair.

'He has been here,' he said, 'and fired a gun.' Turner did not bother to come back to the painting for the next day and a half – and then, in the last moments that were allowed for painting, he glazed the scarlet seal he had put on his picture and shaped it into a buoy.

It wasn't just a blob of paint; it was a bullet across his rival's bows. It was war. What we have here – and not before time – is a proper old rivalry between English painters. We have already seen how London works as a cyclotron of talent: drawing bright people together and then bouncing them off each other in a chain reaction of energy and emulation until – pow – there is an explosion of genius. Fame is the spur, said Milton, and London is fame's echo chamber.

It was the struggle for reputation between Elizabethan playwrights, and the struggle between theatre companies to put bums on seats, that helped to produce the millennial flashpoint of Shakespeare. It was the coffee-house rivalries of the natural philosophers that helped to encourage the inventions and conjectures of Robert Hooke. Now in the Royal Academy the English had found an arena in which men (and I am afraid it was almost always men) could do battle for fame as painters; and we must be honest and confess that London was pretty slow to get there – certainly by comparison with Paris.

Londoners may have been world leaders in drama; they were no slouches at science; but for centuries painting was an art form in which the greatest English exponents had embarrassingly foreign names. Hans Holbein, Sir Anthony van Dyck, Peter Paul Rubens, Sir Peter Lely, Sir Godfrey Kneller – all the greatest names of the Tudor and Stuart period seem to have been born abroad. Cardinal Richelieu founded the French Académie de peinture et de sculpture in 1648, about 120 years before George III got around to founding the Royal Academy.

The first President of that Academy was Sir Joshua Reynolds, the friend of Johnson, and in 1788 he made a speech introducing Thomas Gainsborough, in which he wondered wistfully 'if ever this nation should produce a genius sufficient to acquire to us the honourable distinction of an English school'. There was no English School. There was a cultural cringe, an intellectual subservience before the triumphs of French, Dutch and Italian art.

When rich young men came back from their grand tours, they wanted Canalettos, to remind them with postcard accuracy of where they had been. They wanted works either by or in the style of the Old Masters – and for years Turner had himself laboured to imitate the great continentals. In 2009 the Tate Gallery put on a show called 'Turner and the Masters', in which we were invited to see how Turner took on the giants of the past. It was a curatorial triumph, in which Turner's versions were hung next to the Old Masters who had inspired him. There was even an interactive website where you could vote on who came off better from the comparison. Sometimes – when he was up against Van de Velde or Poussin – you felt Turner more than held his own.

Sometimes he looked distinctly second best. When Turner went to see the Rembrandts in the Louvre, he came away declaring with his customary confidence that they were 'miserably drawn and poor in expression.' He was going to out-Rembrandt Rembrandt, and in paintings such as *Pilate Washing His Hands* he has a crack at it. Critics have been scathing ever since. He can't seem to do faces. His versions of the human form are lumpy and indistinct. A lot of the characters seem to have their backs to us, perhaps because he found them easier to do that way round. Rembrandt he ain't.

Turner did not succeed as an imitator or pasticheur. His triumph was in his original work. His energy and aggression produced a new style of painting that combined the translucence of watercolour with the savagery and grandeur of oil. When I was a child I used to stare for ages at the cover of my Penguin edition of Charles Dickens' *Great Expectations*, not just because I was summoning up the will to read it, but because I was absorbed by the painting.

It was a sunset on a river, with the sun as a ball of flame unlike anything I had ever seen rendered in paint. In the foreground was a curious brown boat or buoy. I was looking at a detail of the right side of *The Fighting Temeraire tugged from her last berth to be broken up*.

I appreciate that this painting is now a visual cliché. We have all stared at it for so long that we can hardly take it in. But it is worth looking at again because it is a supreme English masterpiece – indeed, in 2005 it was voted by listeners of the *Today* programme (and who am I to fault their taste?) to be the single greatest painting now hanging in a gallery of the United Kingdom.

In emotion and style it is part of a revolutionary body of work, the product of a London genius who was decades ahead of the Continent. He was more than just a painter. He was a poet and a thinker. He has summed up in one canvas the volcanic transition of his time, a revolution in technology and society that he echoed in paint.

Let us trace that journey from Covent Garden barbershop to *The Fighting Temeraire*. Let us imagine Turner's mind as a painting, and his mature genius as a vast canvas that has been covered – in true Turneresque fashion – by wash upon wash of colour and ideas and sensory impressions.

We begin with the priming of the canvas, the famous birth above the barber's shop at 21 Maiden Lane. Turner later claimed that his nativity had taken place on 23 April – Shakespeare's birthday, and the most auspicious day in the English calendar; and though we have no proof that either Turner or Shakespeare (let alone St George) had anything to do with this particular day, Turner's claim is an assertion of cultural primacy: what Shakespeare had done for English poetic drama, he would do for painting.

His father, William Turner, had been a wigmaker who had been reduced to cutting hair after wigs went out of fashion in the 1770s (Pitt the Younger imposed a tax on the powder). So it was not exactly the lowest form of barber's shop.

We must imagine a clubby atmosphere in which the infant Turner first gazed about him, with gentlemen coming in for coffee or leafing through the pages of the *Spectator* and even gazing at the paintings on the wall. Turner himself was emphatically not a gentleman. He grew up amid the oaths of costermongers and the calls of whores, and all his life his cockney accent was the subject of mockery – even when he was Professor of Perspective at the Royal Academy.

He never turned into one of the toffs who bought his paintings. He never showed any such pretensions. He remained psychologically rooted in the backstreets of Covent Garden, and if his patrons were lace-cuffed Tory dandies, Turner remained emotionally and politically a radical. He was chippy and insecure to the end, and no wonder, really, when we consider that he had what we would now call a disturbed childhood. His mother was mad, and subject to 'ungovernable rages'.

Poor Mary Turner never recovered the balance of her mind after the death of her daughter, and when Turner was in his early twenties she was committed to the Bedlam asylum in Moorfields. If you want a vision of this hell on Earth, think of Hogarth's image of the Rake's final progress into madness; and yet it doesn't look as if her son even visited her until she died.

By the time he was ten, things were so bad at home that he went to stay with his maternal uncle, Joseph Mallord William Marshall, in Brentford, Middlesex – the same Brentford where Wilkes had fought his famous campaign, and where the cries of 'Liberty' still echoed in the air – loudly enough, some say, for Turner to have picked up their echo. It was here that he employed the sublime displacement for his unhappiness: painting what he saw, and developing a habit he had discovered at the age of eight.

The Thames in those parts was (and to some extent still is) an Arcadian landscape, full of lush meadows and woodland scenes, and from a very young age he drank in ideas – light breaking behind a tree, the play of the sun on water – that he was to reference all his career. Better yet, he went to school the next year in Margate, and now the images of the sea crashed in like breakers on his imagination, and that experience generated so many drawings that his proud father was able to mount an exhibition in the barbershop window.

At the age of twelve he sold his first painting and discovered the joy of making money from art. This was the epoch in which Jane Austen heroines were supposed to knock off watercolours in the longueurs before luncheon, while waiting for Mr Darcy to show up. The boy Turner gave them a hand by doing the background skies, which he sold from a stall in Soho.

His father's barbershop patrons would be offered 'something for the weekend' – a river scene from his manic teenage brush. At the age of only fourteen he had found a job in an architect's firm, colouring in the drawings, and almost certainly through this contact he arrived at this precocious age at the portals of the Royal Academy. On 11 December 1789 he was personally interviewed and admitted by the sixty-six-year-old Sir Joshua Reynolds, the first President. Turner was to remain devoutly loyal to the institution and to Reynolds, and he later asked to be buried next to the man who had spotted his talent.

Reynolds had a theory about painting – that it should be like poetry. A great painting, he said, should have the 'profound humanism, mellifluity of utterance, the aptness of language, measure and imagery, the grandeur of scale, and moral discourse of the most exalted poetry and poetic dramas!'.

In other words, a painting was more than just a souvenir depiction of some place or person. It was meant to engage and lead the emotions, as a poem does. It was a statement. More than any other English painter before or since, Turner tried to turn pigment into pure feeling, and though he was later to shock his fellow Academicians with his techniques, he was always essentially following the ideology of Joshua Reynolds.

But Reynolds was sensible enough to see that you couldn't just invite young ragamuffins into the Royal Academy, and hope that they would become the English equivalent of Rembrandt or Poussin. They had to learn to draw. Under his scheme, pupils spent two years drawing from a sculpture cast gallery; and only then, if they were any good, were they allowed to draw the human form in the nude. Turner was good, and developed a lively interest in drawing naked women that was to last all his life. Even at the age of seventy he was doing graphic close-ups of copulation – hundreds of erotic or just-porno images that later sent his great champion, John Ruskin, into a spin.

You may recall that Ruskin fainted at the sight of his wife's pubic hair (which slightly took the snap out of their honeymoon) and when he opened his hero's notebooks he was so flabbergasted that he pronounced them evidence of Turner's mental frailty, and claimed – falsely, thankfully – to have destroyed them all.

In this desensitised digital age, with electronic images strobing away in the palms of our very hands, it is easy to forget the impact of two-dimensional representational art on the eighteenth-century mind. London was a 'paper culture', in which prints – including erotic prints – sold in their thousands. But for the vast majority of Londoners there was something supernatural in the ability of people like Turner to take a fugitive event – a shipwreck, a frosty morning, a snowstorm engulfing

Hannibal as he crosses the Alps – and make them feel that they were in some sense witnesses.

That is partly why they valued these paintings so highly. By the 1790s, Turner was beginning to get good money – and he acquired the habit of hard bargaining.

In fact, he was to become something of a Scrooge. When Walter Scott later asked him to do some engravings of Edinburgh history, he was amazed at the bill. 'Turner's palm is as itchy as his fingers are ingenious,' he wailed. 'He will do nothing without cash, and anything for it. He is the only man of genius I ever knew who was sordid in these matters.'

Sordid or not, the twenty-five-year-old had achieved a circle of rich patrons. These were men with money to blow from the proceeds of empire, and we must imagine their frustration. They might want a Poussin or a Canaletto to go in the drawing room, but for years the Napoleonic Wars had made it difficult or impossible to source them from the Continent.

They had to make do with home-grown talent; and indeed you could argue that the emergence of Turner in the late eighteenth century – with the Continent effectively cut off by the Royal Navy from trade with the British Empire – was one of the world's great examples of import substitution. A painting by the French master, Claude, might cost £6,000 – a stupefying sum – and they were hard to find. But a French-style Turner could be procured for a mere £150.

The young Turner so venerated Claude that he was once found standing in front of one of his paintings with tears running down his cheeks, in despair that he would never be able to paint like the French Old Master. And yet the last time a big Claude was on the market he fetched a couple of million pounds. The last big Turner fetched £29 million. It's no more after you, Claude.

Already by the end of the eighteenth century Turner was starting to do what all artists yearn to do: to set the trends himself. A commercial painter is generally engaged in a compromise between what he is interested in painting, and what his clients want. On the whole people liked to pay for pictures of themselves, or their estates, or their dogs/horses/wives, or possibly a pastoral view in the manner of some attested foreign artist.

By his mid-twenties Turner had reached the happy state of being able to ignore this convention, and to serve whatever he wanted to his millionaire clients, in the knowledge that they would gobble it up. By 1799 he had orders for sixty watercolours, and had to build a special rotating table to speed up the process of composition.

It would be wrong to say his style emerged from nowhere but his own cockney head. He learned deeply, not just from the Old Masters that were brought to London, but from his fellow Academicians, especially Romantic watercolourists like John Robert Cozens and Richard Wilson. He was in fact a phenomenal sponge of ideas and influences, endlessly looking for new landscapes and new atmospheres. He not only travelled throughout Britain, but as soon as the Peace of Paris was signed in 1802 he raced to the Continent, where eyewitnesses describe this funny little man who would shout for the coach to halt so that he could capture that particular aspect of the dawn or dusk. He spent days at the Louvre, feverishly copying the artistic treasure house that Napoleon had assembled from the rest of conquered Europe. By 1803 he was a full Academician, but already a master of oil as well as watercolour.

He had sold so many paintings that he was able to build his own house near Harley Street, complete with an exhibition gallery – allowing him to exhibit simultaneously at home and at the Royal Academy. With success he grew ever more confident and more adventurous in his style. Some critics attacked his 'dynamic composition' and 'shocking colours'. What they could not fault was his appetite for work and technical mastery.

We have a celebrated insight into his powers of memory, from the niece of one of his patrons. In 1818 he was staying at Farnley Hall near Leeds, the seat of one Walter Fawkes – a descendant of the man who tried to blow up the Houses of Parliament and himself a noted liberal reformer. At one stage he had even held republican views. But like

Turner, Fawkes was a patriot and deeply gripped by England's recent seafaring triumphs.

One morning at breakfast Walter Fawkes commissioned a painting – a rare event, since he normally allowed his famous guest to take it easy. In an age before television, and fifty years before the first photograph, he wanted to be able to feast his eyes on one of the great ships that had beaten Napoleon's admirals. 'I want you to make me a drawing of the ordinary dimensions that will give me some idea of the size of a man-of-war.'

As Fawkes' niece relates: 'The idea hit Turner's fancy, for with a chuckle he said to Walter Fawkes' eldest son, then a boy of about fifteen, "Come along, Hawkey, and we will see what we can do for Papa", and the boy sat by his side the whole morning and witnessed the evolution of the *A First Rate Taking in Stores*. His description of the way Turner went to work was very extraordinary. He began by pouring wet paint on to the paper till it was saturated, he tore, he scratched, he scrubbed at it in a kind of frenzy and the whole thing was chaos – but gradually and as if by magic the lovely ship, with all its exquisite minutia, came into being and by luncheon time the drawing was taken down in triumph. I have heard my uncle give these particulars dozens of times ...'

Have a look at the map of England. You will see that Farnley Hall, Leeds, is nowhere near the sea. Then look at the detail with which he has reconstructed *A First Rate Taking in Stores* – the mass of rigging, the exact number of gunports and spars on the masts, the shape of the prow, the light playing on the waves.

This was a kind of Rain Man, an eidetiker, a human camera, blessed with such creative energy that according to another account 'he tore up the sea with his eagle claw of a thumbnail'. By 1818 he had drawn and painted the sea so many times – and was so gripped by the ships of the line – that he was able to download his brain onto paper in a vast belch of self-expression; and yet the result was harmonious and accurate, and just what his patron wanted.

It must have been an unforgettable experience for that child to sit and watch Turner paint, and the artist loved to show off. Verbally incoherent he may have been, but with his brushes and sponges he was a master, an orator, who could turn the very act of painting into an exhibition in itself.

There was more than a touch of Rolf Harris in his performances. Perhaps his most famous 'Can you see what it is yet?' moment took place in February 1835. Early in the morning the fifty-nine-year-old Turner had arrived at the Royal Institution to find his canvas on the wall – virtually blank except for an indistinct outline of some kind of river scene. A crowd gathered round him, and he started to go through his act, squeezing great gobs from the tubes, chucking them on with his knife, smearing them around with his fingers.

It wasn't long before they had worked it out. On 16 October of the previous year the Clerk of Works of the Palace of Westminster had finally decided to get rid of the tally sticks. These were the medieval systems for recording the payment of taxes – notching two ends of a hazel stick and then splitting it, taxpayer and sheriff each keeping a piece, so that the deal could afterwards be verified by matching the unique irregularities of the split stick. Over the centuries the exchequer had accumulated zillions of these now pointless objects, and it was decided to burn them.

A bonfire would upset the neighbours, so two workmen, Joshua Cross and Patrick Furlong, were ordered to use the underfloor coal furnaces that heated the House of Lords chamber. All day long they went about their work, and soon the furnaces were roaring with the pitiful tax returns of long-dead Englishmen. By 5 pm someone noticed that the floor of the Lords was getting warm, and by the evening the copper flues of the chimney had succumbed to the heat.

The joists of the floor caught fire, the soft furnishings of the Lords went up like paper and that night London was treated to the most spectacular conflagration since 1666. Prime Minister Melbourne was watching, along with the rest of the cabinet, as St Stephen's Chapel – where Wilkes and Pitt had done their stuff – was consumed; and Turner was there too.

He watched from Waterloo Bridge and then he walked round to the south side of Westminster Bridge, recording frame after frame in the photographic cell of his memory. Now the crowd stood behind him to watch the disaster unfold again: he wasn't just Rolf Harris; he was the nearest thing to the television news. He worked all day, as if oblivious to his audience, and when he had finished he didn't even step back to squint and admire his work.

He just shoved his paints back in their box and, keeping his gaze turned to the wall, he just sidled away. Daniel Maclise, an Irish portrait painter, was watching, and he recognised a master. 'He knows it is done, and he is off,' he commented as Turner scuttled out.

Turner painted several views of *The Burning of Parliament*, and there is a striking feature of all of them. You could not say there is any particular sense of horror. We see no arms being waved in despair – as there are, for instance, in the image of Hannibal's army being engulfed by a snowstorm as it crosses the Alps. It is a rather jolly bonfire, with a blue evening sky, and fleecy clouds lit up as if by a spectacular sunset. Which is perhaps how Turner thought of it. He was always an advocate of reform, and if you want parliament reformed, burning it down is a good way to start. Turner's patrons may have been rich Tories but his instincts were reformist, libertarian. He backed the Greeks in their struggle for independence, with a fine painting of the massacre at Chios. And nowhere did his generally libertarian character show itself more clearly than in his domestic arrangements.

He never married, and seems pretty regularly to have found himself in the arms of prostitutes and other ladies of negotiable affections, both at home and abroad. We have a bawdy poem, written in his thirties, to a girl called Molly who was his 'passport to bliss'.

For a long time he had a relationship with Sarah Danby, the widow of a noted songwriter and chum of Turner's. Mrs Danby was ten years older than him, and scholars used to believe that her two daughters, Evelina and Georgiana, were by Turner. But it has recently been suggested that Sarah Danby's daughters were in fact sired by Turner's father, William. Ever since the death of his wife, the old boy had been an important part of the Turner ménage, helping to stretch canvases and varnish paintings. Whether his duties included servicing Turner's mistress we will probably never know, but it was certainly not a conventional household.

In middle age JMW Turner had pleasant flirtations – and possibly more – with the twenty-something daughters of friends, and by the time he was knocking on a bit he found Sophia Booth, who ran a boarding house in Margate. Here in this agreeable Kentish resort he enjoyed terrific views of the sea, and wonderful light, and by means of that new marvel of technology, the steam boat or steamer, it was possible to make fast and regular trips from London.

He would hang over the back of the boat to watch the roiling water, and when Sophia's husband died Turner pursued the widow Danby strategy – and infiltrated himself into her bed. His arrangements now became surreal. When people arrived at his house near Harley Street, they found a Dickensian air of decay. One visitor thought 'it presented the appearance of a place in which some great crime had been committed', paint peeling from the door, 'the windows grimed with successive coats of dust and rain'. The door was opened by a mute servant, her face covered with bandages. The picture gallery itself was in a state of alarming disrepair, with so many holes in the roof and windows that viewers were advised to use an umbrella in case of rain. But the funny thing is that Turner himself was not there. He had taken Sophia Booth to a small riverside cottage in Chelsea, and here he would parade up and down with this buxom illiterate widow twenty-five years his junior – she tall and imposing, he stumping along like a bow-legged old sea dog.

Neighbours and tradesmen in Chelsea learned to call him 'Mr Booth', or 'Puggy Booth', or – as he preferred, 'Admiral Booth', in deference to his nautical air. No one realised that this red-nosed old codger was England's greatest artist, and such was Turner's lust for privacy that he would always make sure, on leaving the Royal Academy or his club in Pall Mall, that no one heard him give his address to the taxi driver.

This was his relationship with Sophia Booth – secret, but more obviously satisfying than any previous affair. So it was that by 1839 we find him chugging back from Margate aboard the steamer, and looking idly to starboard as London came into view. If Turner's genius was a canvas, it is now varnished and complete. Layer upon layer of experience and insight has been applied to one of the most receptive imaginations the world has known.

He has copied the Old Masters, struggled with them, bested them, and forged his own revolutionary and lucrative style. He has absorbed the changes in the landscape of London, changes faster and more shocking than those seen by any previous generation. The population has trebled or even quadrupled in his lifetime, and people's assumptions and way of life have been convulsed by a technological revolution of unprecedented speed and ferocity. He has seen all human life, from the madrigals in the drawing room of Petworth House to the obscene cavortings of sailors' women in the pubs of Wapping. As much as any painter before him, and probably more, he has stared at the impact of sunlight on natural objects, and in London he has seen how that light has become filtered – and its colours made more astonishing – by the smoke and steam of the Industrial Revolution.

He has produced thousands of paintings in oil and watercolour of thousands of objects and people, but none is to do more for his reputation than the thing he now glimpses. It is the hulk of a once great ship, in the dock at Rotherhithe. She has no sails and no masts, but with his piercing eyes Turner can make out the writing on her side. She is the *Temeraire*. For a man of his generation, the name was like a bell.

Called after a French 74-gunner that had been captured at the Battle of Lagos in 1759, HMS *Temeraire* had fought at Trafalgar, and with famous gallantry. She had been badly beaten up as she struggled to protect Nelson's flagship, HMS *Victory*. She had helped to force the surrender of the French ship *Redoubtable* and to capture the *Fougueux* – the flagship of Napoleon's fleet. He was looking, in other words, at one of the most heroic vessels in all the heroic history of English naval warfare.

When he was thirty this boat had helped settle the course of history, and cement the place of England as the greatest maritime and commercial power on Earth. From that engagement, and from the terrestrial victory at Waterloo, there followed the uninterrupted rise of England as the workshop of the world. Everything Turner could see around him from his vantage point on the Thames steamer – the docks, the factories, all the sprawl of human habitation and work – was in a sense the product of the audacity of that ship. And now look at her. Mutilated, about to be ripped up by the forces of capitalism, her brave timbers turned to lumber and scrap. It was like seeing an old broken-down Derby winner being carted off for dog food. Click went the shutter in Turner's retina. Click click click as his steamer chugged round and off upriver; and over the next few weeks and months he meditated a fitting send-off for the *Temeraire*, a funeral pyre of red and gold.

It was only a couple of years since Queen Victoria had come to the throne, in 1837, and her reign had begun with an insult. Constable was dead, and Turner had no rival in English art; and yet the Queen's first honours list included Newton, the miniaturist, Westmacott, the sculptor, and Callcott, a disciple of Turner – but not Turner himself. 'I think it possible he was hurt', said CR Leslie, the Academician. That was an understatement; but the trouble was the Queen apparently thought Turner was barmy.

From the 1820s on he had become more and more controversial. In his refusal to do what people thought an artist should do, that is, represent people and objects in a recognisable way, and in his egotistical obsession with how the light appeared to the eyes of JMW Turner, he was starting to seem perverse. There were some who said he was a con man, toying with the credulity of the public. He was acquiring the same sort of reputation as Damien Hirst. 'Soapsuds and whitewash' was one sniffy response to his unorthodox insistence on so much white paint. There was a theatrical skit in which a baker's boy dropped some red and yellow jam tarts on the floor, put a frame round the mess, called it a Turner and sold it for £1000. It would not be surprising if Turner was in a mood to silence his critics, and avenge his reputation, with a painting that was both obviously representational and yet soaringly Turneresque.

So he took that image of a knackered old prison hulk, and added some inaccuracies. The ship he saw in the dock had no mast or sail. It is doubtful that he saw her being pulled by a tug, and in any case if she was being tugged from Chatham to Rotherhithe then the sun is in the wrong place. And her crew didn't know her as the *Fighting Temeraire*; she was called the *Saucy Temeraire*. But you can see why Saucy didn't quite hit the note Turner wanted.

As soon as she was unveiled, his *Temeraire* was a colossal hit with the public. He liked the painting so much himself that he called it 'My Darling.' Turner had triumphantly fulfilled the precept of Joshua Reynolds. He had created a poem.

As you look at the *Fighting Temeraire*, you are struck not just by the effect and the composition: the sunset on the glassy surface of the water, with the ship and tug off to the left in an artful triangle of blue, and the sinister buoy downstage right – a use of space Turner learned as a teenager, when he painted sets at the Pantheon Theatre, Covent Garden. You sense instantly that there is an argument, a theme, a statement. There was no point in asking the artist what his painting meant, and in any event Turner was famously unintelligible in matters of interpretation.

In the words of George Jones RA, 'Turner's thoughts were deeper than ordinary men can penetrate, and much deeper than he could at any time describe'. There was once a lively discussion in Turner's presence about the identity of a brightly coloured object lying in the water of his painting of *Venice, Ducal Palace, Dogano*, with part of *San Giorgio* (1841).

Was it a buoy? his acolytes asked him. Was it a gorgeous turban? Was it a seaman's cap? 'After one or two twitches of his lips, and as many half hmmms, he replied: 'Orange – orange …'

You don't need any crib from the artist and you don't need the slightest grounding in art history to see the symbolism of *The Fighting Temeraire*. It is about age and youth, the old hero reduced to dependency, blinded Oedipus led by a boy, or perhaps (since all artistic feeling is to some extent autobiographical) it was even about sixy-four-year-old Admiral Turner being tugged up the seafront at Margate by smart, bustling Sophia Booth.

But it is most obviously about transition, about the passing of the great age of sail in favour of the age of steam. On the right hand side the sun is going down, just above the buoy where *Temeraire* will be moored for the last time. On the left we see the silvery light from a waxing moon – a symbol, some say, of the new age of technology.

The legacy of HMS *Temeraire* was a period of unrivalled peace and prosperity for Britain, in which hundreds of thousands of country dwellers came to work in the shops, factories and docks of what had become the greatest manufacturing centre on Earth. In 1824 the Bank of England ended its monopoly of joint-stock banking, and soon great palazzos of finance were being constructed in the City, with Barclays and the Midland among the first.

Banks and insurance companies needed clerks. The hackney carriages of the rich were replaced by large horse-drawn omnibuses, groaning with the weight of everyone who could afford the fare. The concept of the commuter was born. And as soon as mass transit was feasible, the suburbs started to explode. The cartoonist George Cruikshank lived in Amwell Street, Islington, and in 1824 he drew a terrifying vision of urban sprawl. *London Going Out of Town – The March of Bricks and Mortar* shows files of chimney pots forming up to savage the fields, while regiments of houses hurl volleys of bricks, gouging and churning the defenceless turf.

With every new train and chimney stack the pollution grew, and with every new arrival the overcrowding worsened. Londoners suffered repeated outbreaks of cholera, whose cause baffled the authorities. There were many artists and writers who followed William Blake in lamenting the mills and machines and urbanisation; but I am not at all sure Turner was among them.

In 1838, the year he saw the *Temeraire*, they opened the Great Western Railway from Paddington. In 1844 Turner tried to convey his feelings about this development in *Rain, Steam and Speed*. He shows a locomotive shooting towards us over a bridge at Maidenhead, and the painting's 'hero' is the fire blazing in the boiler.

This is not an anti-industrial painting. If anything, it is a celebration of the vision-blurring pace and power of the new machine, unlike anything humanity has seen before. Nor could you say that Turner is exactly hostile to the tugboat in *The Fighting Temeraire*, as she beetles efficiently towards us, flame billowing from her glistening black chimney. Yes, you feel the pathos of the ghostly old superannuated sail ship behind her. But Turner knew nothing of carcinogens or CO_2 emissions.

As far as he was concerned, the steamboat was a wonderful new machine that could convey him speedily to Margate and the arms of Sophia Booth. I would say Turner is basically Promethean, pro-technology. But what really interested him was colour and movement, and the way the light behaved as it shone through the industrial gases of the new epoch, the excuse he found for a style of painting that was ever more impressionistic.

In 1870, long after Turner was dead, Claude Monet came to London. He went to the galleries and saw what Turner had done. He went to the same vantage points on the banks of the Thames, and like Turner, he painted the Houses of Parliament – in this case the Barry and Pugin masterpiece whose £2-million cost Dickens had so deplored. The building was different, the smog was even thicker, and Monet and Co were to go on to become the most fashionable painters of our times, regularly smashing records at auction houses.

But there can be no serious doubt that the first breakthrough was Turner's. He was the first to assert the principle that what mattered was not what you saw, but the way you saw it. He was the father of impressionism.

In 1846 JMW Turner had moved with Sophia Turner to their small house in Chelsea. If he climbed to his rooftop balcony, and looked left and right, he could see two of the finest views of the river to be found in London. On the day he died, 19 December 1851, he was found on the floor of his bedroom, apparently trying to tiger-crawl to the window to look at the river.

Turner's doctor reported how, just before 9 am, 'the sun broke through the cloudy curtain that had for so long obscured its splendour, and filled the chamber of death with the glory of light'. Turner died without a groan, holding the hand of his faithful Sophia – to whom, with typical stinginess, he left virtually nothing.

Another version has it that he offered some famous last words: 'The sun is god.' This was not perhaps as controversial an analysis as you might think. In spite of the efforts of every bishop since Mellitus, London remained, beneath it all, a pretty pagan place, with only 25 per cent of the population turning up to church on a Sunday. Whether he meant it or not, Turner's curious Aztec belief is at least as plausible as any other theory, and it did nothing to dent a popularity that grows to this day.

* * *

In the year Turner died the Victorians went in their millions to the Great Exhibition. A Crystal Palace or 'Great Shalimar' was built in Hyde Park, a temple to the benefits of trade and technological innovation. For a shilling Londoners could see everything from the Koh-i-Noor diamond to a demonstration of the world's first fax machine.

In the same year – 1851 – the first submarine cable was laid between London and Paris, to be followed by a cable to New York in 1866 and Melbourne in 1872. The age of telecommunications was born, and as the telegraph made shipping easier and more predictable, it was possible to cut costs and move to what we would now call a 'just in time' system. More and bigger ships arrived, with bigger cargoes, and speculators dug huge new docks, the Victoria and Albert, at Plaistow levels.

London was now incomparably the richest city on Earth, with a stock exchange more than five times bigger than that of New York (and where the more relaxed approach to settlement deadlines encouraged greater risk and greater reward). All those canals and docks and railroads and bridges and undersea cables – all that Victorian infrastructure – required finance, and hardly any of it would have been possible without the ingenuity and daring of London's leading bankers.

'I was a good deal entertained with Turner – he is uncouth but has a wonderful range of mind.'

John Constable 1813

THE BICYCLE

In its simple brilliance, the bicycle is one of the most fortunate ideas ever to have emerged from the mind of our species – and so I must be scrupulous and record that the first ancestor of the bicycle was not actually invented in London. I am afraid the honour belongs to a German baron called Karl Drais, a forestry official and physics graduate of Heidelberg university, who can also claim to have invented the first typewriter keyboard.

There seems little doubt that the first people to encounter a two-wheeled leg-propelled velocipede were in Mannheim in 1817, when Drais took his Draisine on a country spin. But in less than a year the idea had been filched and improved upon by a London inventor, Denis Johnson. It was in Long Acre, Covent Garden, that Johnson – who may or may not be a distant relative of the present author – made some crucial modifications. If you look at the first image we have of Drais on his Draisine, you can see that it was a pretty agricultural device. The spokes and felloes of the wheels are plainly of wood, and the whole thing was so heavy and unwieldy that any collision was liable to give the driver a hernia.

Johnson was one of the many expert coachbuilders of Covent Garden, and he lightened the contraption with a curved metal frame and metal spokes for the wheels. Unlike Drais, he also found a market for his product. London after 1815 was full of young men whose fathers had grown rich on the proceeds of industry and empire. These were the dandies, the followers of Beau Brummel (*qv*). For the dandies, Johnson's velocipede was not so much a convenient way of getting around. It was like their tumbling white shirt fronts and lorgnettes: it was a fashion statement. In an age of parliamentary reform and industrial strife, it was a frivolous and outrageous assertion of elitism. Denis Johnson made and sold about 320 of his 'pedestrian curricles' – which also went by the name of hobby-horses, dandy-horses and accelerators, and patented his machine in 1818. He was granted Royal Letters Patent for a 'machine for the purpose of diminishing the labour and fatigue of persons in walking, and enabling them at the same time to use greater speed which said machine he intends calling the Pedestrian Curricle'.

By March 1819 he had opened two 'riding schools', on the Strand and Brewer Street, charging a shilling for admission and £8 for purchase. His son took it on a sales tour of the country, and there are some fine prints of young men learning to ride the dandy-horse and coming a cropper. Alas, the roads were so bumpy that the experience was very hard on the lower abdomen, and when they tried it on the pavement the dandies (and dandizettes, as female dandies were called) became even more unpopular.

In a year or two the dandy-horse craze was dying out, and the Royal College of Surgeons pronounced them dangerous. But when rotating pedals were added forty years later, it was Johnson's dandy-horse that served as the basis. The most egalitarian means of transport began as an anti-egalitarian symbol of extravagance, and yet it wasn't as slow as all that.

In 1819 four 'gentlemen' rode Johnson velocipedes over the 60 mile course from London to Brighton in 12 hours. When Mark Cavendish won the Olympic preparation race in August 2011, he covered the 87 miles from London to Box Hill and back in 3 hours 18 minutes – which makes him only about five times faster than the dandies.

Lionel Rothschild

The man who financed the Empire

It is well known and statistically attested that cycling in London is safe and getting safer. But even the most experienced cyclist will accept that there are one or two stretches where you mentally cross yourself and hope that the drivers are paying attention.

It takes a certain sang-froid to hurl yourself down the underpasses of the Marylebone Road; and then there is the *palio* of Hyde Park corner. I don't just mean the bit at the top of Consitution Hill, where you have to launch into the one-way stampede of buses and taxis; the real white-knuckle moment comes after you have puffed up from Knightsbridge towards Piccadilly, and you are held at the lights along with all the Beemers and Maseratis; and when the lights change and you are released, you pedal like the devil, believe me, because you can see the army of cars drawn up on your left at the bottom of Park Lane. It is like passing in front of the cavalry of Crazy Horse or Marshal Ney, as the great beasts paw the earth and prepare to charge. And as you waggle your way into the relative safety of Piccadilly, just ahead of the tide of metal, you may ask yourself how it came about that London has an urban motorway running through what was once a famously lovely and pastoral district of Park Lane.

We must thank a former Tory transport minister, called Ernest Marples. Among other things, this visionary decided that what London needed was big one-way gyratories around Marble Arch (which was called Marple Arch, in honour of the excavations he promoted) and Hyde Park Corner.

In 1962 he turned this attractive area into a scene of devastation, with craters so big that my father used to claim he made use of one of them to inter a clapped-out Austin Healey. In the course of building his five-lane roundabout around the Wellington Arch, Ernest Marples demolished a row of houses at the end of Piccadilly.

These were not any old houses. At least one of them, 148 Piccadilly, had latterly become a bit faded – the headquarters of the Society of Motor Manufacturers and Traders. But it was still a monument of domestic grandeur, built on the scale of a London club. There were cavernous wine cellars and servants' quarters, and vast kitchens with new-fangled gas cookers, and sweeping marble staircases leading up to a *piano nobile* full of masterpieces of Flemish painting and French *cloisonne* and windows with views out over the park.

This was the location of one of the most sensational deals ever done between a bank and the British government. That space now occupied by the roaring traffic was once the home of Lionel de Rothschild, and it was here that he would meet his friend Benjamin Disraeli, the Prime Minister.

It was 1875 and Britain was at the apogee of its power, and London was a great industrial centre. In the East End, the lower Lea Valley, and the area now intended for Olympic rejuvenation, there was a mind-boggling and nostril-assailing array of factories and plants.

Indeed, that was why they were in the East End, because the prevailing wind was meant to carry their vapours away from the sensitive noses of those who lived in great mansions in Piccadilly. There were factories making jute and manure and rubber and fertiliser, and they filled the air with the signature aroma of boiled-up putrid fish. There were businesses that took in the sugar and oranges of the colonies and sent them out again at a vast mark-up as Keiller's marmalade. They shipped in gas tar, and shipped it out again as creosote, naphtha, pitch, anthracene, disinfectant, insecticide and aniline dyes. London took in wool, tea, coffee, sugar, dyestuffs, you name it – and then London firms would process the stuff and package it and send it round the world. They took in cotton from India and then sent it back to clothe the Indians themselves, until it was said that the plains of Hindustan were bleached with the bones of Indian weavers.

Now Disraeli – romantic and opportunistic about the empire and its Empress – saw the chance to extend his country's global lead. By 1871 a French-led consortium had opened the Suez Canal, linking the Mediterranean to the Red Sea, and its strategic potential was obvious. The canal cut journey times to India, because ships no longer had to slog around the Cape of Good Hope. The Suez Canal plainly opened up the whole of east Africa for trade and colonisation – and here there was an opportunity to buy it, and to put British thumbs around this vital new commercial windpipe.

The Ottoman Empire was bust; the Khedive of Egypt was bust; the company that had dug the canal had found – as so often – that the returns on the new infrastructure project did not match up to expectations. The Egyptians wanted £4 million – a staggering sum for those days, equivalent to about 8.3 per cent of the entire UK budget. Disraeli knew where to go.

Lionel Rothschild was the leading British member of the pan-European banking dynasty. In 1870 he had been pictured on the cover of *The Period* magazine as the 'king' of cash and bonds, with the world's rulers paying homage to his supersized bearded person: the Emperor of China, the Turkish sultan, Napoleon III, the Pope, Kaiser Wilhelm 1 and Queen Victoria. He and his family had plenty of experience in financing big transport projects – they had helped to create a network of European railways. He was also a close family friend of Disraeli and of Disraeli's wife.

As soon as the Prime Minister had secured the agreement of the cabinet to the £4 million, the Cabinet Secretary, Montagu Corry, was dispatched to the headquarters of NM Rothschild at New Court in St Swithin's Lane – where it can be found today. He came upon the sixty-seven-year-old financier in a relaxed frame of mind, sitting in his oak-panelled room. 'The Prime Minister wants £4 million tomorrow', said Corry.

Rothschild picked up a muscatel grape, ate it, threw out the skin and said deliberately, 'What is your security?'

'The British government.'

'You shall have it.'

It was an ingenious deal for everyone. The French were confounded to see British influence so manifestly extended. The opposition Liberals, led by WE Gladstone, could not think of any serious objections. 'Will it not give rise to all sorts of international difficulties and questions?' wrote Granville, rather feebly, to Gladstone. 'Ought so great a responsibility to be taken without immediately consulting parliament?' he whimpered.

The patriotic British public was delighted to become the owner of this Middle Eastern jugular, and an elated Disraeli wrote to Her Majesty to break the good news. 'It is just settled: you have it, madam. The French government has been outgeneralled. They tried too much, offering loans at an usurious rate and with conditions which would virtually have given them the government of Egypt.

'The Khedive, in despair and disgust, offered Yr majesty's government to purchase his shares outright – he never would listen to such a proposition before. Four millions sterling! and almost immediately.

'There was only one firm that could do it – Rothschilds. They behaved admirably, advanced the money at a low rate, and the entire interest of the Khedive is now yours, madam.'

Rothschilds hadn't done too badly themselves, as you might expect. Some people said the old grape-peeler had skinned the British government. They objected that it was a bit steep to charge £150,000 for a £4 million loan over three months. That was an annual interest rate of 15 per cent – the sort of rate you would expect to charge the Egyptians, not the English, said men like WH Smith, the bookseller who was also Secretary to the Treasury. Others suggested that Lionel and his family had done some classic insider dealing, buying loads of Egyptian stock in the knowledge that it was bound to rise on the deal.

Lionel was indifferent to criticism. When the stockbroker Arthur Wragg suggested that he should have loaned the cash to the government free of charge, he issued a muscatel-crushing put-down. 'Arthur Wragg, you are a young man and will learn better. I have made £100,000 out of the deal, I wish it had been £200,000.'

As things turned out, this daring decision by the British government to buy an Egyptian waterway was an unexpected bargain for the taxpayer. By January the following year the shares in the canal had gone up 50 per cent. By 1898 the government's stake was worth £24 million – six times what Disraeli had paid for it; and by 1935 it was worth £93 million. The annual dividend on these shares shot up from £200,000 a year in 1875 to £880,000 in 1901.

Disraeli had not only secured Britain's interests in protecting the quickest passage to India – he had made a vast profit on the deal. The Suez Canal was to remain a British interest until 1956, not all that long, frankly, before the present author was born.

As Disraeli noted to Victoria, it was Britain that had the banking system that allowed them to offer the right deal to the Khedive; and it would never have been possible without Lionel Rothschild.

When in 2012 we celebrate the sixtieth anniversary of the reign of Her Majesty the Queen, we modern Elizabethans will feel that we have much to be proud of. The condition of the people has unquestionably improved; London still has a pretty good claim to be called the greatest city on Earth. Real incomes are far higher than in 1952, and we have the internet, the iPod and the Snickers ice-cream bar.

Then someone will inevitably try to take the shine off the festivities, and look back at the last time a British monarch was on the throne for sixty years. Comparisons will inevitably be drawn between the second Elizabethan age and the age of Victoria – and I am not at all sure that the parallels will be comforting.

Man for man, woman for woman, pound of flesh for pound of self-mortifying flesh, I reckon you could argue that the Victorians beat all previous generations for their energy, their ambition and their achievements; and on the face of it you could argue that they beat us, too.

Sometimes I think that the Life of London is like a giant tadpole, and that so far we have been sliding down the long tail of history until suddenly in the last 150 years we have come to the head: the vast bulging dome of Victorian intellect and personalities that made London the *caput mundi*, the modern Rome. It is impossible to do justice to the range of characters or their interests, though others, such as AN Wilson, have done excellent work.

Perhaps because they lived more obviously in the shadow of death, the Victorians seem more gluttonous for life than we are today. They got up earlier, they walked greater distances, they cooked more complicated meals. They wrote bigger novels, they scribbled longer and more confessional diaries, they grew bushier beards and moustaches than any previous generation. They were more scandalised and more hypocritical and therefore (arguably) more excited about sex, and they had more children. They did more watercolours and they played more pianos and generally busied themselves in the lives of others – especially the less fortunate – than the middle classes of modern Britain.

Perhaps because they were at least superficially more religious than any previous generation of Londoners, the Victorians assumed that they were doing God's work; and like the Roman imperialists on whom they consciously modelled themselves, they took their success to be a sign of divine favour. They had conquered huge parts of the Earth because that was what God wanted, and they lorded it over India and Africa because that was – seriously – part of His plan.

Compared to our own times, it was an age of superhuman self-confidence. It was typical of the Victorian era that when in 1854 Isambard Kingdom Brunel built the *Great Eastern*, she was not only a ship of revolutionary design, capable of carrying enough coal to make a round trip between England and Australia. At 19,000 tonnes she was the biggest ship ever built, by a factor of four and – this is the main point – she was bigger than any ship built for the next forty years. It was true that she blew a monumental gasket on her maiden voyage, but never mind: Brunel got ten out of ten for effort.

Under the Teutonic influence of Prince Albert, the Victorian leisured classes were the most intellectually serious people in the world. It was a hedge-bearded Victorian sage, sitting in the London borough of Bromley, who formulated the theory of evolution, perhaps the most significant scientific breakthrough of the last two hundred years. If you have the chance to go to Bromley, and meet its inhabitants, and to behold their physical and intellectual advantages, you will understand how Charles Darwin formulated the doctrines of natural selection and the survival of the fittest.

The Victorians invented or codified just about every form of game or sport. It was Victorian taste and imagination and engineering dynamism that shaped the city we see today. I remember as a student having an argument with a distinguished American professor, at the height of the 1980s boom. I was arguing that Britain, and London, were on their way back. 'Tchah,' he said dismissively. 'You guys are still living on Victorian capital.' He was very largely right.

Look at London's most exuberant architecture, from the Royal Courts of Justice in the Strand to the Albert Memorial or the Natural History Museum. Suppose you want to find a single shorthand image for London, the postcard image of the city that instantly tells a global audience we are talking about Britain. You pick the Barry and Pugin masterpiece that is the House of Commons; and when you look at Victorian architecture, with its colour and intricacy and warmth, it is no wonder that people love it, and will pay ever more for it today.

Look at the gorgeous gilded panelling of the House of Lords – or look at the elegance and ceremony of just about any Victorian town hall – and then look at the sterile grey steel and concrete ovoid that is the present headquarters of the Greater London Authority. Look on it and weep.

We aspire to live in Victorian terraced homes of the kind that Mr Pooter was mocked for, with door scrapers and vaguely classical pediments above the lintel and dinky little gardens at the back. We pump our effluent daily into the titanic Victorian interceptor sewers, groined beneath London by the genius of Joseph Bazalgette. We go down into

Tube stations that were built by the Victorians before anyone else had an underground railway, and we disappear into the very tunnels that they bored. When we arrive at a mainline station in London, we are beholding (in almost every case) a piece of Victorian industrial archaeology.

It was said of some city in America that it was built on rock and roll. Modern London was built on brick and rail – and Victorian brick and rail at that. But there was one resource that made possible this Victorian splurge of construction; one device that allowed the engineers to throw their viaducts across Holborn and dig their tunnels under the river.

It was a piece of technical know-how that was more important than the steam engine or the harnessing of electricity. It was the lending of money at a reasonable rate of interest, in the confidence that the investment would produce a return – and all the associated skills that go with the management of money and risk. There were in London expert people who bought the debt, people who sold the debt and then as now there were people who made money by gambling on whether the debt would be paid.

London's Victorian greatness was built on the City's pre-eminence in banking. As Walter Bagehot pointed out in Lombard Street in 1873, the City's great contribution to the world was to draw private wealth into the banking system. 'English capital runs as surely and instantly where it is most wanted, and where there is most to be made of it, as water runs to find its level.' Thanks to the London merchant banks and discount houses, the savings of Somerset cider-growers or little old ladies in Lincolnshire could be used to build a railway in America or in Prussia – and they were.

London bankers supplied the guarantees that greased the wheels of world trade. In 1858 a select committee was told, 'A man in Boston cannot buy a cargo of tea in Canton without getting a credit from Messrs Matheson or Messrs Baring.' London became the centre of international financial services not just because it was at the heart of a growing world empire, or because it was the biggest city on Earth, or because it was well plugged in to other capitals – with undersea cables at least partly laid by the limping *Great Eastern* herself. All these qualities were important, but the key thing about banking is to be found on every banknote you handle.

It is all about a promise to pay, and that requires trust; and trust is easier when things are calm. London's most attractive quality as the home of international moneymen was that it was the capital of an island that faced no external threat and that enjoyed peace and stability, certainly by comparison with the rest of Europe. It was also in many important respects a thoroughly agreeable place in which to live, with a freedom of expression and association that was hard to find elsewhere.

Ever since the Middle Ages, banking had been very largely the profession of outsiders, in particular Jews; and in the convulsions of the Napoleonic era, increasing numbers of talented newcomers started to arrive in the city. There they found the Barings, who were always keen to point out that in spite of their vaguely Germanic name they were not – repeat not – Jewish, but the descendants of a Lutheran pastor who had first settled in Exeter.

They liked to claim primacy, since John Baring came to London in 1763, and by the nineteenth century his family had no fewer than five peerages, as well as castles, grouse moors, racehorses, elegant wives and unrivalled connections with government which continued right up until 1995, when Barings was spectacularly blown up by a rogue trader in Singapore called Nick Leeson.

Then there were the Sephardic Jews who left Amsterdam after it was conquered by the French in 1795, and there were Jews and gentiles from German cities that had fallen to Napoleon's armies: Schroders, Brandt, Huth, Fruhling, Goschen. There were Greek bankers who came to London in flight from the Turkish persecution. Hambros arrived from Germany and Denmark in 1840, Bischoffsheim and Goldschmidt came in 1846, Kleinwort came in 1855. There were Americans like Peabody and J S Morgan, father of JP Morgan; and there were the Rothschilds.

The Rothschilds were not just a family; they were a joint enterprise, bound together by the ties of religion and DNA. They were an empire, and with a Rothschild presence in all the key capitals of Europe it was not surprising that there were anti-Semitic comparisons to a gigantic octopus wrapped around the globe (an image that has recently been picked up in descriptions of Goldman Sachs, though in today's banker-bashing climate the octopus has become a vampire squid wrapped around the face of humanity).

Through hard work and a grasp of mental arithmetic, the Rothschilds became the richest people in the world. By some calculations they knocked Midas and Croesus into a cocked hat: they were the richest people that had ever been. They made their first millions from the seismic conflicts of the Napoleonic period.

War is the father of all things, says Heracleitus, and war was certainly the progenitor of the international bond market. If Napoleon and Wellington were good at mobilising troops, the Rothschilds were brilliant at mobilising money. In the words of one admiring contemporary, they were the 'finanzbonaparten' – the Bonapartes of finance; and London was their main centre of operations.

The story can be traced back to 1577 when a man called Izaak Elchanan Rothschild lived in the Judengasse, the Jewish alley, in Frankfurt. Jews in those days were severely restricted in what they could do. They couldn't trade in weapons, spices, wine or grain. They had to stay in the Ghetto on Sundays or Christian festivals. They traded coins and lent money, but there were always limits to how rich they could become.

It was the spread of the French Revolution, in 1789, that liberated the Frankfurt Jews from these captivities – and gave one Mayer Amschel Rothschild his chance. Mayer Amschel got rich essentially by acting as the fund manager for the Elector of Hesse-Kassel, who had been exiled by Napoleon, and discreetly but effectively collecting the interest on his assets.

Mayer was a tough old buzzard, and taught his sons various useful precepts such as 'It is better to deal with a government in difficulties than one that has luck on its side'; and 'If you can't make yourself loved, make yourself feared'; and, most spookily, 'If a high-placed person enters into a (financial) partnership with a Jew, he belongs to the Jew'.

One son in particular learned these lessons well. He was Nathan Mayer, who was sent first to Manchester to import textiles and then moved to London in 1804, when he founded the bank NM Rothschild. He was soon helping to finance the British war effort against Napoleon. When Spanish and Portuguese victuallers wouldn't accept paper money to provide for Wellington's troops in the Peninsular War, Nathan smuggled bullion across the Channel. By 1815 the NM Rothschild account with the British government stood at £10 million, and Lord Liverpool described him as a 'very useful friend.'

He was already recognised as a giant of the Stock Exchange, and an anonymous description of the period describes how he would lean against the 'Rothschild pillar', and how 'he hung his heavy hands in his pockets and began to release silent, motionless, implacable cunning.'

On goes this sulphurous account, in the same vein. 'Eyes are usually called windows of the soul. But in Rothschild's case you would conclude that the windows are false ones or that there was no soul to look out of them,' and so on. Nathan, on this version, was the first to hear of Wellington's victory. One of his messengers had hopped on a boat from Ostend; Nathan ran his eye over the opening paragraphs and then went to tell the government what had happened.

Alas, he was not believed, because the London government had just heard of the English defeat at Quatre Bras. He then went to the Stock Exchange. Now another man, it was said, would have bought government stocks – consols – on the grounds that they were sure to rise when the happy truth eventually dawned. Not Nathan: he was too wily for that.

He leaned against his pillar, an unreadable expression in his leaden eyes. Instead of investing in British government consols, he sold. He dumped them. He sold them so fast that a panic started to run round the Exchange. Nathan Rothschild must know something, the traders concluded: he must have heard from his network of agents that Waterloo was lost.

'Waterloo is lost!' went the whisper. Nathan kept selling; the price of consols plummeted, until a second before it was too late, when he switched. He bought. He bought a giant hoard of British consols for an absolute song – like Eddie Murphy and Dan Aykroyd cornering the market in frozen orange juice in the climax of *Trading Places*.

It was only moments afterwards that the news broke of Wellington's famous victory – and consols soared again, and the rollercoaster he had generated earned him between £20 million and £135 million. 'We cannot guess the number of hopes and savings wiped out by this engineered panic', said a sniffy 1960s history of the Rothschild family. This was the version, as you might expect, that was peddled in 1940 by Joseph Goebbels, though he added the detail that the oleaginous Rothschild had bribed a French general to lose.

The reality was somewhat different. Like Aeschylus feasting on the scraps from the banquet of Homer, I am indebted in this account to Niall Ferguson's wonderful one-thousand-page extravaganza, *The House of Rothschild*. Waterloo was very nearly a disaster for the Rothschilds, he points out, because they had amassed huge quantities of bullion in the belief that the war would go on for much longer. It was true that the Rothschilds' intelligence system had enabled them to get the scoop on Waterloo – but it didn't matter when they got the news: it was bad for them.

The armies would now be disbanded. There would be no more troops to victual. The price of gold would slump: they were staring at a shattering loss. So Nathan Mayer Rothschild had another idea – by no means as unpatriotic (he was a naturalised Briton) as the Goebbels version, but just as cunning. He reckoned that the end of the war was basically good news for the British government, since its debts would be reduced; and he calculated that British government stock would therefore rise.

So he bought more consols; indeed he kept buying them long after his rivals assumed that the stock could rise no higher and when his brothers were urging him to be more cautious. He kept buying for a whole year, until the price of consols was 40 per cent higher than at the beginning; and *then* he sold, and then he did indeed make a stupendous profit, of about £600 million pounds.

The Barings looked on in wonderment and respect. 'Money is the God of our time,' said the German-Jewish poet Heinrich Heine, 'and Rothschild is his prophet.' When NM Rothschild died in 1836 he had put his family at the centre of European politics. He had the ear of every prince and prime minister on the Continent, and his role in financing governments was so crucial that it was said that a war could not be begun without the consent of the Rothschilds. His personal fortune was 0.62 per cent of British GDP.

He and his family lacked one thing; and if you think of the smears and slanders that surrounded the coup after Waterloo, it is easy to imagine what it was. He lacked acceptance. There were the casual snubs and slights that successful Jewish bankers had come to expect; and then there was institutional discrimination. By the third generation, the Rothschilds were determined to stamp it out.

Nathan Mayer's son Lionel now spent the next ten years in a campaign for the rights of Jews – starting with himself – to be admitted to the best club in London, the House of Commons. Under ancient custom and practice, it was necessary for new MPs to swear an oath of allegiance of a specifically Christian variety. This plainly no observant Jew could perform. With the support of the Liberal Party and the press, Lionel now decided to test the matter.

In the summer of 1847 he stood for election in the City of London. John Thadeus Delane, the editor of *The Times*, was so supportive as to write his election address. *The Economist* also backed him. The ever-so-slightly bigoted Thomas Carlyle claimed that Lionel had offered him generous remuneration to write a pamphlet in favour of Jewish emancipation, and that he had refused. 'A Jew is bad, but what is a Sham-Jew, a Quack-Jew? And how can a real Jew, by possibility, try to be a Senator, or even a Citizen, of any country except his own wretched Palestine, whither all his thoughts and steps and efforts tend?'

Carlyle's venom was irrelevant. Lionel applied the usual solvent to the problem. Large sums were paid to an electorate that had been intermittently bribed, after all, since the days of John Wilkes and he was returned proudly to parliament, coming third in the multi-member constituency. As his brother Nat said, it was 'one of the greatest triumphs for the family, as well of the greatest advantage to poor Jews in Germany and all over the world'.

There was only one snag. In order to take his seat he still had to take the oath 'upon the faith of the Christians'. It was not enough to get elected as a Jew; Lionel had to persuade parliament to change the system of swearing-in. Now Disraeli took up the cause, with great boldness.

The ringlet-locked novelist and political adventurer had been baptised a Christian at the age of twelve, but he was plainly Jewish by descent and sympathy. He liked Lionel Rothschild. Indeed, there is a passage in *Tancred* in which he expresses admiration for the whole Rothschild empire. Eva asks Tancred:

> 'Which is the greatest city in Europe?'
>
> 'Without doubt the capital of my country, London.'
>
> … 'How rich the most honoured man must be there! Tell me, is he a Christian?'
>
> 'I believe he is one of your race and faith.'
>
> 'And in Paris; who is the richest man in Paris?'
>
> 'The brother, I believe, of the richest man in London.'
>
> 'I know all about Vienna,' said the lady, smiling. 'Caesar makes my countrymen barons of the empire, and rightly, for it would fall to pieces in a week without their support.'

Lionel had helped Disraeli to speculate in French railway stock; and in the very period we are discussing, Lionel was lending Disraeli large sums to pay his debts on his various houses and live the life he felt he deserved. Lionel's pretty dark-haired wife Charlotte had made friends with Disraeli's wife, Mary Anne. In fact, the childless Mary Anne Disraeli had developed a slightly odd fixation with Lionel and Charlotte's five 'beauteous' children.

On behalf of his sponsor and of Jews in general, Disraeli now threw himself into the parliamentary fight, with the unpromising argument that the Jews had done God's work by killing Jesus. They had 'fulfilled the beneficent intention' of the Lord and 'saved the human race', he told boggling MPs. Christianity was the completion of Judaism, said Disraeli, for whom the question had become a chance to express his own complex identity.

The Liberals liked the way he was talking. Many of his fellow Tories were appalled. No fewer than 138 rebelled against the party leadership. Augustus Stafford demanded: 'Must I cheer Disraeli when he declares there is no difference between those who crucified Christ and those who kneel before Christ crucified?' The Tories had bared their primeval instincts. Once again they had appeared to the public as the party of 'No Popery, No Jews'. Their leader Bentinck resigned in despair at the reactionary fumes that rose from his colleagues.

In spite of Tory opposition, the Bill was passed in the Commons; but now the cause of Jewish emancipation received an even more terrible mauling in the Lords. On the night of the debate, in May 1848, Lionel's wife Charlotte sat up waiting for her husband to come back from Westminster, and then at 3.30 am, the men came in. Lionel was still smiling – 'he always had so much firmness and self-control' – but other Rothschilds and their supporters were red-faced with anger and embarrassment. They told her not to read the speeches, because they were scandalous.

'I went to bed at 5 and woke again at 6; I had dreamt that a huge vampire was greedily sucking my blood … Apparently, when the result of the vote was declared, a loud, enthusiastic roar of approval resounded … throughout the House. Surely we do not deserve so much hatred. I spent all Friday weeping and sobbing out of over-excitement.'

The Bishops had spoken against the Bill, especially that Wilberforce who was to go on to make such a berk of himself in denouncing the theory of evolution. The Duke of Cumberland, uncle to the Queen, said that it was 'horrible' to admit to the Commons persons who denied the existence of our Saviour.

In the end Lionel embarked on an audacious (if predictable) course. He just bribed the House of Lords. Don't pay them until the Bill actually passes, his brother Nat advised him. 'You place so much at the disposal of the individual in question upon the Bill passing, and you know nothing more about it.' He even seems to have launched a campaign to bribe Prince Albert, since the Queen's consort was known to be highly influential with their lordships.

In July 1850, only days before Lionel again attempted to take his seat with a modified oath, he contributed £50,000 to subsidise Albert's pet project – the Great Exhibition, whose glories included the Crystal Palace in Hyde Park. When you look today at the 1851 Exhibition's magnificent legacy of Albertopolis – the museums, the Albert Hall – remember Lionel Rothschild, the struggle for Jewish emancipation, and the subtle art of slipping a bung to royalty.

In 1857, after ten years of stubborn engagement with the British Establishment, Lionel was finally allowed to take his seat in parliament. Upon the suggestion of the Earl of Lucan (fresh from orchestrating carnage in the Crimea) it was agreed that the Commons would change its procedures, so that Jews were allowed to swear allegiance while omitting the words 'upon the true faith of a Christian'.

It was the complete and final triumph of Lionel, his family and their resolve. Not that he actually went to the Commons, or made speeches, or anything like that: it was the principle of the thing. The Rothschilds in London had done huge service to their adopted country. They had bankrolled the war effort against Napoleon, and so – in the language of the day – saved the Continent from tyranny.

They had helped to make London the centre of the international bond market and so entrench its position as the financial capital of the world. They had shown how private investment could enable the big infrastructure projects, especially railways, that are so important for long-term growth and competitiveness. They had helped Britain to secure the Suez Canal and an inestimable advantage for the empire.

Thanks to the doggedness of Lionel, they had done something even finer. At a time when other cities in Europe were experiencing a post-

1848 anti-Semitic backlash, Lionel had helped to make a small but overdue change to the law in the cause of humanity and common sense. In a not negligible way, the Rothschilds had boosted the openness, tolerance and pluralism that were to remain vital to the city's attractiveness for the next 150 years – and which were to form such a tragic contrast to events in Germany, the birthplace of Nathan Mayer Rothschild and the country then emerging as Britain's greatest economic rival.

It would be safe to say that the twentieth-century Rothschilds have not quite repeated the success of their ancestors. Somewhere along the line the family failed to make the necessary breakthrough in America, and you might argue that in their struggle for social acceptance they went too far. They not only emulated the Barings in acquiring peerages, they succumbed to the vice of every triumphant merchant in this country, and tried to turn themselves into fully-fledged, tweed-coated twelve-bore-toting members of the landed aristocracy.

The family built colossal pastiche homes and castles all over Britain and the continent – about forty-one of them at the last count – from Gunnersbury Park to Waddesdon to Ferrieres to Cap Ferrat. These things take time. There are horses to be exercised and arboretums to be tended and servants to be sensitively handled. They dissipate the financial energies. Nathan Mayer would not have approved.

Today a young Rothschild can still make the headlines with a knock-out yacht-based party on the coast of the former Yugoslavia. But no one needs his permission to go to war. Gunnersbury Park, Nathan's country retreat, has been turned into a museum. Waddesdon has been sold to the Gettys, and 148 Piccadilly has been vaporised.

And yet those who like the sweep of history will be consoled to know that NM Rothschild is still there where Disraeli used to know it, and still giving good advice on the financing of transport infrastructure. The firm was used by Transport for London in the final dismantling of the disastrous Public Private Partnership, and the establishment of a new and better regime for the upgrading of the Tube.

When I think of the barbaric flattening of 148 Piccadilly, and the lost tranquillity of Park Lane, I am reminded of another great piece of potential transport infrastructure. Somewhere on the shelves of the Department of Transport is a brilliant plan to keep the speed and practicality of Ernest Marples' urban throughways – but to turn Park Lane and the western end of Piccadilly to the happy and distinguished flower-scented boulevard it once was. You could tunnelise Park Lane, and pay for it with the superb real estate you could create on the western side of the street and in the places where Marples swung his wrecking ball.

Of course there would be a big upfront cost, and we would have to go to a bank to help finance it at a reasonable rate of interest. But Lionel Rothschild knew all about how to do that, and there are plenty of bankers in London today who have learned his lessons well.

* * *

In the year of the Exhibition that Lionel had helped to finance, hundreds of thousands if not millions of Londoners lived in poverty, in hovels surrounded by ash-heaps where – in the words of Charles Dickens – the stench was enough to knock over a bullock.

The very poor could hardly afford the entrance fee and contemporary cartoons show round-eyed paupers pressing up against the glass. It may or may not have been much of a consolation to know that they lived in the world's leading city – fated by heaven to rule the waves and to heap the riches of the planet on the altar to Mammon that Prince Albert had constructed in Kensington.

To modern tastes, the Great Exhibition is an orgy of unacceptable attitudes – racism, sexism, colonialism, imperialism, cultural triumphalism and turbo-capitalism.

So it is worth remembering that Victorian capitalism enabled a rise in living standards and a degree of domestic convenience that helped to produce the biggest social revolution since print: I mean female emancipation. By the end of the century, there would be suffragettes on the street, demanding the right to vote. Long before then, there were two women who came to London, took on the men, and refused to take no for an answer – and one of them was from an ethnic minority.

'Money is the god of our time and Rothschild is his prophet.'

Heinrich Heine, *Sämtliche Schriften*, Vol. V

PING PONG

Of all the contributions the Victorians made to the world, the most culturally pervasive today is almost certainly sport. I remember hearing Sepp Blatter, the President of Fifa, shocking the world when he announced that football had been invented in China – when he knows fine well that the game that unites humanity was codified in London in 1863. Whatever the attractions of *cuju*, a third century BC game that involved kicking a leather object through a hole in a piece of silk cloth, it is not Association Football.

The modern Olympic games have their origins in Much Wenlock in Shropshire, where in 1850 a local physician called Dr William Penny Brookes established the Much Wenlock Olympics, an event that involved all kinds of exertion, including wheelbarrow races and singing competitions. The thing was such a success that he bombarded the Greek King, the Greek prime minister and the Greek ambassador in London with fervent pleas that they should revive the Olympic Games themselves, in Athens – somewhat to the mystification of the Greeks. His idea was eventually taken up by the anglophile sports nut, Baron Pierre de Coubertin.

On it went through the nineteenth century, as sport after sport was codified in Britain – usually London. The Athletics Club was founded in West Brompton in 1866, and evolved into the Amateur Athletics Assocation which itself provided the rules and template for all modern athletics. Men have been punching each other in the head since the beginning of time, and you will find references to boxing in the *Iliad*. But it was in London in 1867 that the Marquess of Queensberry gave his name to the modern rules, with their careful stipulations about gloves, holding and so on. In 1871 a group of thiry-two burly Victorians met at the Pall Mall restaurant on Cockspur Street and started the Rugby Football Union. In 1882 the rowers set up the Amateur Rowing Association to formalise the aggressive competitions that had been taking place on the Thames. You can see ancient Greek bas-reliefs of people playing a game that is evidently hockey – but the rules of the modern game were established in 1886 with the foundation of the Hockey Association.

Modern lawn tennis was invented by an eccentric character called Major Walter Clopton Wingfield, and the game was originally called Sphairistike or 'sticky'. In 1888 they changed the court from Wingfield's preferred hour glass shape to a rectangle and the Lawn Tennis Association was born. Rackets was first played by inmates of London debtors' prisons. The world's first squash court was in Harrow. The global home of cricket is in Marylebone. The world's first organised swimming competitions seem to have taken place on the Serpentine in 1837.

In case after case we see the Victorians taking a long-standing sporting activity, playing it obsessively, and then deciding on the rules – partly because rules were a vital part of the public school concept of 'fair play' and partly because rules were essential for deciding who had won the betting on the outcome.

But there was one game that seems to be wholly indigenous to Britain: not just the rules, but the very idea. The Victorians were so energetic that in the 1880s they came up with a new after-dinner entertainment. They cleared the table and balanced a row of upright books down the middle, so as to form a barrier. They then fashioned a ball made of a sawn-off champagne cork s or string or anything they had knocking around, and then with the help of other books or cigar box lids they biffed that projectile to and fro across the table.

In 1890 there was the first patented version, which involved a 30 millimetre rubber ball covered with cloth, strung rackets and a low wooden fence all around the table. A year later the games company John Jaques of London introduced their 'Gossima' game with a 50 millimetre cork ball, a foot high net, and bats made of parchment – hence the ping pong noise.

Soon other variants were on the market, with names like Whiff-Whaff, Pom-Pom, Pim-Pam, Netto, Ping Pong, Parlour tennis and Table Tennis. It was not long before Ping Pong and Table Tennis were the two survivors, and since they had different rules they agreed in 1903 to end the confusion and form the Table Tennis Association.

The interesting question is why the miracle took place on English dining room tables. It may be something to do with the embarrassment of trying to maintain after-dinner conversation. It may be to do with a lack of interest in food, or rain stopping play of tennis outside. It may be that Victorians were simply richer than any other society on earth – and had the leisure to hit champagne corks at each other.

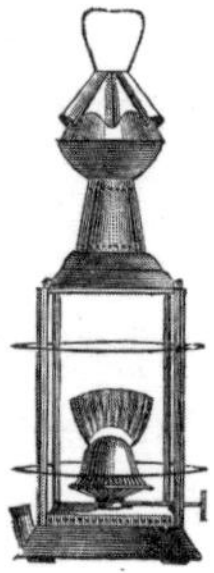

Florence Nightingale and Mary Seacole

Who pioneered nursing

On the whole it must have been a wearying evening for Florence Nightingale. She didn't really do banquets. She didn't get drunk. Indeed, she disapproved of alcohol.

Here she was on 25 August 1856 in the Royal Surrey Gardens, Kennington, and the noise was deafening. Around her were two thousand roaring, red-faced, tail coated soldiers drinking her health with an intensifying ferocity; and their songs reverberated around the wrought-iron pillars and balconies of the newly-built music hall.

They were delighted to have survived the madness and carnage of the Crimean War. They were proud of the little lace-capped angel who occupied the place of honour, and again and again they toasted her name until they became as magnificently plastered as the ceiling of the music hall itself.

Then there was an even greater commotion. There was another woman in the company – almost as famous, just as much loved. Amid tremendous acclaim she was hoisted aloft, and the very chair she sat in was carried on the shoulders of four large men; and we should not be surprised if Nightingale saw this gross manoeuvre and shuddered at the exposure of the lady's petticoats.

Now the rival heroine was being borne through the crowds, and two burly sergeants went with her, to push aside anyone attempting familiarity with the hem of her garments. And the face of Mary Seacole turned beaming in the light of the gas lamps, and everywhere she looked there was a cheer.

She radiated the simple joy of a nurse who had always loved her 'boys', and who was no stranger to a piss-up; and she shone with the pride of knowing that for the first time in England and indeed in the Western world there was public adulation being paid to a woman who was patently black.

High up on the podium, in the seat of honour, Florence Nightingale looked down her beaky nose. She watched the lionising of Mary, her fellow nurse from the Crimea. She watched and wondered.

It must be about eight years ago now that I went to a morning assembly in an Islington primary school, and saw one of my children appear in a historical pageant about the Crimean War. The child was playing Queen Victoria, and her role was to pin medals on the breasts of two other children, playing Florence Nightingale and Mary Seacole. Queen Victoria's line, which I had heard rehearsed many times, was 'Well done, Florence and Mary! Without you we would not have won the war.'

I am afraid to say I snorted a bit at this. Pshaw, I said to the Islington mums after the assembly had ended. Whoever heard of Mary Seacole? We were never taught about her when I was a nipper, I said, with revolting assurance.

She's just been added in there for the sake of political correctness, I said, half hoping to shock them.

One of the parents must have objected, because I went away and looked up Mary Seacole, and it didn't take me long before I realised I had been wrong. Not only did I find a description of the Royal Surrey Gardens banquet, but discovered that she was so huge that the following year the same venue saw a 'Seacole Fund Grand Military Festival.' There were over a thousand artistes, including eleven military bands and an orchestra conducted by some French maestro. They charged an ambitious eight shillings a head for the first night, and yet the audience was forty thousand.

Mary Seacole's bust was carved by Count Gleichen, who also did King Alfred. She published a racy and amusing two-hundred-page 'autobiography' – the first such document ever published by a black woman in this country. If you read it – and I can thoroughly recommend it – you will see that she was a very remarkable woman indeed.

'See, here is Mary Seacole,' says Salman Rushdie in *The Satanic Verses*, 'who did as much in the Crimea as another magic-lamping lady, but, being dark, could scarce be seen for the flame of Florence's candle.'

That was more than twenty years ago. No one could now say that Mary was 'unjustly neglected' or 'half-forgotten'. The Seacole industry is in full-throated roar. Her place on the curriculum is assured. But what I find fascinating is that she really did fade from the story, and for about a hundred years. I was wrong to say that she was unimportant; I was right to say that we didn't hear much about her forty years ago.

By 1877 the Royal Surrey Gardens had been burned down, and the park sold for development. The memory of the Mary Seacole fundraisers was lost with the music hall. It is partly, as you might imagine, a tale of racism and sexism. To these we must add the suspicions of some modern scholars that poor Mary was the victim of the prejudices … of the Angel of Scutari herself.

To appreciate the joy of the soldiers, and their sincere worship of Seacole and Nightingale, you have to remember what they had just been through. They had seen their comrades snuff it in staggering numbers, at the hands of an enemy more lethal than the guns of Sevastopol, more vicious than the sabres of the Cossacks.

Like all Londoners of the mid-nineteenth century, they had learned to have a terror of disease. No one had a scientific grasp of what caused the outbreaks of cholera that ravaged the city, but everyone had seen the speed with which it carried off its victims. They knew that within the space of a day a hale and hearty human being could be transformed into a Stilton-cheeked wraith with sunken eyes and wrinkled skin and a humiliating and terminal dysentery. The typhus louse ran riot in the rookeries and fever-nests of Clerkenwell, Holborn and St Giles.

For the millions of the working poor there was no hope of medical treatment, and no idea of nursing whatever. They died in such droves that the very graveyards overflowed, and the burial grounds themselves became a source of contagion. In the richest city on Earth, the heart of the greatest empire ever seen, life expectancy fell to thirty-five – lower than in the days of Hadrian.

Mid-nineteenth-century London was the victim of its own success. The population grew by about 20 per cent in every decade that Florence Nightingale was alive. At the apex of the pyramid were certainly people of astonishing wealth. As ever in the history of the city, there were bankers who made money so fast that their fortunes soon equalled those of the landed aristocracy. There were Barings and Rothschilds – and then there were figures of ruthlessness and cynicism, satirised by Trollope in the figure of Augustus Melmotte; a man first hailed as a great financier, drumming up excitement in a Latin American railroad – and then exposed as a dirty, bullying, ignorant charlatan. Of the forty richest men who died between 1809 and 1914, fourteen were merchant bankers.

For every such tycoon there were a thousand Pooters – the lower middle class clerk of *Diary of a Nobody*. And ranged beneath every Pooter-like clerk were the legions of the poor, their numbers swelled and their misery intensified every month by fresh additions from countryside.

In his book *Ragged London*, John Hollinghsead calculated that a third of the city's population lived in filthy and ill-constructed lanes and courts. The French writer Hippolyte Taine described his shock at seeing life in the alleys behind Oxford Street, the stifling lanes encrusted with human exhalations, the troops of pale children nestling on the muddy stairs. Henry Mayhew saw elderly people living on hard, dirty crusts they picked out of the road, washing them and steeping them in water before eating them.

The greatest connoisseur of urban squalor was Charles Dickens himself, and the pages of *Bleak House* and *Oliver Twist* must be among the most powerful pieces of campaigning literature ever written. He created a landscape by which we identify and remember the worst of Victorian London; and yet even Dickens failed sometimes to do justice to the brutality of nineteenth-century capitalism.

Henry Mayhew interviewed a 60-year-old woman who had once had a good education, but was now widowed and penniless. She lay exhausted and feverish at the end of her labours, trying to recover her strength on a cellar floor. She had become one of London's 250 pure-collectors. That is, she literally scoured the streets for dog turds, and took them to Bermondsey to sell them to the tanners. She had no understanding of the risks she was running with her health – and nor, frankly, had Mayhew.

As an organism, London was sick, and getting sicker.

In 1815 it was decided that homes should be allowed to make use of Joseph Bramall's increasingly popular water closet and discharge their waste directly into the sewers. By 1828, 140 sewers emptied directly into the Thames. By 1834 people started to appreciate the full horror of waterborne pollution. In the words of Sydney Smith, canon of St Paul's, 'he who drinks a tumbler of London water has literally in his stomach more animated beings than there are men, women and children on the face of the globe.'

But still the link between sewage and disease was misunderstood. It was the sheer smell, the 'miasma', that sickened people, they decided. They called it 'pythonogenesis'. Edwin Chadwick tried to address the stench by commanding yet more of London's filth to be pumped into the Thames – with disastrous consequences.

In 1849 there was another outbreak of cholera, in which 14,000 people died. By 1854, when Nightingale and Seacole were preparing to leave for the Crimea, the mystery was still unsolved. They were both deeply ignorant of what we would now call basic hygiene – and yet that was the least of the barriers that they faced.

In their different ways, both women had conceived a burning desire to consecrate their lives to helping the sick. They were both important in creating the idea of the professional nurse.

To achieve her ambition, each woman faced prejudice and discrimination of a kind we find outlandish today. Let us trace their lives, as they converge on that momentous encounter in a hospital in Turkey. I hope I will not be accused of political correctness if I say that Nightingale's career was a triumph of the will; but Seacole's advance in some ways was even more amazing.

Florence Nightingale's maternal grandfather had made his fortune from lead mines. The family had both an estate in Derbyshire and a mock-Tudor schloss in Hampshire called Embley Park. They took their holidays abroad in Florence (her birthplace, in 1820) and Paris, where she caught glimpses of celebrities. As soon as she was able to think about her future, Florence concluded that she was going to disappoint her parents.

Her fate ought to have been to marry an eligible young man. She had no such intention. She wanted to be a nurse. She practised her arts on her sister, on her dolls, and even set the paw of her doll in splints.

As she grew older, the feeling became stronger. She wanted to be esteemed for doing something, for practical action. She tried to slope off to become a nurse at Salisbury Hospital, and was frustrated by her parents. She had a visionary scheme to found a kind of Protestant sisterhood, without vows, for women of educated feeling. No dice, said Mama.

A nurse in the Victorian lexicon was either Juliet's nurse, a sentimental old milch-cow; or else she was a Mrs Gamp, slurping liquor and hiccupping; or else she was too free with the male patients. No, said Mr and Mrs Nightingale to their daughter: nursing was not a suitable activity for a nice young gel. 'It was as if I wanted to be a kitchen maid,' she wailed.

For eight years she struggled to overcome this rejection. She pored over vast reports by medical commissions; she devoured pamphlets about sanitation; in the intervals of the London season she would bunk off to ragged schools and workhouses, drinking in the atmosphere of destitution. One minute she would be with her mother and sister as they strolled through some foreign capital; the next she would pop up in the slums.

She was courted by an ineffably suitable cravat-sporting poet and politician called Richard Monckton Milnes – and turned him down, much to the chagrin of Mama. Not that Florence was incapable of lustful thoughts. 'I have a passional nature which requires satisfaction, and that would find it in him,' she mused. But she concluded: 'I have a moral, an active nature which requires satisfaction, and that I would not find it in his life.'

It was one of the tragedies of the Victorian age – admittedly a fairly minor tragedy – that it does not look as though Florence Nightingale ever fulfilled the 'passional' side of her nature. She never had sexual relations with a man.

This was not, perhaps, because she was a lesbian or because she was unattractive to men (she inspired the devotion of all sorts, including the romantic feelings of the great Master of Balliol, Benjamin Jowett). The problem surely was that any such entanglement would have amounted in her own eyes to a surrender, a submission, a loss of that autonomy she yearned to express.

'To be nailed to a continuation and exaggeration of my present life ... to put it out of my power ever to seize the chance of forming a full and rich life' – that would be suicide. It was appalling, she wrote in her torrential memoirs, that a talented and energetic young woman should face that choice: between fulfilling her professional dream, or marrying some dope with mutton-chop whiskers.

'The thoughts and feelings I now have I can remember since I was six years old,' she said. 'A profession, a trade, a necessary occupation, something to fulfil and employ all my faculties, I have always felt essential to me, I have always longed for. The first thought I can remember, and the last, was nursing work ... Everything has been tried, foreign travel, kind friends, everything. My God! What is to become of me?'

God answered the question soon enough. One day she was travelling in Thebes in Egypt, when the Almighty 'called' her. Those of us who have never been lucky enough to take a call from God can only wonder what it is like.

Perhaps it is like the interruption of normal programming by a party political broadcast; or maybe there is literally a kind of ringing in the head. Hello, switchboard here, I have God on the line. Will you take the call?

At any rate, she said, 'God called me in the morning and asked me would I do good for him alone.' Florence assented, with the massive seriousness of the Victorians. She went to work in a hospital in Germany, and in 1853 her determination paid off.

She became Superintendent of the Institute for the Care of Sick Gentlewomen in Upper Harley Street. Mrs Nightingale wept. 'We are ducks, who have hatched a wild swan,' she said. Her mother was wrong. In the phrase of Lytton Strachey, it was not a swan her mother had hatched, but an eagle. The following year she spread her wings and soared. Britain may have possessed the greatest empire the world had ever seen, but that did not make London complacent. The government was chronically nervous of Russian intentions towards India, and when some argy-bargy arose between Russia and Turkey over the management of the Holy Places of Jerusalem, it seemed a good moment to teach the Bear a lesson.

But where? They consulted their maps. Big place, eh, Russia. Battle was eventually joined in the Crimea, a large peninsula in the Black Sea, and by September 1854 a British force was on its way to Turkey.

It wasn't long before the troops were hellishly ill, with eight thousand suffering from either cholera or malaria. *The Times* ran a letter heavily criticising the medical facilities. The eagle's eye locked on her target.

She wrote a letter to Sidney Herbert, the Secretary for War, offering her services. It shows how plugged in Nightingale was to the Establishment that Herbert had already written to his friend Florence to invite her to do just that. The letters crossed in the post.

She took a detachment of thirty-eight nurses, including her aunt Mai, and soon they were bouncing across the Bosphorus, looking up at the vast and mouldering barracks of Uskudar (Scutari) and debating which of the gels should be charged with getting the troops into the bath.

It was thanks to the miracle of newspapers that these events were brought to the notice of a chubby fifty year old as she sat on the veranda of her hotel in Panama. Despite her age (she was fifteen years older than Nightingale), her stoutness, her skin colour, her complete lack of any formal qualifications and her ignorance of Russia, she knew she had to be there. She decided to travel to England to volunteer as a nurse – and to 'experience the pomp, pride and circumstance of glorious war'.

Mary Jane Seacole had been born in 1805, the year of Trafalgar, in Kingston, Jamaica. She was the daughter of a female 'doctress' or healer and a Scottish army officer called Grant. So she was not entirely black – indeed she boasted that she had 'good Scots blood' coursing through her veins; but she looked Afro-Caribbean, and all her life she sympathised and identified with black and coloured people.

It was her mixed race, she speculated, that gave her the natural buoyancy and energy that propelled her around the globe, in an age when respectable women were supposed to be chaperoned wherever they went. 'Some have called me quite a female Ulysses', she boasted.

As a young woman she travelled to Britain, the Bahamas, Cuba and Haiti. She married a mysterious Englishman called Edwin Horatio Hamilton Seacole, who was supposed to be the illegitimate offspring of Horatio Nelson and Emma Hamilton. Whoever Edwin was, he lacked his wife's robust constitution, and died in 1844. Their nine years of marriage rate barely a mention in her autobiography.

Mary lived by her wits. She was an accomplished cook. She made curries, she picked guavas and made jellies. Like her mother, she was in Jamaican parlance a 'doctress' who learned to treat all sorts of dreadful tropical plagues. She was a hostess, who ran a series of hotels-cum-convalescent homes, the first of which was in Kingston where 'one of the hardest struggles of my life was to resist the pressing candidates for the late Mr Seacole's shoes.'

We have a watercolour portrait of Mary from about 1850, and though she is a bit on the plump side we can see that she is very pretty, with a sweet and honest expression. When her first hotel burned down, she built another, and then went off to run a riotous establishment in Panama. She went prospecting for gold. She roasted and ate iguanas. She had a (possibly fictitious) encounter with Lola Montes, the noted sexpot and adventuress.

She cared throughout for the many who were afflicted by cholera. 'I used mustard emetics, warm fomentations, mustard plasters on the stomach and back, and calomel first in large and then in gradually smaller doses,' she said. She took pride in the apparent success of these decoctions, but such was her mental vigour that she was always prepared to learn.

There was a fearful cholera epidemic in Panama in 1849, and when a year-old baby died in her care, Mary was sufficiently inquisitive to steal down to the banks of the river, take out a scalpel and perform an autopsy.

'I need not linger on the scene, or give the reader the results of my operation; though novel to me, and decidedly useful, they were what every medical man knows.' She had a bout with the sickness herself, survived, and in 1852 she decided to return to Jamaica. Her optimism and dynamism are all the more interesting when you consider that she was not only female, but black, and sensitive to racism all her life.

In 1821 she had travelled to London with a young female friend, a few shades darker than herself. They were teased by the street urchins, she recorded, and without any police to reprimand the little beasts 'our progress through the London streets was sometimes a rather chequered one.' Yet she came back to London the following year, in the hope of selling her stock of West Indian pickles.

She always maintained that the racial prejudice in Britain was nothing like as bad as it was in the Americas. One evening before her return to Jamaica, she was attending a Fourth of July dinner when an American stood up and made a speech of death-defying crassness. 'God bless the best yaller woman he ever made,' he said, in what he imagined to be a compliment.

'I imagine, gentlemen, that you're as vexed as I am that she is not wholly white – but I do reckon on your rejoicing with me that she's so many shades removed from being entirely black.' He went on to say – and please remember that this cretin thought he was making himself pleasant to Mary – that 'if we could bleach her by any means we would and thus make her acceptable in any company as she deserves to be'.

The man may have been drunk; the occasion may have been a party in a hotel in Panama; but Mary was not going to be spoken to like that. She made a fierce reply. She would have been happy to have a complexion as 'dark as any nigger's', she said, and called for 'the general reformation of American manners'.

This 'autobiography' is not a straightforward text. Though her voice and character ring true to me, there is no doubt that her account has been very substantially edited by 'WJS', the London hack who buffed it up for publication. Never forget that the purpose of the book, like the dinner for the troops in Royal Surrey Gardens, was financial. It was intended to excite the admiration and support of the public, who might be in danger of forgetting her role in the Crimea. There was therefore no harm in reminding her British readers what good and unprejudiced chaps they were – unlike those slave-driving Yankees.

Mary was being generous to her British readership, but she also gloried genuinely in the name of Briton. She was a proud child of empire, and in both Panama and the Crimea she called her establishment the 'British Hotel'.

She spoke of her instinct to cure and help English soldiers; and it was with a mixture of patriotism and commercial opportunism that she decided to offer up all her energies to the service of the British army in the Crimea.

She was bitterly disappointed by the response. In the autumn of 1854 both Nightingale and Seacole were in London. Nightingale was preparing to set out, aged only thirty-four, as Superintendent of the Female Nursing Establishment of the English General Hospital in Turkey. In spite of the clamour for nurses, in spite of the golden stream of public donations for Crimean medical care, Mary Seacole experienced a series of rebuffs.

She went to the War Office, and tried in vain to see Sidney Herbert – he who had despatched Nightingale. She was fobbed off by a series of amused young men; so she applied to the quartermaster-general's department, where another man listened to her with polite enjoyment, before she went to the medical department; and when that failed, she decided to apply directly to be one of Nightingale's nurses.

She began to stalk Sidney Herbert, sitting in his hall while scores of people passed in and out, the flunkeys smirking at this 'yellow woman whom no excuses could get rid of nor impertinence dismay'. At length she gave up this route, and went to see one of Florence Nightingale's companions. 'She gave me the same reply, and I read in her face the fact that had there been a vacancy, I should not have been chosen to fill it.'

As a last resort, she went to the manager of the Crimean Fund, to see if they would simply send her out to the camp. Once there, she was sure that something would turn up. The Crimean Fund said no.

No one had been interested in her credentials or her manifest experience in treating cholera. She stood in the wintry twilight and succumbed to despair. 'Doubts and suspicions arose in my heart for the first and last time, thank heaven. Was it possible that American prejudices against my colour had some root here? Did these ladies shrink from accepting my aid because my blood flowed beneath a skin somewhat duskier than theirs?

'Tears streamed down my foolish cheeks as I stood in the fast thinning streets; tears of grief that anyone should doubt my motives – that heaven should deny me the opportunity that I sought.' There was nothing for it. Mary Seacole decided – with enormous pluck – to go under her own steam.

If she couldn't join Nightingale's nurses, she would go as a sutler – an army camp-follower or victualler, who sells provisions to the troops in the field. She sailed to Constantinople via Malta, and on her way she came across a doctor who gave her a letter of introduction to Nightingale.

Clutching this document she then chartered a caique for the Selimiye barracks, where the hospital was housed. The water was choppy, and it was tricky to get in and out of the boats. 'Time and trouble have left me with a well filled-out, portly form – the envy of many an angular Yankee female – and more than once I was in no slight danger of being too intimately acquainted with the temperature of the Bosphorus.'

Soon the boat was approaching the dull-looking barracks, where Nightingale had been working for many months, and the stately Caribbean lady began the steep climb to the gate.

When Florence Nightingale had arrived at Scutari, she found a vision of hell. There were four miles of beds, in which men mutilated by Russian cannon lay so close to one another that a nurse could not pass between them. The place was crawling with rats and other vermin. The floorboards were rotten. The soldiers had no elementary comforts such as basins, towels and soap. Worst of all, the hospital basement contained vast cisterns of sewage, so that the place of so-called healing was pervaded by an awful smell.

Using her knowledge of statistics and mathematics – which her father had taught her in defiance of her mother – Nightingale worked out that if the soldiers kept dying at this rate there would soon be no army left. Brushing aside the protests of the sexist army medical officers – who referred to her slightingly as 'the Bird', and called her appointment 'droll' – she insisted on giving the men newspapers, properly cooked food and toothbrushes.

'What does a soldier want with a toothbrush?' said one of her opponents. Nightingale crushed him. If someone said something couldn't be done, she would say, 'But it must be done', and though she never raised her voice, she found that it was done.

She tried to beat the smell by throwing open the windows. She fixed the plumbing. She cut the red tape that stopped the supplies getting through. Before she arrived the hospital had managed to wash a grand total of seven shirts. Nightingale set up a laundry.

It would be nice to say that the death rates started to fall in the way that Lytton Strachey suggests – from 42 per cent to 2 per cent. The reality is that Florence hugely improved conditions in the hospital, and doubtless saved many lives. But she still did not understand – any more than Edwin Chadwick – the full relation between hygiene and disease.

John Snow had come up with the right answer in 1854, shortly before she set out, and postulated that the cholera agent was borne in water; but the breakthrough was not widely understood. The awful truth seems to be that the death rate actually increased in the six months after Florence arrived, and Scutari was the most effective slaughterhouse in the region – with 4077 people dying there in her first winter.

This was the house of death at which pilgrim Seacole now arrived, determined to make her mark with the Angel of Scutari.

The door creaked open; a nurse admitted her with a whisper. The injured soldiers may have been equipped with newspapers and toothbrushes, and they may have given up swearing in the presence of Nightingale – but they were still in pretty bad shape. Mary Seacole now began to walk round the beds, and by her own account she started to weep at the state of the men.

Some of them were veterans of the West Indies who recognised her from her Kingston hotel. An Irish sergeant shouted out 'Mother Seacole, Mother Seacole!' and held out his feeble arms before flopping back on the pillow, a fearful wound on his shaven head. Mary did not want to seem presumptuous, but since no one seemed interested in her she started to do a spot of nursing – replacing a slipped bandage here, easing another bandage there.

Where was Nightingale? She finally found a nurse who was willing to read the letter. Mrs Seacole, she asked, turning over the document in her hand, what is your purpose in coming here? Well, said Mary, she wanted to be of use (and she thought, as she spoke, that she would have worked for the wounded soldiers in return for nothing but bread and water).

Then it came: another soft slap in the face. 'Mrs Nightingale has the entire management of our hospital staff, but I do not think that any vacancy ...'

Mary interrupted her before the rejection could be completed, and said that she was off to the front in a few days. At which her questioner looked more puzzled than ever, and went off, leaving her in the hospital kitchen. After half an hour she was ushered into the presence of Florence Nightingale herself – 'that Englishwoman whose name shall never die, but sound like music on the lips of British men until the hour of doom.'

Mary described a slight figure, resting her pale face lightly on the palm of one hand. She had a keen, inquiring expression, and the only sign of impatience was the tapping of her right foot. 'What do you want, Mrs Seacole? Anything we can do for you – if it lies in my power, I shall be very happy.'

What was Mary to say? She plainly wasn't wanted in the hospital. She blurted something about not wanting to travel back to Constantinople by night, the perils of the caique.

Was there room for her anywhere in the hospital? At last she was found a billet in the washerwomen's quarters, where fleas feasted on her plump person. 'Upon my word,' she joked in her memoirs, 'I believe the fleas are the only industrious creatures in all Turkey.'

She left Nightingale's empire with a flea in her ear and just about everywhere else. Soon she was hundreds of miles away, on the dockside of Balaclava itself – a busy bumblebee in a bright yellow dress, ministering to the mutilated men as they were loaded on to the ships.

Stump-limbed victims gave joyous shouts (so she boasts) at the mere sight of Old Mother Seacole, and vowed patriotically to get back into the fighting. 'Never fear for me, Aunty Seacole,' said one man with *Monty Pythonesque* enthusiasm, 'I'll make the best of the leg the Russians have left me. I'll get at them soon again, never fear.'

Within weeks she had found a site at Spring Hill, about two miles from Balaclava, and in spite of floods, theft and the incompetence of her Turkish carpenters, she had constructed her latest 'British Hotel' – a Heath Robinson affair of scrap iron, old packing cases and driftwood, with a large Union Jack floating from the roof.

Inside it was all comfortable and warm, and by the Christmas of 1855 Old Mother Seacole's place was the most popular address in the Crimea. There were raucous plum-pudding feasts, washed down with claret and cider cup. Her rice pudding was so popular that maimed soldiers would lurch and hobble from their bivouacs to get it; officers would try to prise her tarts, still warm, from the oven. When she wasn't earning the undying love of the troops with her cooking and her potations, Mother Seacole was showing physical bravery far beyond that expected of her sex.

To be sure, Florence Nightingale was brave herself. She eventually came to the front to see the hospitals, and spent whole days in the saddle. She would stand for hours in the heavy snow. She would scramble through ravines and only reach her hut at dead of night, almost delirious from fatigue. But for sheer recklessness Nightingale is comfortably beaten by Seacole.

Such was her lust for excitement and her indifference to danger that Mary Seacole was frequently in range of the Russian guns – huge ships' cannon fixed to the ground and trained on the British positions. Shots would come ploughing into the turf in front of her little mule, and the soldiers would shout, 'Lie down, mother, lie down!'

At one point a shell whizzed overhead and she flung herself with such force to the earth that she bent her thumb permanently out of shape. She saw the Battle of Tchernaya as it happened, and attended on the spot to the injuries of the French, the Sardinians and the Russians themselves. One Russian had been badly shot in the jaw, and as Seacole instinctively shoved in her finger to remove the bullet his jaws clamped shut in the agony of death.

A slow smile spread over his face, and with Seacole's digit stuck fast in his mouth, the Russian died. She would bear the scar for the rest of her life. She was the first civilian to enter Sevastopol after the siege. She was one of life's adrenalin-chasers; she was wily (she once tried to sell some French troops a mangy horse by covering its bald patches with flour); and she was seemingly very successful at medicine.

Whatever her doctress mother had taught her about mustard emetics, it worked. We have abundant testimonials from officers and men who claimed that she had solved their enteric crises. 'She doctors and cures all manner of men with extraordinary success,' said William H Russell, the *Times* correspondent who was so important in bringing Mary to a wider public.

By the end of the war it is clear that her fame was immense – almost as great as Nightingale's. Shortly before the great dinner at the Royal Surrey Gardens, *The Times* announced that 'copies of the admirable likeness of the Mother of the British Army' were on sale at the Royal Polytechnic Institute in Regent Street, priced at five shillings, ten shillings and £2. She was famous not because she was an amiable eccentric, but because of what she had contributed to the war.

British nursing was born amid the horrors of the Crimea, and it looks as though Seacole and Nightingale – at least at first – were jointly associated with its beginnings. The concept of nursing includes systematically dealing with the symptoms of epidemic disease, and it is now understood to be an essential part of city life.

The triumph of Victorian capitalism had brought a boom in the population, and a consequent explosion of disease. Nursing was part of the fightback. In 1855 Florence and Mary were trying to cope with the evils of infection in the army, and in the same year Londoners were starting to deal with some of the most appalling sources of contamination in their city.

Smithfield Market had long been a shambles of dung, gore and the bellows of dying animals. In the name of hygiene the operation was moved to Islington. In the same year parliament tried to deal with the selfish squabbling of the various sewage authorities by setting up the Metropolitan Board of Works, the first modern attempt to create a central municipal body in London – the ancestor of today's Greater London Authority.

By 1858 the smell from the river was so mind-bending that MPs could take it no more, and Joseph Bazalgette was commissioned to produce the immense system of sewers on which the city relies to this day.

The penny had finally dropped with London's rulers. If you let poor people live in conditions of squalor and penury, then their diseases could be transmitted to the rich. The slums began to be cleared. In 1867 Dr Barnardo launched his superb movement to help children in the East End. In 1870 Royal Doulton Ware produced the porcelain toilet, on which filth could be more easily spotted.

The concepts of hygiene and ventilation informed the legal ratio of windows to walls in the spreading terraced houses that are still so loved and prized by London's middle classes. In 1875 the Public Health Act ordained that parks should be laid out in such a way as to boost physical fitness.

There were a thousand innovations in the name of human health: but none was as far-reaching as the simple idea promoted by Nightingale and Seacole: that when people were sick, their chances of living were greatly improved by a professional nurse. It was only about forty years after the death of Florence Nightingale that Britain produced the NHS, whose central principle is that everyone – like the soldiers of the Crimea – should receive medical attention according to their need and not their ability to pay.

It is perhaps not surprising that by that stage – the mid-twentieth century – Mary Seacole had been forgotten. In the post-Crimean years she was hailed as a grand and spunky old dame. She toured barracks and received ovations from the troops who remembered her. She was adopted by various minor members of the royal family, and served one of them as a personal masseuse.

After a while, however, her legend faded with the fickleness of the news. She eventually died of 'apoplexy', at the age of at least seventy-six, in Paddington.

It was Florence Nightingale whose lamp burned brighter and brighter, and who publicly continued on her march to sainthood. She retired to her bed in Mayfair, where she lived to a huge old age and terrorised the various men who worshipped her (notably Sidney Herbert and the poet AH Clough). She produced encyclopaedic volumes on nursing; she introduced professional nurses to workhouses – hence her claim to be the grandmother of the NHS – and she produced sanitary designs for hospitals.

Mary Seacole had nothing like her theoretical visions or ambitions. She was not rich. She was not well connected. She had no education in statistics. All that helps to explain the relative decline in her reputation; and yet it does not quite justify one striking omission in the post-war celebrations that were held in her honour.

Her Seacole fund was supported by the Prince of Wales (£25) and by his brother the Duke of Edinburgh (£15). But she was never accorded the recognition that was enjoyed by so many others. She was never invited to meet the Queen.

That touching medal ceremony we saw at the Islington primary school – it never happened. There can be no suggestion that race was any bar, not with Victoria. As Helen Rapaport has convincingly shown in her book, the Queen was remarkably colour-blind. She met and congratulated people of all races from across the empire. In Victoria's own prodigious letters and journals we find references to Josiah Henson, Mrs Ricks, Sarah Forbes Bonetta, Duleep Singh and Prince Alamayou – all of whom she met.

When you consider the fame and popular sentiment excited by Mary Seacole, and her support among other members of the royal household, it is amazing that she was given no kind of audience at all. Someone, says Rapaport, must have poisoned the mind of the Queen against Mary Seacole – and that someone (so says Rapaport) was surely Florence Nightingale.

The Lady of the Lamp was summoned to Balmoral almost as soon as she returned from the Crimea, and there was a series of dinners at which the two women discussed the war and the difficulties of nursing. At some stage in those conversations the Queen must have asked about Mary Seacole, and at some stage it looks as if Florence slipped in a bad word.

We have a letter from Nightingale to her brother-in-law, the Liberal MP Sir Harry Verney. It is marked 'burn' at the top, suggesting that other such comments would have been incinerated. Seacole was 'very kind to the men', said Florence, and 'did some good'. But the trouble was alcohol.

Mary had 'made many drunk', and though she would not go so far as to say that Seacole's 'British Hotel' was a 'bad house', it was 'something not very unlike it.' She added the killer: 'Anyone who employs Mrs Seacole will introduce much kindness – also much drunkenness and improper conduct wherever she is.'

The suspicion is there, even if we will never prove it now. Poor sweet Mary Seacole was deprived of that crowning tribute – an audience with Her Maj, some tender words, a tin enamel trinket pinned on that curvaceous bosom – because she had been surreptitiously dished by Florence Nightingale.

So what if she got the men drunk with her 'first-rate' claret cup? So what if she had a comely illegitimate daughter to help her in the 'British Hotel'? So what if some of the French officers became so drunk as to attempt a bit of slap and tickle?

She was a dynamic and enterprising lady, who did many sick men a power of good. And yet I think we can nonetheless forgive Florence Nightingale, if indeed she is guilty as charged. With all the heaven-sent self-belief of the very greatest Victorians, she wanted to change the world. She wanted fundamentally to adjust the way that people looked at nursing and at women, and that meant above all that they and the profession had to be taken seriously.

It wasn't so much that she was a Queen Bee, or that she wanted to be unchallenged as Mother of the British Army (though there may have been an element of that). It wasn't that she was personally censorious about alcohol and sex (though that may have affected her attitude).

The reason she worried about the whiff of booze and fun from Mary Seacole was that it might detract from what she was trying to do. If you want evidence that she did rather admire her rumbustious black counterpart, it has been shown that Nightingale herself contributed quite generously to Seacole's fund – but anonymously. Appearances mattered in those days.

Today the supporters of Seacole are proposing to erect a statue in her honour in the grounds of St Thomas' Hospital, where Nightingale started her training school for nurses.

* * *

And it was the Seacole view of alcohol that was supported by most Londoners. The capital did not boast quite as many pubs per head as the seriously sozzled Birmingham or Manchester, but you only had to walk down Whitechapel Road to encounter forty-five hostelries. There was one on every street corner; and pubs were not just places of alcoholic refreshment.

You went there to find medical advice, credit, work, bargains, union activity, political debate – as well as prostitutes, gossip, warmth, food and drink. You also went there for newspapers, which were read in vast numbers across the city.

People read them on buses and on the amazing new underground trains, and over their tuppenny breakfasts in the coffee rooms and dining rooms that started to multiply around town. London's press had played a glorious role in the tumults of the eighteenth century, with cartoons so scatological and disrespectful that most newspapers would not carry them today.

By the mid- to late nineteenth century, however, it would be fair to say that most London papers had become a bit on the heavy side. WH Russell and *The Times* had played a part in exposing the scandal of Scutari that brought Florence Nightingale to national prominence. But on the whole a Victorian worthiness had descended on the press.

One man did more than any other to revive London reporting. He was a pioneer of the muckraking and exuberant style of journalism that survives – despite all the threats of politicians – in London today. He was the world inventor of the great big quivering tabloid exposé, complete with slavering headlines, dodgy quotes, reporters passing themselves off as others, and the whole thing followed by a delicious public hoo-ha about journalistic 'ethics'.

'Lo! In that hour of misery
A lady with a lamp I see
Pass through the glorious gloom
And flit from room to room.'

Santa Filomena, Henry Wadsworth Longfellow

JOSEPH BAZALGETTE AND THE SEWERS

It was great to see the comedian David Walliams earning all that cash for charity by swimming the length of the Thames. He was brave to do it. But if he had done it in the middle of the ninteenth century he would have been suicidal. The place was worse than a sewer. It was biologically dead. Not a newt, not a fish, not a duckling could hope to survive the vile discharges of the growing city. And the river that gave life to London had become a source of deadly poison for human beings.

In the autumn of 1848, more than 14,000 Londoners died of cholera in the worst ever outbreak to hit the capital. While Florence Nightingale and others persisted in their belief that the infection was borne by air or dirty sheets, a London doctor by name of John Snow had other ideas. Using a dot map, he worked out that all the victims in Soho had been living near or using a certain water pump in Broad Street – and he concluded that the pump was the source of the contagion.

It was contaminated drinking water that was causing the problem, he suggested – and it was no coincidence that the cholera outbreak had taken place just after the cesspools were systematically flushed into the Thames. That project had been led by the Metropolitan Committee of Sewers, and the assistant surveyor on the project was one Joseph William Bazalgette (1819–1891), grandson of a French protestant immigrant and a promising engineer.

Eight years later Bazalgette had become the chief engineer of the new Metropolitan Board of Works, and he found himself in agreement with Snow. The existing system of London sewers carried off surface water, full of unspeakable things, and washed it down to the Thames. He proposed a bold solution: a network of new self-cleaning underground sewers including 82 miles of larger sewers fed from over 1,000 miles of new street sewers. It was an engineering plan on an unprecedented scale. As one would expect, the government turned it down on five separate occasions.

In the summer of 1858 MPs suffered the olfactory onslaught of the Great Stink, and his case was made. The vapours rising from the river were so awful that MPs had to flee the city. The authorities capitulated to Bazalgette, and having secured approval for his plans the extravagantly moustachioed engineer showed his genius and resolve.

He took his plans and doubled them. He looked at the density of the population of the city, and then carefully calculated the width of the pipe that would be needed to carry away the effluent. He then spoke words that should have been used by the builders of the Tube tunnels and indeed whoever first decided on the location of London's hub international airport.

'Well', he said, 'we are only going to do this once, and there is always the unforeseen'. He multiplied the width of the tunnels by two. Recent studies have shown that if he had kept to his original calculation then the network would have reached capacity in the 1960s. As it was, Bazalgette's masterpiece was used as a blueprint for urban sewer networks across the globe from New York to New Zealand.

A network of sewers designed for 2.5 million people has survived to deal with the sewage of 7.7 million people. It is a tribute to the Victorian that it is only today that we are building again on his scale. Once we have completed the Thames Tideway Tunnel – a *cloaca maxima* running underneath the bed of the river – we will finally be able to deal with the unmentionable consequences of what happens when the Bazalgette interceptors overflow. The river will not only be safe for trout but for charity swims of all kinds.

WT Stead

The inventor of tabloid journalism

On Saturday 4 July 1885 the readers of the *Pall Mall Gazette* were given a taster of what was to come in the paper the following week. It wasn't so much a puff as a blood-curdling warning.

'All those who are squeamish, and all those who are prudish, and all those who would prefer to live in a fool's paradise of imaginary innocence and purity, selfishly oblivious to the horrible realities which torment those whose lives are lived in the London inferno, will do well not to read the *Pall Mall Gazette* of Monday and the following three days.'

Unlike so many newspaper plugs, the ensuing copy more than lived up to the strangled excitement of the trailer. On Monday 6 July, before the eyes of a palpitating nation, the *Pall Mall Gazette* flipped up one of the great big flat rocks at the centre of Victorian society.

In six marmalade-dropping pages, the paper exposed the reality of Victorian prostitution. Or at least it exposed the reality as conceived by the editor, a bushy bearded, northern Bible-basher by the name of William Thomas Stead.

Over the previous weeks Stead had expended prodigious energy in researching this article, which he entitled 'The Maiden Tribute of Modern Babylon.' The Modern Babylon was London. The Maiden Tribute was paid by fifty thousand young women of London. They were sacrificed to male lust, said Stead, as the Athenian maidens were sacrificed to the Minotaur.

Down the mean streets of Victorian London went Stead and Co, shoving their notebooks under the noses of anyone involved in the vile trade …

'For days and nights it seemed I had to drink the purulent matter that flows from the bodies of the damned,' he gasps. He talks to pimps and to procuresses, and to the miserable alcoholic parents who are forced to sell their daughters as sex slaves. He talks to an old goat of an MP who tells him without shame that he regularly traffics in young virgins.

He finds an experienced police officer at Scotland Yard, and asks him how to get hold of an underage girl. 'Is it or is it not a fact that if I were to go to the proper houses, well introduced, the keeper would in return for money down supply me in due time with a maid – a genuine article, I mean, not a mere prostitute tricked out as a virgin but a girl who had never been seduced?'

'Certainly!' replies the officer of the law, without a moment's hesitation.

'How much would it cost', he asks. The policeman thinks about £20. Now Stead comes to the key question, the scandal he intends to expose.

'These young women,' he asks the policeman, 'do they consent to their horrible seductions or are they … raped?' Well, says the copper, they are generally unwilling, as far as he knows.

'Then do you mean to tell me,' says Stead, the headline forming in his mind, 'that in very truth actual rapes, in the legal sense of the word, are constantly being perpetrated in London on unwilling virgins, purveyed and procured to rich men, at so much a head, by keepers of brothels?'

'Certainly', says the obliging policeman, and bingo – Stead has his story. It is the crime of rape, illegal then as now, that gives him the excuse to regale his readers with tales of prostitution and throw himself with such gusto into the underworld.

We are looking at mass rape, he tells his mainly middle-to-upper class readers, and it must be stopped. It is an abuse of the common people by the privileged classes. It is a systematic violation of the daughters of the poor that will lead to unrest or even revolution.

'It is the one explosion which is strong enough to wreck the throne.' All he must do – in order to save the nation, and the Queen herself – is prove that he is right.

To say that Stead's style is salacious is an understatement. It fails to do justice to the operatic intensity with which he focuses the reader's mind on the issue of female virginity – how much it is worth, how it is verified, and the awful circumstances in which it is lost.

In this amazing issue of the *Pall Mall Gazette*, we see the birth of that technique most beloved of the best and most powerful tabloid papers. You put the reader morally in the right by issuing a foaming denunciation of some human failing or sexual habit. But you secure that reader's pop-eyed devotion (and subscription) by titillating him (and indeed her) with a detailed account of the very vice you purport to denounce.

To put it more snappily, Stead had worked out that sex sells, and that the best way to talk about sex was to veil it in a moral campaign. He had found a manoeuvre to discuss what would otherwise have been forbidden.

He visits the women who issue the certificates of virginity, and one of them informs him that 'you can soon find out, if you are in the business, whether a child is fresh or not.' He tells us of an old roué whose jaded appetites can only be stimulated by fourteen-year-old girls – and then only when they have been strapped to the bed. He goes and shakes his head at the various crime scenes – noise-proof rooms and basements where the rapes take place.

Sometimes the house of ill fame looked innocent from the outside, a villa in west London – one of those lovely stuccoed houses that now tend to be the homes of international bankers. 'To enjoy to the full the exclusive luxury of revelling in the cries of an immature child, it is not necessary to have a padded chamber, a double chamber or an underground room.'

The neighbours will not dream of interfering, he says, and informs the drooling public that 'you can enjoy the screams of the girl with the certainty that no one hears them but yourself.' In spite of all his interviews and quotations, it is clear that Stead feels he must do more to satisfy his readers.

He needs to show beyond doubt that girls as young as 13 are bought and raped. He needs to give his readers the ocular proof, the blow-by-blow eyewitness account. He needs to supply the smoking gun. So he does – and shoots himself spectacularly in the foot.

He brings his account of London prostitution to a juddering climax with his story of Lily, a cockney girl of thirteen. He informs us grandly but mysteriously that 'I can personally vouch for every fact in the narrative.'

Lily is pretty much at the bottom of the social pyramid. She is one of those who by the thousand develop into the servants of the poorer middle class, says Stead. She is an 'industrious, warm-hearted little thing, a hardy English child, slightly coarse in texture, with dark blue eyes and short, sturdy figure'. She is able to read and write, and even composes little poems about her dreams. None of her talents, alas, is to be allowed to flourish.

Her drunken mother sells her to a procuress for a sovereign; her drunken father is indifferent. She is taken to a midwife who checks that she is virgo intacta, and Stead reports that the youth and innocence of the girl extort the pity of the old abortionist.

'The poor little thing,' she exclaimed to the reporter. 'She is so small, her pain will be extreme. I hope you will not be too cruel with her.' To mitigate the procedure she supplies a phial of chloroform, for which she charges £1 10 shillings – many times its true value, and £1 1 shilling for the certificate of virginity.

The girl is taken to a house of ill fame near Regent Street. All is quiet and still, says Stead, about to spring the hideous denouement on the world.

'A few moments later the purchaser entered the bedroom. He closed and locked the door. There was a brief silence. And then there rose a wild and piteous cry – not a loud shriek, but a helpless, startled scream like the bleat of a frightened lamb. And the child's voice was heard crying, in accents of terror, 'There's a man in the room! Take me home, oh, take me home!'

'And then all once more was still.'

You will not be surprised to discover that this stuff went down big with Londoners. WH Smith refused to stock the paper out of disapproval at the subject matter, but crowds formed outside the offices of the *Pall Mall Gazette* in the hope that more copies would be printed, and feverishly prised apart the bundles when they arrived.

The circulation of the *Gazette* soared to 13,000 as men stole off to read it in the privy or placed top hats over their laps as they read it in the train. For the thirty-six-year-old Stead, it was the most notable triumph of his vertiginous career.

The progenitor of the tabloid shocker was born on 5 July 1849 in the Northumberland village of Embleton. The son of a Congregationalist minister, he could read Latin fluently by the age of five. On winning a school prize for an essay on Cromwell, he was given the poetical works of the American James Russell Lowell, and in combination with a profound adolescent religious experience the works of Lowell seem to have inspired in Stead a messianic belief that he was to right the wrongs of the world.

Lowell had written that the mission of an editor was to be the Moses of society: to 'find the tables of the new law among our factories and cities', and 'to become the captain of our exodus into the Canaan of a truer social order'.

This was a revelation, said Stead, and his personal editorial manifesto. 'I felt the sacredness of the power placed in my hands to be used on behalf of the poor, the outcast and the oppressed.'

At the age of only twenty-two he became the editor of the *Northern Echo*, and launched his first great polemical campaign: against Britain's passive acquiescence in the Bulgarian atrocities – the 1876 massacre of 12,000 Bulgarian Christians by the Turks, an issue on which Gladstone relaunched his career.

By 1880 his irrepressible energy and talents had brought him to London, where he believed the daily papers were hopeless. They were badly laid-out, full of close-packed type, and woefully lacking in zing and fire. They were 'drivelling productions', he said, 'without weight, influence or representative character.'

In 1883 he mounted a sensational attack on slum housing, prompting new legislation. The following year he ran a campaign called 'The Truth About The Navy', and so embarrassed the government that £3.5 million was found to upgrade British warships.

Not everyone liked the 'New Journalism', as it was called. The poet Algernon Charles Swinburne called the *Pall Mall Gazette* the 'Dung Hill Gazette'. Matthew Arnold called Stead 'feather-brained.'

More dangerously, Stead was earning the jealousy of rival papers. On making their own inquiries into the tragic story of thirteen-year-old 'Lily', reporters from *The Times* discovered that things were not quite as they seemed.

As soon as the story broke, parliament came under terrific pressure from the press and public to raise the age of consent from thirteen to sixteen – exactly as Stead wanted. Some MPs were dubious about this, whether because of their personal predilections or because they objected to being stampeded by the media.

Sir William Harcourt, the Home Secretary, begged Stead to lay off. Not until you pass the Bill, said Stead, and ordered the presses to roll again. On Wednesday 8 July, only days after the publication of Lily's story, parliament took up the Bill again, and on 7 August it was passed into law.

Yes, the press is powerful today, and yes, it retains an ability to bully politicians over questions of sex and morality (one thinks of the *News of the World* and its onslaught on paedophiles). But not even Rebekah Brooks, at the zenith of her power, could compare with Stead in his ability to bend the government to his will.

His glory, however, was short-lived. Big chips of paint had started to come off the story of poor little Lily and her 'rape'. First her mother came forward and said that she had no idea that her daughter – whose real name was Eliza Armstrong – was to be sold as a prostitute. Then her drunken father told the exultant media that no one had consulted him, either.

Finally it emerged that the satanic male 'purchaser' of Eliza, the man who had descended upon her terrified form in that climactic scene, was none other (of course) than Stead himself. A lifelong teetotaller, he had apparently fortified himself with a whole bottle of champagne before entering her room.

There was hilarity, scandal and outrage. It wasn't just that Stead was guilty of a put-up job, he appeared to have violated the very law for which he had just successfully campaigned. Though he had not touched Eliza (he just wanted to show what *might* have happened) he and various other plotters, including the midwife and the procuress, were accused of abducting an underage girl.

The heroic campaigner against prostitution was convicted of abduction and procurement and sentenced to three months, which he served mainly in Holloway. He would afterwards claim that he had a perfectly splendid time, and edited the *Gazette* while in prison. But his journalistic career never quite recovered.

He left the *Pall Mall Gazette*, which then declined and was eventually folded into the *Evening Standard* in 1921. He founded and edited *Review of Reviews*, in which he pioneered character sketches of the current celebrity and such immortal headlines as 'baby killing as an investment' and 'Ought Mrs Maybrook to be tortured to death?' In 1893 he launched his own 'Daily Paper', but his reputation was starting to suffer from his opposition to the Boer War.

He had become more and more preoccupied with spiritualism and campaigns for world peace – for which he was several times nominated for the Nobel Prize – and he was starting to lose that supple feel for the pulse of the reader.

If we strip away his occasional absurdity, and the bungle of the Maiden Tribute, there is something irresistible about Stead. He loved and cared about journalism, and with his interest in interviews, in colour, quotation, personality and sensation he revolutionised and (for my money) improved his profession.

What other editors can claim to have personally founded two papers, forced the government to legislate on at least three occasions, and to have recruited Oscar Wilde and GB Shaw as reviewers? He worked phenomenally hard, taking the train in from Wimbledon to be in the office from 8.20 am. By that time he had read everything in the papers down to the inquests – even though he had begun the day out on the Common, in his dressing gown, giving each of his little children a ride on the donkey he owned.

Of course he was lubricious, in the classic Victorian way. Mrs Lynn Linton even said that he 'exuded semen through the skin', whatever she meant by that. But he was hardly wrong to conceive the exercise of the Maiden Tribute.

If his techniques were faulty, we must surely enter in his defence that this was one of the world's first efforts at investigative journalism. Even if the story of little Lily was stunted up, Stead had exposed real cruelty and abuse, and done society a service.

Stead's life ended on 15 April 1912, in what was to remain one of the biggest news stories of the twentieth century. He didn't need to fabricate any quotes; he didn't need anyone to play any role for him; he didn't need to stunt up the mise-en-scene. The entire event was enacted before his boggling eyes.

The only pity was that he was unable to go over to copy. He was off to New York in pursuit of world peace (and, some said later, the Nobel Prize that awaited him) and had somehow managed to book a passage on the maiden voyage of the *Titanic*.

With typical prescience he had already published articles about what might happen if a mail steamer went down in mid-Atlantic with too few boats, and about a White Star liner rescuing the survivors of a ship that hit an iceberg. He was last sighted, said the survivor Philip Mock, clinging to a life raft with John Jacob Astor IV, until their feet became frozen and they had to let go.

Another account says that earlier in the evening he had heroically helped several women and children into the lifeboats. He had then gone into the first-class smoking room, lit a cigar, and started reading a book. I like to think that he was urged to follow the example of some less principled men, who had found places in the boats; and that in the tradition of some of the very greatest reporters he made his excuses – and stayed.

* * *

Anybody who has seen James Cameron's excellent film of the disaster will know that the *Titanic* was heavily segregated by class. The white-tied millionaires floated with their partners in the ballroom; the loveable twine-belted third-class passengers stamped and scraped their fiddles in the steamy belly of the ship.

It is a broadly accurate representation of a world that had only two years of life left in it. In 1914 Londoners were caught up in the first of two connected World Wars that were cumulatively disastrous for Britain and for the commercial and political dominance she had established in the world. From London alone 124,000 young men were sent to be slaughtered, mainly in the strategic idiocy of the Western Front. One in ten of London males in their twenties or thirties was killed. There was scarcely a family in the city that was not affected by the catastrophe.

It was a shock that accelerated – of necessity – the emancipation of women, and that fatally undermined the old culture of deference and respect. The pre-war class system could not survive such carnage. The world of *Downton Abbey* (if it ever really existed) was no more. As Winston Churchill was to discover in the Second World War, British troops no longer assumed that their generals must be wise and justified when they invited them to die for their country.

In other ways the First World War was rather good for London. Employment was near capacity, with thousands of women employed in munitions factories. As for the inter-war period, it was almost a golden age. Remember Betjeman's elegiac poems about the Metroland of the 1930s. Or think of the *Just William* stories, about a young boy growing up in a sylvan Elysium where he could tickle trout in streams and roam with his faithful dog Jumble and play in tumbledown barns. That was inter-war Bromley, a world where young girls could go for a tramp in the woods – as the old joke goes – and the tramp had nothing to fear.

London was growing ever vaster, propelled to all points of the compass by swish new electric underground trains and trolley buses and big red omnibuses going boggler boggler boggler down leafy lanes. Suburban Londoners lived in huge peaceful developments, the garden cities of mock-Tudor or pebbledash semi-detached houses, and they were speedily carried in the morning and evening to the centres of an economy that was remarkably diverse and robust.

While much of Britain suffered in the depression of the 1930s, London remained strikingly buoyant, manufacturing everything from Smiths crisps to Hoovers, to rifles, to motor cars. By 1939 the city was six times as extensive by geographical area as it had been in 1880, and the population stood at an all-time high of more than 8.7 million people – and that is about a million more than there are today.

And then history threw its second big punch of the twentieth century. London had soaked up the force of the first blow pretty well. This punch the city took full in the face.

THE TUBE

It was in August 1900 that a portly American with a silvery walrus moustache stood on Hampstead Heath. He saw the smoke rising from London, a population straining to break free to new neighbourhoods – but without the transport they needed. He saw the pleasant and still underpopulated suburbs of north London. He knew how he was going to join them up.

His name was Charles Tyson Yerkes (pronounced to rhyme with turkeys), a sixty-three year old financier and self-confessed crook from Philadelphia. He was about to transform the London Tube network. By then the London Underground was getting on for forty years old, and it was starting to run into trouble.

It had all begun when a London solicitor called Charles Pearson had a brainwave in a traffic jam. (Actually a lot of people have brainwaves in London traffic jams. In 1933 a Hungarian physicist called Leo Szilard was stuck in motionless cars in Southampton Row, Bloomsbury, when he formulated the principle of the nuclear chain reaction.) Such was the volume of horse-drawn traffic that this Pearson was wishing he was on a train ... and then it came to him. 'Trains in drains, by God!' he cried.

By 1845, his drain trains had evolved into a full-blown plan for an underground railway linking London's main terminals at Paddington, Euston and King's Cross. His timing could not have been better. Everybody was following the heroic progress of Marc Brunel's Thames tunnel – the first under a river in a capital city – between Rotherhithe and Wapping. The famous engineer, father of the even more famous engineer, was trying out his newly-invented tunnelling shield – and the theory was that after digging under the Thames, a network of underground railways would be a cinch.

The tunnel took longer than expected, so when Parliament did pass the Subterranean Railway Bill in 1852, MPs rejected the deep bore in favour of the simpler 'cut and cover' – an exposed trench with a lid on. The Metropolitan Line, completed eight years later, was soon carrying around 26,000 passengers a day.

The trains were specially built by the Great Western Railways Company and consisted of steam-powered locomotives pulling uncovered rolling stock. Other lines soon followed until by the early twentieth century there were eight lines and six different independent operators.

In theory, the underground was a triumph. The free market had responded to demand and London had a comprehensive new transport network. In reality, the operators and passengers found the system neither cost effective nor convenient. Users became impatient with changing trains and tickets between one privately-run company and another, while for operators the costs were considerable.

The answer for these companies lay in aggressive expansion and modernisation. By extending their tracks into the suburbs they could challenge the traditional rail networks for commuter custom. They could lead the construction of a new London, spreading in great whorls and loops and terraces of Metroland. They could use the wonderful new electric trains. The only problem was that they lacked the capital.

As London entered the new century, the race was on for which operator would first have the gumption to carry London's transport into the twentieth century. The race was won by Yerkes. Visionary, robber baron, art pseud and notorious shagger, Charles Yerkes is the embodiment of the United States at a time between cowboys and skyscrapers. By the age of forty-four he had already made and lost a fortune, blackmailed politicians, been imprisoned for larceny and pardoned on the orders of the President. He had managed to rebuild his fortune by financing Chicago's transport system and it was this success that convinced him of the potential returns in London's growing underground network.

He came down from that height on the Heath and by October, Yerkes had secured the rights to build the Charing Cross, Euston and Hampstead Railway (today also part of the Northern Line), and by March the following year, he effectively took control of the District and Metropolitan lines as well. Then he secured rights to the Great Northern and Strand Railway; the Brompton and Piccadilly Circus Railway followed quickly, together with the moribund Baker Street & Waterloo Railway in March 1902, which together formed our present-day Piccadilly Line.

The unstoppable Yerkes went on to buy tram and bus companies, creating London's first integrated transport network. Reflecting on his life, the old tycoon commented that, 'the secret of my success in business is to buy old junk, fix it up a little and unload it upon other fellows'.

He died in 1905, but his company continued until the 1930s when they eventually 'unloaded' it to the newly-created public corporation, London Transport.

Winston Churchill

The unsung founder of the welfare state – and the man who saved the world from tyranny

If you have not yet done so, can I suggest that you go immediately (upon finishing this book) to the Cabinet War Rooms. I mean the bunker whose entrance is to be found to the right of the Clive Steps, between the Foreign Office and the Treasury. You may have unconsciously dismissed it as a tourist-trap, a money-spinning shrine to the cult of Winston Churchill. You only have to go under the sand-bagged lintel and down the steps to see that this is no gimmick.

This isn't some Tussaud's-style animatronic Churchill experience: this is the real thing. You are taken down and back seventy years to the moment when London and Britain faced their supreme trial; and as your eyes adjust to the low-watt lighting of the former command centre, you begin to grasp something about being a Londoner in the Second World War. You will find it easy to ignore the global Churchill-worshipping pilgrims, with their wide eyes and audiophones pressed religiously to their ears.

The rooms have been so meticulously preserved that you can almost believe you are back there in the 1940s. You can hear the rattle and purr of the oversized bakelite telephones – red, white and green – that link this tiny warren of interconnected offices with British forces around the world. You can imagine the soft mutter of the uniformed service johnnies, their waxed moustaches drooping in the heat, as they stick their round-headed coloured pins into the maps: here the sinking of another capital ship, there another humiliating Japanese breakthrough.

You can see the dark patches widening under the nylon armpits of good-looking shorthand typists, as they tap tap tap to keep up with the blistering pace set by whisky-fuelled lucubrations of their chief client, and you can hear the pathetic efforts of the 1940s gizmos that are charged with keeping them cool – the wall-mounted fans or the solitary and newfangled mahogany air conditioning unit, made by Frigidaire and donated by the Americans.

If you are lucky, Gerry McCartney, the Director of Operations, will make an exception and allow you into the War Cabinet Room itself; and here you can almost taste the gulfs of tobacco taken in and exhaled by the nut-coloured lungs of its most famous denizens – Eden, Beaverbrook, pipe-puffing Attlee, and Churchill himself, each with his square metal ashtray in front of him.

I have never been anywhere so instantly redolent of a dead historical figure, and of his personality. I can almost sense him padding around behind us in the corridors in one of his red boiler suits, calling for a secretary or a fifty centilitre bottle of Pol Roger; or pouring himself one of his tall glasses of whisky and water before addressing the nation on the set that is still mounted on his desk.

When you go into his bedroom, you feel his physical presence in the neat little Civil Service-issue bed with its plain headboard and blue quilted counterpane; in the white ceramic potty underneath; in the authentic Romeo y Julieta lying like a desiccated dog-turd in the metal canister on the bedside table. You can draw the curtains on the wall-maps opposite his bed, and you can see the very sight that greeted Churchill when he woke from one of his frequent power naps – a detailed depiction of Britain's defences and vulnerabilities; the places where it would be easy to guard against a German tank break-out, and the places where it would be trickier.

Then you suddenly catch a whiff of the dominant emotion of this place. It is not so much the bustle, or excitement, or even the tension. It is the desperation.

When they first started to fortify this government furniture store in the summer of 1938, London was at the heart of what was still the mightiest empire the world had ever seen. In a few short months all that power and might had been chivvied and contracted into these few shabby rooms, with their dowdy brown armchairs and ugly curtains – the whole thing somehow reminiscent of one of those local paper stories about council staff opening a flat and finding the mummified remains of a forgotten old age pensioner.

You can see the desperation in the primitive information technology: the yellowing dockets and files, the fridge-sized scrambling devices, the pitiful pot of glue – now reduced to an oily black sludge – in front of Churchill's desk; glue he would use physically to cut and paste his briefings into an order he liked. You can see the desperation in the little wooden sign that informed these light-deprived war-voles what kind of day it was outside. Above all, you can understand their fear and urgency when you consider the concrete slab, between three and nine feet thick, that has been placed above the ceiling.

The cause of desperation was simple. London was under attack, bombarded with an indiscriminate sadism that it had never known before. Among all the other noises – Churchill's growlings, the phones, the fans – you can imagine the noise of high explosive falling on London, and trying to work with the knowledge that even this bunker could probably not withstand a direct hit.

Looking back at the Second World War, it is pretty clear that it was a disaster for Britain and for British standing in the world. For my generation of post-war softies, brought up to fear nothing more than the sporadic campaigns of the IRA or al-Qaeda, the Blitz seems an unimaginable horror. It was more terrifying and vastly more lethal than the Great Fire of London (which killed how many? That's right – eight people); and it went on so long – night after night, month after month, from the autumn of 1940 to the spring of 1941, and then with a resumption in 1944 and a series of deafening false climaxes like a hideous parody of a Beethoven symphony.

Everyone knew that it was coming, and that London was all but defenceless. When Neville Chamberlain came back from Munich in 1938, he tried to justify his appeasement of Hitler by telling the cabinet of his fear as he flew upriver towards London, and he saw the thousands of vulnerable rooftops beneath him. It was the aerial threat to London that wound Churchill up in 1934, when Hitler had come to power and was boosting the German air force. 'It was the greatest target in the world,' he warned, 'a kind of tremendous fat valuable cow, tied up to attract the beasts of prey.'

He had issued dreadful warnings about what would happen if they failed to listen to him. There would be thirty or forty thousand people killed in only a week or ten days of intensive bombing, and three to four million panicking Londoners would be driven into the open country. 'The flying peril is not one from which we can fly. It is necessary to face it where we stand. We cannot possibly retreat. We cannot move London. We cannot move the vast population that is dependent on the estuary of the Thames.' By 1939 people had seen the newsreels of what happened when the Japanese bombed Shanghai. They knew what the Condor Legion had done to Guernica in 1937.

The terror must have been all the greater for the slow drum-roll build up. Tens of thousands of children were evacuated in 1939, only to come back to the city when the bombing failed to start – many of them East End kids only too happy to flee their strange middle-class families and their prissy habits. Theatres and cinemas had closed down and started up again. Then, on the evening of Saturday 7 September 1940, the bombing started in earnest. Fighter command and the British chiefs of staff were caught napping as a force of 320 German bombers, accompanied by more than 600 fighters, flew virtually unopposed towards key industrial and commercial targets. They bombed Woolwich Arsenal, Beckton gas works, West Ham power station, and they pounded the docks and slums of the East End.

Soon the blaze was so great that it was like an orange false dawn, a convenient beacon to attract the next force of 250 German bombers that came over to continue the work. Stephen Inwood records that by morning there were a thousand fires burning, three main railway stations closed, 430 Londoners dead and 1,600 injured. The docklands was full of speciality blazes from the goods whose import and export had helped to make London great.

There were pepper fires whose fumes made firemen think they were breathing fire itself. There were barrels of rum exploding like bombs; paint that went up in sheets of white hot flame, asphyxiating black clouds from the rubber and a sweet sickly aroma from the burning tea. On it went through the autumn, intensifying in the spring. On 16 April 1941 the Junkers 88s came screaming through the night. They blew such a gash in the Admiralty Arch that Churchill claimed flippantly he now had a better view of Nelson's column. There were countless vignettes of a horror-film quality: a much-loved local vicar, killed on the steps of his church as he invited people to take shelter; the bursting of the Fleet sewer, and the release of smells that Londoners had not endured for two hundred years; a corpse a century old blown from its lead-lined casket, and the head bouncing before people's eyes.

On 10 May 1941 the city was so pounded that by morning Londoners awoke (those that had managed to get to sleep) to find the Law Courts, the Tower of London and the Royal Mint had all been hit. The bridges were down, the stations were closed, 250,000 books had been burned in the British Museum, Westminster Hall had been set on fire and the House of Commons gutted. A bomb had even crashed through Big Ben, pocking and scarring the clock face. Even if the tempo died down for the next couple of years, the climax was horrendous.

By 1944 new jet and rocket technology enabled Hitler to launch the V1s and V2s, causing such a stampede to leave the city that one wag reversed the aphorism of Dr Johnson: only he who was tired of life chose to stay in London. By the end of the war the city had sustained catastrophic and in many cases irreparable damage. Eighteen city churches were ruined, including fourteen by Wren, and there were swathes of destruction around the City and the East End. Almost 30,000

Londoners were killed and another 50,000 badly injured, while 116,000 homes were destroyed and another 288,000 in need of major repair. About a million other buildings – half the entire housing stock – were in need of repair of some kind.

The Blitz was not just physical in its destruction. There were psychological impacts. It would be nice to report that all Londoners behaved well in adversity, but it is pretty clear that there were some shameful exceptions. Looters prowled around the floors of shattered night clubs, as Philip Ziegler records, ripping open handbags and tearing rings off the dead and unconscious. Gangs of looters would send out spotters during the raids, and try to get to the scene before the emergency services arrived. Though the crime of looting bombed premises was technically punishable by death, the magistrates began by being quite tender-hearted. By 1941, the panic over looting was so great that sentences of five years penal servitude were common. Young culprits were birched.

Scotland Yard set up a special anti-looting squad, and the police of 1941 had no compunctions about physically chastising the thieves. Henry Green describes the condition of one man who had been collared by the cops, 'with most of his clothes torn off, heels dragging, drooling blood at the mouth, out on his feet from the bashing he had been given'. There is perhaps no need to belabour the contrast in what is legally acceptable in the police handling of looters today.

In spite of these punishments, the incidence of looting was actually higher in the 'Little Blitz' of 1944, when the bombers returned. In West Hampstead the stock of a wireless shop disappeared within twenty minutes of a bomb falling. A resident of Agamemnon Road complained, 'The looting that went on that night was something hawful. When the greengrocer's wife found 'er 'andbag, every penny 'ad been taken out of it.' Under the stress of the Blitz some Londoners even succumbed to the virus of anti-semitism – the very prejudice that raged uncontrolled in Nazi Germany – as though the bombs had opened the floorboards and exposed the spores of an ancient disease.

Jews in wartime London were accused of hogging space in the air-raid shelters. The Home Office was so concerned by reports of anti-semitism that it commissioned weekly studies of the flare-ups. Of course there was no evidence whatever that Jewish people were being selfish in the use of air-raid shelters, but even an author as fastidious as George Orwell noted of the queues, in language that may disappoint some of his fans, 'What is bad about the Jews is that they are not only conspicuous, but go out of their way to make themselves so'.

One of the most tragic incidents of the war took place on 3 March 1943, when people were filing to get into Bethnal Green Tube station. A salvo of rockets was fired in nearby Victoria Park, a woman stumbled at the top of the steps, and within seconds a panicked stampede had claimed the lives of 178 people who were either crushed to death or suffocated. Some said it was the work of Fifth columnists or German agents, but more Londoners – though not in Bethnal Green, where they knew the truth – blamed the Jews. They were so terrified that they stampeded: that was the story told over the city. According to a poll of the time, the proportion of those hostile to the Jews rose to 27 per cent.

It was odd, and unpleasant. And since we are looking at the morally discreditable aspects of British wartime performance, we might as well face another awful truth – that the ostensibly heroic British armed forces were sometimes accused of lacking the stomach for the fight; and their most notable accuser, in private if not in public, was Winston Churchill himself.

On 16 January 1940 – reinstalled at the Admiralty – he wrote a fierce memo to the First Sea Lord, Admiral Dudley Pound. 'Our army is puny as far as the fighting front is concerned; our air force is hopelessly inferior to the Germans.' His words seemed to be borne out by events. Of all the military manoeuvres that the military were called upon to execute, the one at which they excelled was evacuation: the abject scuttle, the headlong flight.

They evacuated Namsos in Norway in May 1940, in a humiliation that brought Churchill to power as Prime Minister. Nor did their performance palpably improve with his hand on the tiller. They were driven from France, and it is one of those miracles of self-deception that we still refer to Dunkirk as a triumph, when in fact this chaotic withdrawal was only made possible by the gross tactical error of the Germans, who halted their armour and allowed the British to get away. In May 1941 the British were conclusively bested in Crete, bullied off the island by the skill and daring of the German paratroopers in an episode bleakly and bitingly immortalised by Evelyn Waugh. But Norway, Dunkirk and Crete were nothing next to the disaster in Singapore.

On 10 February Churchill cabled Field Marshal Wavell, the poetry enthusiast who was then Commander-in-Chief, India, and warned him of what was at stake. Look here, said Churchill, you ought to know how we see this thing here in London. There were more British forces in Singapore, he noted, than the Japanese had in the entire Malay peninsula. 'The battle must be fought to the bitter end, at all costs. The 18th Division has a chance to make its name in history. Commanders and senior officers should die with their troops. The honour of the British Empire and of the British army is at stake. I rely on you to show no mercy to weakness in any form. With the Russians fighting as they are, and the Americans so stubborn at Luzon, the whole reputation of our country and race is involved ...'

Alas, the generals decided that on the whole there was no need to follow Churchill's exhortations. Given the choice between death and dishonour, they plumped resoundingly for dishonour. On 15 February 1942 Singapore surrendered, and the event seemed to confirm a sneaking anxiety that had been growing in Churchill's mind: that the British troops, man for man, did not have the same stuff of battle in them as the Germans or indeed the Japanese. He was worried, he wrote to Violet Bonham Carter, 'that our soldiers are not as good fighters as our fathers were. In 1915 our men fought on even when they had only one shell left and were under a fierce barrage. Now they cannot resist dive bombers. We have so many men in Singapore, so many men – they should have done better.'

Alan Brooke, the Chief of the Imperial General Staff, took the same view as Churchill. He noted in his diary on 18 February 1942, 'If the army cannot fight better than it is doing at present, we shall deserve to lose our empire'. It may seem a bit much for brandy-swilling politicians and absent generals to criticise our troops, but even the Japanese felt lucky to win at Singapore. In 1992 the victorious general Yamashita noted in his memoirs that his attack was a bluff. 'I had thirty thousand men and was outnumbered more than three to one. I knew that if I had to fight for long in Singapore, I would be beaten …'

If Churchill was embarrassed by the tapioca-like performance in Singapore, he was mortified by what happened next at Tobruk. He was actually sitting with Roosevelt, in the Oval Office, when the news came through that a garrison of 35,000 had surrendered the Libyan town to a smaller force of Germans. 'Defeat is one thing,' he mused later in his diary; 'disgrace is another.' But if Churchill doubted the levels of spunk and pluck in the British soldier, others were beginning to have their doubts about Churchill, and his leadership of the whole effort.

The government started to lose bye-elections, and on 25 June a motion 'of no confidence in the central direction of the war' was placed on the order paper of the Commons. When the debate was held, in July, MPs of all parties laid into Churchill, including Lord Winterton (an Irish peer, and therefore able to sit in the Commons), who said: 'We are getting close to the intellectual and moral position of the German people … that the Fuhrer is always right … During the thirty-seven years that I have sat in this house, I have never seen such attempts to absolve the Prime Minister of ministerial responsibility'.

Aneurin Bevan said the problem was nothing to do with the fighting spirit of the average Tommy. It was the useless officer corps! The army was riddled with class prejudice. 'Had Rommel been in the British army, he would still be a sergeant!' – a blistering crack that glided over Rommel's graduation from an officer cadet school. Rommel was never a sergeant.

In the end, of course, British troops redeemed themselves convincingly at El Alamein. Montgomery duly assembled a two-to-one advantage in men and tanks, hit Jerry for six, and stopped the German advance to Cairo. Churchill hailed the moment (not the end, not the beginning of the end, but the end of the beginning), and even in the 1970s I remember being taught – by good men who were themselves veterans of the Second World War – that this was a turning-point.

These days I am not so sure. The real turning-points, surely, were the German failure at Moscow, or American entry, or Stalingrad. Monty faced three German divisions at El Alamein; the Russians defeated thirteen German divisions at Stalingrad. We are talking about events on a different scale, and as the war went on it is clear that Churchill – and Britain – had diminished in relative importance.

Even as the allies were preparing for 'Overlord' and the liberation of Europe, Churchill seemed to be strategically off the pace, continually suggesting peripheral feints and ruses, in the manner of Gallipoli, as if he were leery of a frontal attack. He was teased by Stalin about the prowess of the British navy, and it is a measure of the relative decline of British influence that when the Russians mistreated two British sailors – sentencing them to long periods of imprisonment in Siberia after a brawl in Murmansk – there was nothing that Churchill could do.

Stalin and Roosevelt made jokes about shooting thousands of German officers, while Churchill seemed to be the gooseberry, fuming pompously on the sidelines. It was the Russians and the Americans who shook hands across the Elbe, and they must take most of the credit for the German defeat. Churchill was only as powerful as the country behind him, and Britain was simply exhausted, while London was on its knees.

The industrial base of the city was smashed, with capacity reduced by about 40 per cent; and as a manufacturing centre London never recovered to pre-war levels. Even office space only crawled back up to pre-war volumes by 1954. Children's education had been badly disrupted. Literacy declined. Bermondsey, Finsbury and Southwark lost 38 per cent of their population. Poplar, Shoreditch and the City lost 45 per cent and Stepney lost a half. Buddleia and willow herb sprouted in the bomb sites. The Americans ruthlessly cancelled Lend-Lease as soon as the war was over, and Britain struggled to pay the interest on her debts.

On 10 November 1942 Churchill had told the Lord Mayor's Banquet: 'I have not become the King's First Minister in order to preside over the liquidation of the British Empire.' And yet that was precisely what took place – largely at American behest – in the immediate post-war years. Churchill had spent much of his 1930s wilderness years campaigning against Gandhi and Indian independence. In one of his speeches that has emphatically not stood the test of time, he had in 1931 denounced Gandhi as a seditious Middle Temple lawyer, and said it was 'alarming and nauseating to see this fakir striding half-naked up the steps of the Vice-regal palace to parley on equal terms with the representatives of the King-Emperor.' He had prophesied mass unemployment if India was given independence. When India was afflicted by a cruel famine during the war, and Churchill was asked permission to divert food supplies, he sent back a brutal reply. Things couldn't be that bad, he said, if Gandhi was still alive.

Churchill made a lot of good jokes in his career, but that was not among them, and by 1948 the joke was on him. India was given independence and there was not a thing he could do about it – because in 1945 he had been crushingly ejected from office.

On 16 July 1945, *Time* magazine did an eve of poll colour piece in which its reporter followed the seventy-year-old premier to Walthamstow dog track. He arrived to cheers, with Clementine in tow; and then the booing began. 'We want Attlee!' they cried. 'In a free country like ours ...' Churchill began to remonstrate, before – as *Time* put it – 'Boos blitzed him out.'

They booed him when he talked about housing, and increased food production, and the general lèse-majesté continued the following day when a seventeen-year-old tossed a lit firecracker into his face. Churchill may have persuaded himself that the booers were a minority – just as they had been a minority when he toured the areas that had been bombed – but when the ballot boxes were finally opened, it was clear that they spoke for the country. The great war leader had lost by miles.

A revisionist account of Churchill's leadership might (and probably does) therefore go as follows: that his ceaseless 1930s warmongering was intended not so much for the good of the country, but to put Churchill at the head of the nation's affairs. Having got Britain into an avoidable war with Germany, he presided over one military debacle after another while London's citizens, especially the poor, were mercilessly bombed. After six years of fighting Britain found herself so weakened and impoverished that she had no choice but to run down the flag, relinquish the empire and accept a much diminished global role; and that after these vicissitudes it was hardly surprising that the great British public decided to kick Churchill out in one of the biggest landslides of the twentieth century.

I am sure there are other charges that are laid against him: that he was a racist and a sexist and a believer in eugenics, or that he cynically allowed Coventry to be bombed rather than betray Britain's knowledge of German codes (a lie), or that he failed to do enough to stop the Holocaust (another lie); and so on and so forth. These are the kind of accusations that tend to be made by revisionists – Charmley, Ponting, Irving, Buchanan and the like – and yet the interesting thing is how little difference they have made. We still love him – I love him; and we all know instinctively that the popguns of revisionism have left not a scratch in the supercolossal Mount Rushmore of his reputation.

Like all members of the human race, the British are an instinctively hierarchical people. They tend to rank things and individuals and they like to argue about it. But in two important categories you will find agreement in just about every pub in the country: that Shakespeare is our number one author, and Churchill is our number one politician. There are about 430 British roads, avenues, streets and cul-de-sacs that bear his name. Madame Tussauds has made 10 effigies of him.

We may now have forgotten how much effort Churchill poured into his speeches, spending up to fourteen hours on their composition, and practising his pauses and flourishes in front of the mirror. We do remember many of the things he said, not least because Churchill grasped that if you want to speak directly to the hearts of English people, then you should use short Anglo-Saxon words. 'Never in the field of human conflict was so much owed by so many to so few,' or, 'I have nothing to offer but blood, toil, tears and sweat.' I make that three Latinate words to twenty-seven Anglo-Saxon. That's why they stick. Or take this one: 'We shall fight on the beaches, we shall fight on the landing-grounds, we shall fight in the fields and in the streets, we shall fight in the hills; we shall never surrender.' The only Latinate word is surrender, of course.

Mind you, with a vocabulary of more than sixty thousand, Churchill could play any shot he liked, and he was skilled at mixing the short with the flowery, the punchy with the bombastic. Chinese-indentured labour in the Transvaal, he famously said in 1906, could not be classified as slavery in the extreme acceptance of the word, without some risk of terminological inexactitude. Which was soon taken up as a delightful parliamentary euphemism for a lie.

He mobilised the English language, said John F Kennedy (trying to make up for his father), and sent it into battle. In 1953 he was awarded the Nobel Prize – not for 'peace', the traditional gong for politicians, but for Literature: 'for his mastery of historical and biographical descriptions, as well as for his brilliant oratory in defending exalted values'. Whatever you may think of the taste of the judges (who passed over the claims of WH Auden, DH Lawrence, Evelyn Waugh, Ezra Pound, and so on) that seems to be an achievement unlikely to be equalled, in the near future, by any other British politician.

His character is still so talismanic in British politics that almost any foible or course of action can be justified if it can be shown to be 'Churchillian'. Newspapers once teased the gentle figure of Bob McLennan MP, after he was seen to shed a tear on being deprived of the leadership of the Social and Liberal Democrats, a now defunct centrist party. He explained that he had a 'Churchillian' tendency to weep. If people are saying you are getting a bit long in the tooth for front-line politics, you can always point out that Churchill was sixty-five when he first became prime minister. If you get drunk before lunchtime, you can point to Churchill's vast potations of champagne, whisky and brandy. If you must smoke, you reply to your critics that Churchill was hardly ever seen without a cigar. If someone tells you that you can't combine writing and politics, you can remind them that Churchill wrote journalism throughout his career, and – for heaven's sake! – he continued to write the *History of the English-Speaking Peoples* after Hitler had invaded Poland and he was in charge of the entire British navy.

If you make a terrific goof, you can point to Churchill's recovery from the debacle of Gallipoli. If you are making a speech and suddenly lose your place and freeze, there is always the example of Churchill, who once dried up so badly in the House of Commons that he simply sat down and put his head in his hands. If people have a tendency to make jokes about you, don't forget Roy Jenkins' insight about Churchill (and also, of course, about Roy Jenkins) that all truly great men have an element of comicality about them. If you were a flop at school, and you couldn't handle maths, let alone Latin, Churchill is your model. He is the perpetual Chancellor of the University of Life.

He remains uniquely popular with all voters not just because he led a wartime coalition, but because his political identity was so protean. There is something there for almost everyone. Take the eternal debate on 'Europe'. A British Euro-sceptic can point to his 1930 speech in which he insisted that Britain, like the Shunammite woman, would always dwell apart from the rest of Europe. A Euro-enthusiast, on the other hand, has plenty of shimmering post-war rhapsody about the need to create a United States of Europe. He invokes God (I am ready to meet my maker; whether the Almighty is ready for the ordeal of meeting me is another question), and yet he could hardly be called a Christian.

His judgments swoop and veer. He began the 1930s by saying that Mussolini was 'the Roman genius … the greatest lawgiver among men'. Which was not exactly the stuff to give the troops in the 1940s. He hated Soviet communism as much as he hated fascism, and once said that he had tried to strangle the Soviet Union at birth. But at a summit in Moscow he toasted Stalin in the following emetic terms: 'I walk through this world with greater courage and hope, when I find myself in a relationship of friendship and intimacy with that great man, whose fame has gone out not only over all Russia but the world.' He straddles political divides, with complete incorrigibility and lack of embarrassment.

If you go into the lobby of the House of Commons, you can see one of Oscar Nemon's great statues of Churchill, in the act of straddling, and you will notice something about the left toe. While the rest of the statue is a dark brownish black, the toe has been buffed and polished to a golden brilliance. That is because Winston Churchill's left toe is like the shiny bosses on the Gates to the Heavenly City in Tienanmen Square, or the much-rubbed rock underneath the altar of the Church of the Holy Sepulchre in Jerusalem. It is a sacred object, which politicians of all parties have got into the habit of caressing, with trailing fingers, as they make their way into the Chamber. It is as if they hope that some of that astral genius will flow through the toe end and up their arms, fortifying them for their statement about the Educational Maintenance Allowance, or Housing Benefit, or whatever it happens to be.

The Serjeant at Arms has asked MPs to stop the habit, because the bronze is wearing thin. But still they frot and rub, MPs of all parties. Liberals claim him because in 1904 he defected from the Tory party, announcing, 'I hate the Tory party, their men, their words and their methods, and I feel no sort of sympathy with them'. Tories can obviously claim him, because he then re-ratted and became a rather too purist Chancellor of the Exchequer in the 1920s. He led the nation as a Tory and died a Tory. Margaret Thatcher was so keen to demonstrate an affinity with him that she once referred to him familiarly as 'Winston', though there is no evidence that they ever met.

Labour has traditionally claimed that he was put in power with Labour votes in 1940, and that they can therefore boast paternity of his wartime premiership. Roy Jenkins says that this is a myth, and that Attlee would equally have settled for Halifax – who might well have been tempted to make some sort of accommodation with Hitler. What is certainly true is that Churchill's politics – imperialist, quixotic, traditionalist but basically soft-hearted – were not as much at variance with Attlee's socialism as is sometimes supposed.

Let us go back to that chaotic event at the dog-track, on the eve of his electoral humiliation, in July 1945. Churchill has been booed about housing and food production, and he tries to rescue the occasion by making his central pitch against Labour and socialism. 'All these plans will be nullified by foolish faction fights about idiotic ideologies and philosophical dreams about absurd Utopian worlds which will never be seen except by great improvements of the human heart and the human head.' There was a roar of laughter, reported *Time* magazine, and Churchill said, 'I am sorry if that hurts.'

It isn't clear from the report what they were laughing at. Perhaps it was his Tory supporters showing their relief and pleasure at hearing the old alliterative whoosh and whack of his rhetoric. Perhaps they liked to hear him give the lefties a kicking. Or perhaps there were some who were laughing at him, who thought he sounded frankly parodic and out of touch. There were people in that crowd who remembered the unemployment of the 1930s, and who were willing to give Labour a go at building a Utopian world, whether or not Churchill said the project was absurd.

Churchill's attack on Labour was a variant of his ill-fated 'Gestapo' broadcast of about a month earlier. The gist of his criticism (and it is a point that continues to be made to this day) is that Labour has an unrealistic interpretation of human nature, and will require all sorts of bureaucracy for the government to enforce its will. In other words, it is the old 'nanny state' argument; and it was a bit rich, frankly, coming from Churchill.

He had just spent the last five years in the biggest exercise in top-down government the country had ever seen, with himself on top. Think of the famous Low cartoon, of the serried ranks of men behind him, rolling up their sleeves and marching in step, and the caption, 'All behind you, Winston'. It wasn't just a question of 'let us go forward together, with our united strength'. It was turn off those lights, melt down those railings, give up your books to be pulped, and no, we have no bananas.

AJP Taylor begins his wonderful history of Britain between 1914 and 1945 with the remark that before 1914 a sensible law-abiding Englishman could pass through life and hardly notice the existence of the state beyond the post office and the policeman. By 1945 Londoners had got used to a world where they were told what they should wear, what they should eat, how they should cook it, and what sort of things they should talk about in public. When in 1944 the first V2 rocket landed in Chiswick, the government tried to pretend it was a gas explosion.

Some have tried to maintain that Churchill was somehow estranged from this expansion in the functions of the state, and they cite his merry boozing, or his Falstaffian memo to Lord Woolton, the Minister of Food. Woolton was trying to deal with the meat shortage by persuading people that they might enjoy a kind of meatless pasty known as the Woolton pie. 'Almost all the food faddists I have known have died young after a long period of senile decay,' Churchill wrote. 'The British soldier is far more likely to be right than the scientists. All he cares about is beef. I do not understand why there should be these serious difficulties about food, considering the tonnages we are importing. The way to lose the war is to try to force the British public into a diet of milk, oatmeal, potatoes, etc, washed down on gala occasions with a little lime juice.'

This is all good knockabout stuff: but it was surely nanny who prevailed in the coalition government. It has suited both sides of the argument – Labour and Tory – to pretend over the years that the coalition was a yoking together of opposites, or that Churchill was the flamboyant bellicose frontman for a left-wing domestic administration, a camp Conservative carapace for a socialist mollusc. This does not do justice to Churchill's instincts and record. It was Attlee's view that he had 'sympathy, incredibly wide sympathy, for ordinary people all over the world'. Indeed it is the view of Andrew Roberts, the most eminent of modern Churchillians, that 'he was unremittingly left-liberal all his life'.

In 1908 he was one of the first British politicians to call for a minimum wage. In 1910 he refused to allow troops to be deployed against the Tonypandy rioters. In 1911 he wanted a referendum (of male voters, naturally) on the issue of female suffrage, and was turned down by Asquith. Above all, it is just not right to imagine that Churchill was somehow ignorant of or uninvolved in the wartime genesis of the welfare state. He gave a broadcast on 21 March 1943, called *After the War*, in which he foresaw a four-year plan of post-war reconstruction, 'to cover five or six large measures of a practical character'.

These were to include 'national compulsory insurance for all classes for all purposes from the cradle to the grave'; the abolition of unemployment by government policies 'which would exercise a balancing influence upon development which can be turned on and off as circumstances require'; 'a broadening field for state ownership and enterprise'; new housing; major reforms to education; largely expanded health and welfare services.

There is Churchill, in the middle of the war, mapping out the very shape of the new Jerusalem that Attlee and Co were to try to create, up to and including greater nationalisation. No wonder people were disappointed, in the General Election campaign, by his prophecies of a socialist 'Gestapo', with vast bureaucracies of civil servants who were no longer servants and no longer civil. It seemed so inconsistent with his own key selling-point, that he was capable of uniting people in a great national effort. He seemed to be desperately exaggerating the threat of state control in order to create a greater sense of difference between himself and Labour.

His attacks misfired because he sounded like a party hack when people had been used to hearing him speak as the *Pater patriae* and the saviour of his country. Which, by the way, he certainly was. Churchill's enduring grip on the imaginations of today's public and politicians can be attributed to two vast and interconnected achievements.

He led Britain through the transformational experience of the Second World War, a time of agonising trial in which barriers of class and sex (and to some extent race) were broken down more effectively than in any previous epoch, and in which people could see the job-generating role the government had played. He is therefore one of the key makers of the modern epoch, and the outlines of the post-war settlement – the welfare state, the NHS, comprehensive education – can be clearly seen in his administration. A Tory might point out that the original Beveridge plan was for an insurance-based system, designed to avoid the welfarism and poverty traps of today. But that is a quibble.

Churchill helped to build our post-war existence, and more important still he helped to ensure that Britain had a post-war existence to enjoy. He helped ensure that Britain won the war. If Winston Churchill had not taken over in 1940, it really looks as if the outcome might have been different.

It is easy to forget how bad things looked. Britain was alone. The Russians had behaved with nauseating cynicism, joining the Germans to carve up Poland and conspiring to supply Hitler's war machine. France had folded with dizzying speed. So had Denmark, Norway, Holland, Belgium; in fact the whole of continental Europe was under the Nazi jackboot in one way or another, and some were positively licking the leather.

The American ambassador in London, Joseph P Kennedy, had made the cheering prediction that democracy in Britain was finished. The more Churchill learned about the military position in the summer of that year, the more desperate things seemed. According to his chiefs of staff, it all depended on the RAF, and if they lost control of the skies to the Luftwaffe, it was not at all clear that Britain could hang on.

With the benefit of hindsight, it can appear to us now as if all Britain had to do was survive, stick it out until the Americans did the right thing in the end (having exhausted the available alternatives), and came in to pull our chestnuts out of the fire. No one could have known in the summer of 1940 that the Japanese would make the mistake of bombing Pearl Harbor, or that the Germans would simultaneously declare war on America, or that Hitler would be so deranged as to attack Russia. There were people in London who remembered the dreadful losses of the First World War, and argued that it might be possible to cut a deal with Hitler – perhaps using Mussolini as an intermediary. Perhaps British possessions in the Mediterranean and Africa could be traded for peace, it was hinted.

Churchill was having none of it. There are still some historians who contend that his 'finest hour' was in fact a disaster for Britain. It doesn't take much imagination to see how that counterfactual world – in which, say, Halifax had sued for peace in 1940 – would have been a total political and moral eclipse, a plunge into darkness, for this country and for the world.

Yes, Britain might have hung on for longer to parts of the empire. But it is frankly hard to see why Gandhi and his supporters should have desisted in their campaign for independence in the face of a pusillanimous capitulation by Britain to Germany. More important, the European continent would have been lost to a barbaric Nazi system, and Britain would have been a pathetic bobbing offshore creature that depended on maintaining good trading relations with a revolting and racist regime. It was Churchill who saw that threat most clearly, and he had done so for years.

He was right about rearmament in the 1930s, when the Labour Party was hopelessly pacifist. He was right to object to appeasement, when most of the Conservative Party supported it. It was not politically cost-free to take this stand, incidentally. There was a concerted move, led by some local toad, to deselect him from his seat.

It was Churchill who found the words that emboldened the British people. When he spoke of fighting on to the end they believed that he, Churchill, would fight on to the end. His courage was contagious, and it was important that in so far as people knew anything of his background, they knew that his life was littered with tales of spectacular derring-do. He first came under fire in Cuba in 1896, where he acquired his habits of cigars and siestas. In 1897 he repeatedly saw action on the North West Frontier of India, riding his grey pony along the front line and almost getting killed. In 1898 he took part in the last cavalry charge launched by the British army, at Omdurman in the Sudan, writing afterwards to his mother, 'I shot five men for certain and two doubtful. Nothing touched me. I destroyed all those who molested me.'

In 1899 we find him working as a newspaper correspondent in the Boer War – but a journalist determined to become the story. His train is derailed in an ambush; he heroically organises a counter-attack; he is captured; he escapes from prison, jumps from a goods train, hides in a wood and is hailed by cheering crowds in Durban. In the run-up to the First World War he not only championed the airplane – when the thing had been barely invented, and must have seemed insanely dangerous – but went up a hundred and forty times himself and was on the verge of taking his pilot's licence when he acceded to Clementine's entreaties.

After engendering the disaster of the Dardanelles, he atoned by leaving office and going out to the Western Front, to take personal charge of the 6th Royal Scots Fusiliers – and made more than a hundred expeditions to No Man's Land, prowling around at night in the barbed wire and corpses. Throughout the Second World War there was something prodigious about the physical energy and recklessness of a man in his late sixties. He travelled more than 110,000 miles on his desperate missions of shuttle diplomacy between Stalin and Roosevelt and others, enduring jolting, freezing, cattle-class conditions. In 1943 he spent a hundred and seventy three days out of the country. Planes he had used were shot down; ships were sunk after he disembarked.

As a veteran of the Western Front, he may have been nervous about the consequences of a full-frontal attack on Nazi-held Europe, but when D-Day came around George VI himself had to write to him to beg him to abandon his plan to attend the landings in person. I suppose a psychologist might want to understand the origins of this volcanic appetite for risk-taking and self-promotion. One might conjecture that he was compensating for some insecurity. There is that curious and malicious accusation (pursued by a fatuous Liberal MP and journalist called Henry Labouchere) that as a young officer he had buggered another subaltern.

Although the accusation was false it was quite widely publicised, and Churchill and his mother Jenny sued for damages of £20,000 – a big sum in those days – to get the thing corrected. Did he set off for Cuba, and other macho adventures, with the partial objective of expunging this falsehood once and for all? Or was it all about a subconscious desire to please and impress the shade of his father?

Much more likely, he was just made that way. He was built on a bigger and grander scale than we are today. Don't forget that he became an MP while Victoria was still on the throne. He imported into the twentieth century that Victorian confidence, that aristocratic desire for glory on the widest possible stage.

Londoners responded to the confidence he showed, and there was a kind of psychic continuum between the leader and the led. As Philip Ziegler has shown, there was no 'myth of the Blitz'. It truly was a remarkable time in the life of the city, when people felt more alive, more special, sometimes more 'unmarried', as the novelist Elizabeth Bowen put it – when they did countless acts of kindness for their neighbours. When a bomb went off, most Londoners neither panicked nor looted.

A Hungarian doctor was at Bank, when the Underground shelter was hit. 'You English cannot comprehend the discipline of your people,' he said. 'I have not found one hysterical, shouting patient. It does not happen in other countries.' Preparations had been made for a network of psychiatric clinics, to deal with all the cases of bomb-induced neurosis. They were all shut down for lack of patients. Even under provocation, Londoners behaved with stoical reasonableness. When a man began kicking a captured German bomber pilot, the crowd did not object. But when it looked as though he was going to take the airman's revolver and shoot him, the crowd intervened and held both men until the police arrived.

It was the constant presence of death and danger that tinged events with greatness, and tinged the individuals most closely associated with those events. Churchill not only benefited from that effect, but articulated the spirit of the country. 'I was not the lion,' he later explained, 'but I was privileged to give the roar.' By the end of his career it was as if his special characteristics were morphing into the special characteristics of the country as a whole. As Enoch Powell was later to put it: 'By 1955 it was given to Winston Churchill to have become the living embodiment of the nation through the accumulation of its past in his one individual person ... he enjoyed an enormous span of public life which made him, at the end of it, the incarnation of the British people'.

It was like a much-loved pet and its owner. You couldn't say who was imitating whom.

Look at his features: the bulbous nose and cheeks, the slightly jutting chin, the protuberant lips. He is a Toby jug, a John Bull. He had a hundred horsepower mind (as a contemporary put it, in the days when a hundred-horsepower was a lot), and yet he was no intellectual. He had a long and happy marriage to Clementine, with four children, and not a whiff of scandal has been detected in his relations with the good-looking shorthand typists, which suits the generally no-sex-please approach of the British.

He had become symbolic of the country, and also of the city he defended – magnificent, eccentric, traditional but obsessed with technological progress and above all resilient – so that it was entirely fitting, on his retirement in 1955, that the Queen should offer him the Dukedom of London. It turns out, rather disappointingly, that Her Majesty's Private Secretary had previously ascertained that Churchill would turn it down.

Which was the right thing to do, of course – not just because the title would have been passed on to Randolph Churchill, and his heirs and successors. Fiercely though Londoners admired Churchill, I am not sure how they would have reacted to the idea that he was now their Duke; many with enthusiasm, but by no means all. London and Londoners had changed in the Blitz, and Churchill was well aware of it.

I was talking to Gerry McCartney in the Cabinet War Rooms, standing just behind the place where Cabinet Secretary Sir Edward Bridges used to sit. I was trying to imagine what it must have been like to be there, while so many treasures of the city were being smashed, so many lives lost, in the course of a bombardment that at least some of the victims and the dispossessed would blame partly on Churchill himself. I wondered what it must have been like to sit there in the mornings as the lists of casualties and disasters were brought in, waiting until Washington had got out of bed, so that you could get on the scrambler and see if they were getting any nearer to helping out.

At once I knew what I must do. 'We don't normally allow people ...' said Gerry. 'The Churchill family are reluctant ...' It was too late. I was sitting in the chair from which he directed the war, my elbows polishing the very wood that his sleeve had polished seventy years before. I wish I had felt a charge of Churchillian dynamism, or the wit to bark some brilliant piece of defiance. I am afraid that I felt nothing but a pathetic incongruity and a nervousness that one of the tourists would snap me on their cameraphone through the glass pane, and reveal my pretentiousness on Twitter. I got up hastily. All I can report is that the chair and desk are very small and ordinary for a man who helped save the world from tyranny – and that, I suppose, is in keeping with the attempt at equality of the post-war world that he helped to create.

* * *

On 30 January 1965 Sir Winston Churchill staged his last great manoeuvre. He had planned it meticulously, down to the very hymns that he wanted sung. It was called Operation Hope Not. For three days his coffin had lain in state in Westminster Hall, and 321,360 people had filed past to pay their respects to the greatest Englishman of the twentieth century.

Then he was loaded on to a gun carriage, and taken through vast crowds to St Paul's for the funeral. The coffin was then loaded on to a launch, the Havengore, at the Tower of London, and taken back upstream under London Bridge to Waterloo, where a special steam train conveyed the dead leader to his burial place at Bladon in Oxfordshire.

The crowds were wearing coats, silent, and sometimes weeping. A flight of sixteen English Electric Lightnings swooped over London as the little launch nosed upriver. But in perhaps the most touching gesture of all, the cranes dipped in salute as he went through the Pool of London – the bit between the Tower and London Bridge.

Ten years later those cranes would be almost all gone. The docks would be no more. After nineteen centuries, since Aulus Plautius first created a port at the site, that port could no longer compete.

As the 1960s and 1970s wore on, it was clear that London had entered a period of stagnation or decline. Old industries collapsed; the population fell. Humiliated by America at Suez, spurned by de Gaulle in her

1963 bid to join the Common Market, Britain was starting to feel down on her luck.

And yet there were still some wonderful things that London was to give the world. If I look closely at the footage of those people watching the Churchill funeral, I can see that in some ways they appear to be from another epoch from my own. The men outside St Paul's are in top hats. People lift their bowlers and blink stoically at the cameras.

But when I study the women I can see from their clothes – the boots, the knee-length coats – that the 1960s are in full swing. They look like some of the earliest photos I have of my mother. By the time Winston Churchill died the Beatles had already conquered America, and just four months after the funeral the Rolling Stones released a song that came to Keith Richards in the middle of the night, and went to number one around the world. It was called '(I can't get no) Satisfaction'.

'There is no finer investment for any community than putting milk into babies.'

Winston Churchill, Radio Broadcast, 1943

THE ROUTEMASTER BUS

When Transport for London announced in 2005 that they were finally going to banish the Routemaster buses, a great cry of lamentation went up over the city. It was as though the ravens were to be evicted from the Tower. Newspaper petitions were got up, learned pamphlets were written in defence of a machine that was already pretty ancient.

The last Routemaster had left the Chiswick production line in 1968, and those still left on the streets throbbed and heaved through the traffic like wounded battle elephants. They had no airconditioning, and Brussels had condemned the bus as an insult to contemporary health and safety standards.

But they were loved. They not only stood for London in the twentieth century. You only had to show a glimpse of one in a film to establish where you were. They were the only splash of colour in the grey of the post-war world, and they kept their chic for the next fifty years, and for one fundamental reason. They were the last bus on London's streets to be built by Londoners, for Londoners, in London, and with specific regard to the needs of London passengers.

The Routemaster story began in 1947, the year Britain was also meditating such popular revolutions as the NHS. Wartime bus production in Chiswick had been given over to the manufacture of Handley Page Halifax bombers, and memos began to circulate wondering whether there was anything that could be learned from that experience. It was decided that there was. In fact it was decided, in a rare post-war burst of confidence, that London Transport was going to use everything they had learned over the years about buses and their passengers to create a masterbus. It took years of research, design and planning – indeed it took the Russians less long to put Sputnik in space – but by 1956 the bus was ready. They copied the riveted aluminium fuselage of the wartime planes to create a bus that could be assembled and taken apart like Lego.

There was a special new cubby hole where the conductor could stand, out of the way of passengers hopping on and off via the open platform. It had a heating system – a big advance for the times; the wheels had their own independent suspension; and there was a fully automatic gearbox for a smoother ride. Mainly, though, it was a masterpiece of urban design.

Before he died in 1941, London Transport's legendary Chief Executive, Frank Pick, had decreed that buses must look good. They must be pieces of 'street furniture', he said. Like policemen's helmets or Giles Gilbert Scott's telephone box, they were to catch and hold the eye. It was Douglas Scott – who also did Potterton boilers and Rediffusion radio sets – who gave the Routemaster its curved roof, and the lovely rounded windows. He specified the 'Burgundy lining panels, Chinese green window surrounds, and Sung Yellow ceilings' of the interior. He created the tartan moquette of dark red and yellow for the seats, and London Transport expended so much thought and energy on the designs because they wanted bums on those seats.

Buses were in increasing competition with private cars, whose numbers doubled in London between 1945 and 1960. The trolley buses – clean and green and popular – were (sadly) taken off the streets to make way for the car; and the Routemaster was meant to be the replacement for the trolley buses.

It was a great success. They built 2,875 of them between 1954 and 1968, and there were so many vacancies for crew that London Transport actively recruited for drivers and conductors in Barbados, Jamaica and Trinidad. Yes, the Routemaster bus played a part in the Caribbean immigration that was to transform and diversify London. On they chugged through the 1970s and 1980s, and even if there were only 600 left by the 1990s, they were still landmarks of the city, each of them, as Travis Elborough has put it, a burly red diesel-powered Beefeater that stood for London.

If there was one thing that doomed them to their final execution in 2005, it was the government's fatal 1960s decision to pour money into British Leyland buses – in the hope of keeping that doomed business alive – instead of investing in the development of London's own bus.

The result is that the machines on the streets today have lorry engines and lorry gearboxes, and would be frankly more suited to carrying 32 tonnes of gravel than a complement of passengers. It is therefore only fitting that the New Bus For London has been designed as a bus for the streets of the city, with clean, green technology; and it restores the Routemaster's hop-on hop-off platform that was so essential to its appeal.

Keith Richards

He (and Sir Mick) gave the world rock music

The ancients were familiar with the notion of a Bacchic frenzy. They knew what happened when you combined music and alcohol. Euripides tells us how a bunch of otherwise good-natured women were turned into sex-crazed groupies who laid hands on a chap called Pentheus and tore him limb from limb.

They took off their stays and let their hair down. They were free from all cares and self-consciousness and behaved very badly indeed – and I cannot believe there is anyone out there reading this who has not done the same.

Of course you need to have drunk just the right amount of alcohol – enough to retain some primitive sense of rhythm. You also need the right music. It was some time in my late teens that I found myself in a student house – and even now I hesitate to give the location for fear of reprisals – when someone put on 'Start Me Up' by the Rolling Stones.

I can hear you snicker.

I am fully aware of what sophisticated people are supposed to think about those first three siren-jangling chords. My old friend James Delingpole once wrote a supercilious piece about 'Start Me Up', how corny he thought it was. But I can tell you that noise came out of that bashed-up old tape deck and seemed to vibrate in my rib cage.

Somewhere in my endocrine system something gave a little squirt – adrenal gland, pituitary, hypothalamus, I don't know; and pow, I could feel myself being transformed from this shy, spotty, swotty nerd who had spent the past hour trying to maintain a conversation with the poor young woman who was sitting next to me …

… And then I was hit by the second bar, the same crashing three-note electric tocsin, and in a second it was pure Jekyll and Hyde. It was Clark Kent in the phone kiosk. I won't say that I leapt to my feet and beat my chest and took the girl by the hand. But I can't rule it out, because frankly I can't remember the details, except that it involved us all dancing on some chests of drawers and smashing some chairs. I remember the feeling, the psychic rush that music gave.

To this day I have only to hear that opening riff by Keith Richards, and that feeling comes back. That is how it is for billions of human beings. It is these hundreds of snatches of rock/pop music that remain on our mental iPods to intensify our experience and provide the soundtracks of our lives.

I would argue – no, there is no argument; I would assert without fear of contradiction that rock/pop was the most important popular art form of the twentieth century and continues to occupy that rank today. It has no serious challenger from the visual, plastic, poetic or literary arts, and is far more culturally pervasive than film. It is therefore one of the greatest triumphs of British culture that rock/pop had its most beautiful and psychedelic flowering in London in the 1960s.

It was, on the face of things, a surprising triumph. We have seen so far that London has produced some of the world's greatest poets, playwrights, novelists, painters, architects, scientists, libertines, orators and lexicographers. But in the almost two thousand-year history of the city, there aren't that many moments when we could say that native Londoners were the acknowledged global leaders in music. There were plenty of people who came to London to perform their music, because that was where the money and the patronage was. But they had vaguely foreign-sounding names like Haydn or Handel.

In the second half of the twentieth century, however, the musical scene was like the sixteenth century cyclotron of theatrical talent that produced William Shakespeare. There were at least two flashes, two supernova explosions that were seen around the world. There were the Beatles, the most musically influential group of the last hundred years (OK, OK, they were from Liverpool, but almost all of their songs were recorded in London, and London was where they made their name). And then there were the Beatles' fractionally more energetic rivals, the Rolling Stones – the biggest and most successful touring act in history.

True, there were many other constellations that rose over the London suburbs and were hailed around the world. But we are relatively safe in saying that the Beatles and the Stones were the two brightest.

All this is to some extent a matter of taste. People will dispute my verdict, just as they will dispute precedence between the Beatles and the Stones or between individual Beatles and Stones. Middle-aged Stones fans tend to be either votaries of Mick Jagger (like Tony Blair), or else they think Keef is the really cool one. Since quite a young age I have believed fiercely that Keef was the man.

Someone who claimed to know about it told me at a critical moment in my adolescence that Mick was the front man, the Orphic show-off, while Keith was the better musician. He did more than his share of creating the aching, plangent, slow stuff: 'Angie, Fool to Cry'. He was equally adept at the sublime swooshing choral stuff like 'You Can't Always Get What You Want'. And he was definitely the go-to man for the volcanic intro, the double-triple crump of chords that make your eyes dilate, your lips go green and your twitching hands reach for a chair to break.

Think of the opening artillery of 'Satisfaction', or 'Brown Sugar', or 'Jumping Jack Flash'. That's all Keith, I was told. He was a man who knew all about how to start with an earthquake and work up to a climax. It was Keith I pathetically aimed to emulate at the age of about sixteen when I bought a pair of tight purple cords (a sheen of sweat appears on my brow as I write these words) and tried with fat and fumbling fingers to plink out 'Satisfaction' on a borrowed guitar; and my abysmal failure to become a rock star only deepened my hero-worship.

My understanding of the Mick-Keith arrangement was that Keith was the genius of the Glimmer Twins, who managed for years to hold the Number One spot on the *New Musical Express* list of Rock Stars Most Likely to Die – and yet who contrived to sleep with some of the most exotic women of the Western world: Uschi Obermaier, Anita Pallenberg, Patti Hansen, you name it.

Keith has spent decades slurping, shooting and snorting such prodigious quantities of chemicals that he looks as though the stuff has taxidermied his tissues, like some Inca mummy; and all that while he has produced work of such quantity and originality that he has changed the face of rock music as decisively as he has changed his own physiognomy.

He has become very rich. Between 1989 and 2003, for instance, he helped the Rolling Stones to earn £1.23 billion. And yet he still fizzes with so much energy – well into his sixties – that Johnny Depp borrowed his camp, be-ringed and bangled style for the blockbusting *Pirates of the Caribbean*. At the time of writing he is thinking of yet another tour. If he didn't look so epically raddled, you might be tempted to say that he was an advertisement for the health-giving properties of very pure heroin and cocaine.

In the course of years of brooding on this chapter, I have been all over Richards' London. I once went to open a riverside park in Twickenham, and looked over towards the cottages and houseboats of Eel Pie Island. I gazed at the dank mud flats, and tried to imagine the scene before the famous Eel Pie Island Hotel was mysteriously burned to the ground – those magical sixties evenings when the air was full of the yowling of Keith's guitar and the scent of dope and patchouli while the girls in brightly patterned cheesecloth dresses gambolled in the shallows. I have been to the 100 Club in Oxford Street, and even tried to help a campaign to keep it open.

I have nosed around the chewing gummed alley off Ealing Broadway where Alexis Korner had his famous club and where fifty years ago – 12 July 1962 – Mick and Keith first played with Brian Jones, and the Rolling Stones effectively came into being. Many times I have cycled up and down Edith Grove in Chelsea, and looked out for number 102, and the kitchen window of the flat that Keith shared in the early days with Brian Jones, a place of such indescribable squalor that in the end they gave up on the contents of the kitchen, left it all piled in the sink, and sealed the door shut with gaffer tape.

For years I have snuffled on his spoor, but never come across a trace of the man himself; until not so long ago, when fate dealt me the most incredible slice of luck.

I was due to attend a ceremony in Covent Garden, where the objective was to make a short speech in honour of the noble and learned Lord Coe and to give him a prize.

When I reached the Royal Opera House, the road was jammed with huge limos, glossy black Bentleys and Maybachs. Even though it was well after 10 pm there were still large crowds of autograph hunters, cheering and yelling at anyone who went through.

Within was taking place the most important and mystic rite of the national cult of celebrity. I went into the atrium, shaped like a giant arched greenhouse, and watched as the roving spotlight played on the tuxedoed crowd.

These weren't just A-listers. They were A-star. It was a triumph of sycophantic bidding-up by the organizers, in which you tell Bono's people that Sting is going to be there and you tell Sting's people that Bono is going to be there – and bingo – they both come; and you have a roiling slebfest of mutual congratulation, in which Salman Rushdie is to be seen explaining his next plot to Kylie Minogue, and Bill Clinton has Madonna perched on his knee while Mother Theresa of Calcutta whispers a dirty joke in his other ear – you get the point. The rest of us B-, C- and D-listers feel a kind of insane helium pleasure just to be allowed to share the same airspace, or to quaff some Jacob's Creek from the same chalice or grail that has touched the lips of the gods.

That was how I felt when I had found my seat and made my salutations to A* politician George Osborne and A* theatre impresario Trevor Nunn and their gorgeous A* womenfolk.

'I am sorry I am so late,' I gasped to an impossibly tall, thin, and yet somehow curvaceous, hostess who appeared at my side.

'It's all right,' she said. 'Stephen Fry spoke for so long that we are running a bit behind.'

'Oh fine,' I said. 'When am I on?'

'Not long now. You are speaking after the Writer of the Year, which is going to be Keith Richards. He's just over there,' she said, in answer to my hoarse exclamation of disbelief.

'Where?' I goggled.

'There – right up at the front,' and she pointed towards an unmistakable grey bird's nest of hair.

For the next few minutes I fixed my gaze on my prey until he turned his head to show his famous profile, a magnificent Roman profile. A Roman profile? Wait a mo: that wasn't Keef. That was Sir Tom Stoppard, another man with a grey heron's nest on his head.

Where was Keef? But the girl had gone, and as I kept trying to pick him out I ran through the options. In my experience they are very hard to pull off, these impromptu interviews with an uberceleb. I once spent three days tailing Jacques Chirac across France, after one of his staff assured me that he would give an interview 'in the margin' of one of his campaign visits. After repeated disappointments I had managed to put myself in his path as he swept out of a rally towards his vast Citroën.

'President Chirac,' I cried, holding out my hand. 'Boris Johnson, from London!' He paused for a nanosecond; he gripped; he beamed. 'Jacques Chirac, from Paris!' he said, and then I felt like a quarterback being hit from both sides as a pair of bodyguards terminated the conversation, and Chirac was gone. I tried it all sorts of ways, but I couldn't make much of that quote.

So I knew that if I was to make the most of my time I had better boil it down to one single, overwhelming question. As the awards ceremony churned on into the night, I thought about what I knew, and what I wanted to know.

I am a keen student of *LIFE*, the autobiography that has earned Keith his award for writing. On reading it over and again, I reckon I have an inkling about how it all happened. The Rolling Stones are landmarks of our culture, as weatherbeaten and venerable – and central to the story of modern London – as the lions of Trafalgar Square.

As I say, they are still rocking at the age of about sixty-eight, even if Bill Wyman seems to have opted out a bit lately. They have generated billions in revenue streams of all kinds (not much of which, thanks to adroit planning, has come the way of the UK taxpayer). Their lolling tongue is recognized by admen as one of this country's most powerful brands. I am serious. I have seen presentations in which this fat-lipped symbol is rated one of the strengths of UK PLC.

More important, they have created an imperishable anthology of great rock/pop songs, and you don't produce so much work, over so many years, without some mania that impels creativity. It is obvious that this fertility is all about Mick Jagger and Keith Richards, and their avowed love–hate relationship. To find the defining moment of that friendship, you have to go back more than half a century; before their 1962 gig at Alexis Korner's club in Ealing; before the historic December 1961 encounter at Sidcup railway station, where Keith found Mick on his way to study at the LSE with a bunch of records by Chuck Berry and Muddy Waters under his arm.

To understand what is going on between Mick and Keith, you need to go right back to their primary school in what is virtually the London suburb of Dartford – Wentworth – and what happened when they both hit the age of eleven. The critical fact is that Mick Jagger passed his Eleven plus and went to Dartford Grammar School, on the glide path to university. Keith failed, and might have gone to a secondary modern if he had not shown some aptitude for drawing and music.

So he went to a technical school in Dartford, and even there his work was deemed to be so bad that he was forced – to his fury – to repeat a year. You only have to watch him being interviewed, or read *LIFE*, to see that Keith is a very thoughtful and intelligent man; not only one of the top ten guitarists in history (says *Rolling Stone* magazine) but a reader of military history with a handsome library in Connecticut. And yet at the tender age of eleven he was informed by the emanations of the

British educational establishment that he was made of different intellectual timber from his little chum and neighbour.

Under the shaming sheep-and-goats separation of the 1944 Butler Act – against which the British middle classes were soon to rebel – he was deemed to be less capable of abstract thought, less suitable for a bourgeois profession than Michael Philip Jagger. He was the one who supplied the riffs that made the hordes of teenage girls begin to moan like maenads; and yet Jagger was officially the clever one.

It was this unresolved issue – of intellectual and creative primacy – that was the motor of the Rolling Stones. At the heart of the group are two colossal talents, competing and collaborating at the same time. It was a competition that took many forms, and in some ways, after fifty years, it is Sir Michael who has emerged ahead.

Take the battle for female company, the primal struggle of life. In a sense it began by being even stevens, and Keith makes clear that he was quite capable of getting girly action, if I can use the blatantly sexist language of their first number one.

He does not spare us in his account of how he snaffled Anita Pallenberg from Brian Jones (it took place, if you want to know, on the back seat of his 'Blue Lena' Bentley, during the watershed summer of 1967, as they were being chauffeur driven down through Spain towards Morocco); and though Keith accuses Mick of having his way with Anita sometime after the filming of the bath scene in *Performance* (an allegation I think the lady still denies), Keith gets the ball back over the net by going to bed with Marianne Faithfull at a time when she was meant to be faithfull to Mick; and at one point, he tells us, he was forced by Mick's return to make such a rapid leap from the bedroom window that he forgot his socks – still the subject, we gather, of a running gag between himself and Marianne.

Again, both men seem to have gone to bed with brooding Bavarian bombshell Uschi Obermaier, who then does Keith a favour by announcing her verdict to an expectant planet. Mick is the 'perfect gentleman' but Keith is adjudged the better lover because he knows a woman's anatomy. Of course there was also Bill Wyman, who was earning a reputation for his metronomic success with groupies, and though Keith acknowledges this reputation he also observes a bit disparagingly that most of the young women who were ushered into Wyman's room were treated to nothing more than a cup of milky tea.

The point is that Keith is competitive and wants us to know that he has had more than his fair share of women of all shapes and sizes, and yet most casual observers would think – probably rightly – that Mick has been the final winner in this crazed marathon exhibition match of heterosexuality. In the end it is Mick whose name is linked with the longer and more glamorous list of women, and who seems to inspire the most uncalled-for behaviour in the female sex.

Many years ago a girl I was going out with came back from a party (to which I had not been invited) and said that she had met Mick Jagger. 'Of course I kissed him,' she said. 'Why?' I asked. 'Only on the cheek. It just seemed the right thing to do'. It isn't clear that Keef would have produced the same instinctive reaction. And so throughout his discussion of this kind of thing, he makes plain in *LIFE* that this is not a contest he particularly wanted to win, and that he was actually pretty bashful with girls (it was Anita who made the running in the back seat of the Bentley); and unlike the ancient satyr Jagger he has spent the last few decades in happy monogamy with Patti.

Nor did he try to compete with Jagger in what you might loosely call social climbing. Both of them were in fact pretty middle class: Jagger the son and grandson of teachers, Keith the grandson of the Lady Mayoress of Walthamstow (who was almost certainly at the dog track to hear Churchill get booed in 1945). Cool London in the 1960s was meant to be a mixture of the 'new aristocracy' and the old. There was the soaring cockney talent – film stars, designers, gobby photographers; there were suburban rock stars and models; and then there was a bunch of effete and more or less aristocratic Old Etonian drug fiends and art dealers.

It was Mick, who once considered a career as a politician, who seems on the whole to have liked the company of toffs. The pair of them were asked in a magazine questionnaire to name their heroes. Mick put down

'Dukes.' Keith put down 'the Great Train Robbers.' In 2003 there came the moment of ultimate betrayal, when Mick rang Keith to say that he had accepted a knighthood from Tony Blair. He didn't really see how he could turn it down. 'You can turn down anything you like, pal,' said Keith brutally.

The award was 'ludicrous', he later complained. He wasn't going on stage with someone 'wearing a coronet and sporting the old ermine', he raved.

Jagger fired back by saying that Richards was 'an unhappy man'. What do you mean, he's unhappy? asked the interviewer. 'What I say,' said Mick. 'He's unhappy. If you can't understand that you can't understand anything.'

You can see why Keith might have been unhappy about this lop-sided tribute to the Stones. It wasn't as if Mick could be held up as a shining example to young people, with Keith the old drug-fuelled reprobate.

They had both been busted for drugs. They had both been (briefly) imprisoned. As for their contributions to society, let's face it, Mick got his knighthood because Blair venerated him, in the manner of so many ex-public school wannabe rockers, and Alastair Campbell probably decided they needed some stardust for the honours list.

Whatever he claimed, Keith must have felt hacked off not even to be offered parity of recognition. In *LIFE*, Keith is full of praise for Mick's talents as a musician and as a fast and highly effective writer of lyrics. He can do bawdy, decadent, satirical, sentimental, soulful, mock-soulful and satanic. He writes with terrific punch and economy and some times absurdity. Think of 'Brown Sugar', which involves a 'scarred old slaver' who apparently enjoys whipping some women 'just around midnight', to a chorus of 'Ah, brown sugar, how come you taste so good, uh-huh':

The reason this verging-on-the racist and sexist material is not more widely denounced is that frankly most of us spend our lives barely able to work out what he is saying. I have met all sorts of gin-soaked bar-room queens at Tory gatherings, but it was only after decades of listening to 'Honky Tonk Women' that someone put me out of my misery and explained that the singer begins by claiming to have met a gin-soaked bar-room queen in Memphis.

I always thought the opening line of 'Wild Horses' was 'Tired of living', though I now discover that it is 'Childhood living'. What I am getting at is that the words are certainly important in creating the general climate of emotion, but it is the tune that always gives the words their potency. It is the tune you hum and dance to, and most of the ideas for the tunes seem to have come from Keith.

Mick may have sung 'Satisfaction' and written the words, but Keith discovered the tune when he woke up one morning and turned on his cassette recorder to find that the Muse had imparted it to him in a dream; and that he had got up in the middle of the night and cracked it out. To a non-expert like me there is something spine-tingling about reading his disquisitions on the right way to play and tune a guitar, and the open 'G system' (or whatever it is) that he pioneered. He talks about his toil to make the instrument produce exactly the sound he has in his head, and you feel in the presence of a connoisseur.

It is like the privilege of hearing a top-class artist talk about his technique, as you watch the first enigmatic lines of the sketch. There is something dotty-professorish about the way he hooks up amps and extension leads and cassette recorders in the hope of capturing some elusive effect. Sometimes he spends so long in the recording studio, striving to perfect a song, that everyone else has conked out on the floor and it is just drug-fuelled Keith chuntering on through the night until he has got it.

In other words there is something a little bit paradoxical about Keith's self-portrait. In an interview in 2005 he tried again to suggest that Mick was the swot, and that he was relatively unambitious. 'Me I wake up, praise the Lord, and then make sure that all the phones are turned off. Mick has to get up in the morning with a plan.' This strikes me as classic British false modesty and pretence of amateurism.

It is absolutely clear that Keith is not some laid-back loon-panted druggie. He is a creative stakhanovite. There is a message in the long technical expositions in *LIFE*, the confident analysis of how the blues evolved into rock and roll, and the place of the Stones in the story. The message is that Keith is at least the intellectual equal of Mick, and that the verdict of the Eleven plus was wrong.

It is the rubbing of two sticks that makes the flame. It was the constant competitive urge – to impress the other guy – that produced the flash of genius. That was the internal dynamo that powered the Stones; and as if that was not enough, there was the immense external pressure from their rivals. Just as there is a Mick faction and a Keith faction, so the human race is divided into those who go for the Beatles and those who prefer the Stones (with a large chunk of us prepared to support both of them, depending on our mood).

Both groups were all-male; both benefited from the creative tension between the lead pair. Both set out to conquer America and triumphantly succeeded; and though they collaborated on some of their songs – and even coordinated their releases so as to avoid spoiling the other's publicity – the idea from the outset was that they were avowed rivals.

The peculiar Andrew Loog Oldham was a former Beatles publicist who somehow made himself the manager of the Stones, and he saw that if Mick and Keith were to make it big they couldn't just cover Chuck Berry records. They would have to follow the lead of John and Paul. So he locked them in a room and made them write their own stuff, and for the whole of that glorious decade the Beatles and the Stones were in a kind of semi-official competition. Loog Oldham saw that it was vital to distinguish his acts, so the suggestion was that the Beatles were the wholesome ones while the Stones were leering, troglodytic and more overtly sexual.

The Beatles went out with nice girls like Cynthia Lennon or Jane Asher. The girl friends of the Rolling Stones were busted for drugs wearing nothing but fur coats, with semi-eaten Mars Bars arranged nearby – leading the police to make prurient but unfounded suggestions to the media. The Beatles did psychedelia; the Stones did psychedelia with more than a hint of devil-worship.

The Beatles produced *Sergeant Pepper's Lonely Hearts Club Band*. The Stones aped it with *Their Satanic Majesties Request*. If artistic success is to judged by public approval, it is clear the Beatles are still some way ahead. Though they had broken up before 1970, they produced more top ten hits, more number ones, more top ten albums and more number one albums than any other band, including the Rolling Stones. But even the Beatles were the product of their time, and in so far as they wrote hits they were at least spurred by the knowledge that others were capable of beating them to the top of the charts.

By the end of that decade the suburbs of London were blooming with talent of all kinds. A new generation had emerged, nurtured by the NHS, free dentistry, good drains, higher per capita incomes and above all decent publicly funded education in grammar schools and art colleges. In bedrooms and garages across the city, acnoid teenagers twanged and morphed into gaudy apparitions with silk bandanas and leather vests and dirty sheepskin coats.

Of the remaining Stones, Bill Wyman came from Lewisham, Ronnie Wood from an old family of canal bargees in Hillingdon, Charlie Watts from Islington, and Brian Jones, never let it be forgotten, began his career as a sales assistant at Whiteleys in Queensway.

Jimmy Page of Led Zeppelin came from Wallington near Croydon. The Who were almost all educated at Acton County Grammar School. Ray Davies and the Kinks came from Hornsey. The Dave Clark Five came from Tottenham. The Small Faces came from East Ham.

The clubs they played in were suburban clubs, with a notable emphasis on the south west of London. There was the Crawdaddy club in Richmond, as well as the Station Hotel and the Richmond Athletics Club; and of course there was Eel Pie Island and Ealing and many others. London is 607 square miles, by far the most extensive city in Europe, a vast network of well-connected villages and urban centres, and it was the sheer scale and diversity of the available talent that helped to produce the rock/pop boom.

Americans were certainly the pioneers of rock and roll – Chuck Berry, Muddy Waters, Elvis. But to understand the unique contribution of London, you must remember that very few American cities were anything like as big. There were many American centres of musical revolution: New Orleans, Nashville, Memphis, Detroit, LA, San Francisco, New York, and so on. And yet there was no single metropolis in which so much talent was concentrated.

To get back to our nuclear metaphor: there were just more uranium rods in the nuclear pile of London than there were in any single American city. When the thing went bang, it was more likely to produce a flash that lit up the world, as it did in the case of the Beatles and the Stones. There is a final reason why London played a pivotal role. Young white Londoners could play black music – the twelve-bar blues – in a way that young white Americans might have found embarrassing.

You only have to look at a video of Chuck Berry singing 'Johnny B Goode' to see where the whole thing began. But for decades black American jazz and blues musicians had accused white musicians of effectively ripping off their ideas and using them to make more money; and since this accusation was well-founded, white American musicians came to be hesitant about simply taking a piece of blues music and playing it in the style of a black performer.

White middle-class Londoners such as Richards and Jagger, on the other hand, had no such hang-ups. They saw nothing ridiculous or disrespectful about singing how they woke up this morning and their woman done gone left them, etc. It was just a tribute to the music they loved. So what happened with rock and roll in London was really the supreme example of the import-export process that made the city great.

People like Mick Jagger and Keith Richards got their hands on records by Muddy Waters and Chuck Berry. They sat listening to them in their bedrooms and art college lavatories. They imitated them with religious devotion, singing and playing in (what they hoped was) a plausibly black way. After a while – about 1964 – they started branching out into psychedelia and pop and then, with 'Jumping Jack Flash', pure rock music. But when they went to America, and played those blues-derived songs, the Rolling Stones were effectively introducing a mass American audience to a musical genre that originated in America.

That was the triumph of London, and that, I concluded, as the Awards ceremony neared its climax, was the point I needed to put to Keith Richards. By now it was getting on for 11 pm, and the black-tied crowd was getting tired. So many top-notch celebs had been hailed on stage that it seemed the appetite for fame was nearly glutted. Then Keef was finally announced, and as he sauntered swayingly on stage – jacket sleeves rolled up to expose his sinewy wrists, headband making him look like an ancient John McEnroe – we were all lifted spontaneously to our feet.

His speech was short, droll, modest, and as soon as he had gyrated back to his seat I knew that this was it. This was my moment. Quickly I did my own turn on stage, introducing Seb Coe, and then with some pushfulness I persuaded Keith's agent Barbara Charone (a kindly person I had come across before) to let me station myself by his side. 'Just five minutes, Barbara, just three,' I pleaded.

At last Keith came back from having his photo taken and there took place a vicious contest for the honour of sitting next to him. I was later informed that Keith's people had somehow rebuffed Stephen Fry in the mistaken belief that he was Prime Minister David Cameron.

After decades of hoping, I found myself sitting inches from the kohl-eyed demigod, and I noticed that though his face was as lined as Auden's, his teeth were American in their whiteness. We began with some small talk about how much I had enjoyed *LIFE*, and about his grandparents, and what it was like growing up in wartime Dartford, where a doodle-bug explosion had famously lobbed a brick on to his cot.

But the crowd around us was jostling and jabbering ever more insistently, and I knew that I must blurt it out.

'Er, Keith,' I stumbled.

'Mr Ma-yor', he said, in his courtly way.

'I've got this theory that, er …' and as I tried to get it out assorted supplicants descended like harpies, begging him to sign their napkins, their £20 notes, their left breasts, etc.

For a moment or two they were repulsed, and I gasped out the story, as told by Joe Walsh, the god-gifted guitarist of the Eagles.

Joe Walsh revealed that he had never even heard Muddy Waters until he went to hear a Stones concert, right?

'That's right,' said Keith, nodding.

And so, I went on, you could argue that the Stones were critical in the history of rock and roll – by now I was half-shouting – because they *gave back* the blues to America!

'I'll go with that', said Keith with infinite affability.

And I'll go with it, too, Keith. It's more than enough to go on. It may not have been the longest and most probing interview in the history of rock journalism, but it was a good deal more useful than my conversation with Chirac.

I didn't need to waste any more of his time, forcing him to sit there amid his caterwauling fans and regurgitate the supermasticated anecdotes that are to be found in his book. He had affirmed my key point. Without the Stones, a great American band like the Eagles would never have been turned on to Muddy Waters. Without the intermediation of Keith Richards, Joe Walsh would never have come to play such epic guitar solos as diddle-ee diddle-ee diddle-ee diddle-dee did did did diddle-ee diddle-ee DEE, the climax of 'Hotel California'.

As nineteenth-century London took in sugar and oranges and sold them back to the world as marmalade, so twentieth-century London imported the American blues and re-exported them as rock/pop. It was a great trade.

Now it was time for Keith Richards to make his royal progress from the Opera House, and I followed him out at the back of his tide of admirers. I watched the flashguns pop like Chinese New Year, and as his entourage climbed into some vast limo, I thought how much had changed in London since he first hit the scene.

When Keef was growing up, one of the most important points about rock and roll was that it was subversive; it was disapproved of. *Melody Maker* said it was 'one of the most terrifying things to have happened to popular music.' When a hundred and twenty Teddy Boys were thrown out of an east London cinema, and danced on the municipal flowerbeds, top conductor Sir Malcolm Sargent harrumphed that 'this music is nothing more than primitive tom-tom thumping. I think if rock and roll is capable of inciting young people to riot then it is obviously bad'.

The film *Rock Around the Clock* was actually banned. It was a world of vicious laws against homosexuality, and censorship of plays by the Lord Chamberlain, and a ban on *Lady Chatterley's Lover*, and where the Vice Squad was so dur-brained that in 1966 they raided the Victoria and Albert Museum postcard shop in order to seize some pictures by Aubrey Beardsley.

It is this climate of disapproval that helps to create a counter-culture, where so much of the fun is in the fact of rebellion itself. With his drugs and his women's clothes, Keith was obviously part of that counter-culture, and a vibrant phenomenon it was – while it lasted.

The 1960s counter-culture could survive police raids and bourgeois hysteria and draconian magistrates. Indeed, it thrived as long as there was an effort at repression. The one thing, logically, that it could not survive was establishment approval.

I would say the rot set in on 1 July 1967, when *The Times* published a leader about the infamous Rolling Stones drugs bust at Redlands. Like some Victorian beldame loosening her corset and beginning to jive, *The Times* opined that the sentences were too harsh. 'Who breaks a butterfly upon a wheel?' was the headline William Rees-Mogg rather brainily put on his piece.

It was *The Times* – the Thunderer! – siding with these snake-hipped drug-snorting rapscallions; and for the 1960s counter-culture it was downhill all the way from there. As the years went by, ever more liberal laws were passed in favour of gay rights or gender equality or freedom of expression, to the extent that today the idea of a counter-culture is very largely defunct.

Counter-culture values have been mainstreamed, folded into the lilac-scented bosom of the Establishment and celebrated at awards ceremonies. When I made this point recently on the radio, I came in for some flak on the internet from some people who said indignantly that they were still into S&M and necrophilia and other things – and therefore proud upholders of a counterculture in that their values are still rejected by polite society. Fair play to them, I say, though I suspect they will remain a happy and defiant minority.

Then there is obviously one group of young people (mainly men), who inspire apprehension in the rest of society, and who angrily reject some of the very values – sexual tolerance and freedom, for instance – that were espoused by the 1960s rebels. Perhaps there are some who would argue that the new counterculture is the intolerant version of Islam.

But the old counterculture has been adopted and expanded and has permeated society in a way that is good for London and the London economy. Where once we had Mary Quant hacking away with her scissors in a bedsit, we now have a London fashion industry worth £21 billion and employing 80,000 people. Instead of the debauched figures of William Burroughs and Francis Bacon, we have the 'young British artists' charging quite fantastic sums – and getting them – for diamond-studded skulls, and we have the brilliant Tracey Emin having no shame whatever in telling the world that she is a Conservative.

The Colony Room is still going, but it is now supplemented by the Groucho Club and dozens of other posh-washroomed venues occupied by people with some sort of creative talent: advertising, media, PR, TV production, film editing, you name it. There are all sorts of reasons why London is one of the world's most important centres for these 'creative, culture and media' industries.

We might mention the English language, the proximity of a dynamic financial sector and associated legal and accountancy services, with their endless requirements for creative work of all kinds. There is the dual relationship London enjoys with the EU and the USA. But there is one art form that serves more than any other to intensify our emotions, that creates an atmosphere or a feeling by sheer power of association. One art form more than any other helps to make a city cool, and that is the music; and if the music makes your city likeable, then people from all kinds of vaguely cultural sectors will be confident that it is the hip and jiving place to be.

London has more live music venues – about four hundred – than any other city in the world, and there is more happening in London every night than there is anywhere else. In the 1960s London became the rock/pop capital of the world, and as the driving force behind the Rolling Stones, Keith Richards played a big part in that achievement. A knighthood? The least the man deserves.

The Midland Grand Hotel

Since my dinner companion is unavoidably late I have loads of time to study the restaurant and its staff. What a swell place it is. About three blond women take care of my bike helmet and rucksack, and show me to a relatively quiet table where I slump down and look about me.

The walls are a rich mustard yellow; a deep tasteful tone, that somehow intensifies the gold of the writhing beech leaf capitals on top of the slender marble pilasters. The ceiling is a riot of twiddles and volutes, like some mad wedding cake; and the whole room curves in a wave, as if you are already drunk.

Still my companion fails to show but my mood improves as a bunch of semi-inebriated IT consultants celebrate some contract by sending me a glass of wine. When she finally appears I am so thrilled that I would eat almost anything that the kitchen produces. As it is – and I am no restaurant critic – we can soon tell that this is posh tucker.

For no reason at all someone brings us a little ceramic beaker of something yellow. Is it soup? Is it a mousse? We can't tell whether it is tomato or vanilla ice-cream or a fusion of the two. But an hour or so later it is in a fairly exalted frame of mind that we head for the exit, where we are waylaid by a man called Tamir. He wants to give us a tour. He keeps saying that it is an incredible place to work, and we can see why.

We go up the double staircase, like a DNA helix, and we pass symbolic Victorian paintings of seated women in classical drapery with names like 'Industry' and 'Forbearance'. The walls are a noble red, hand-stencilled with golden fleurs-de-lys. The oak of the banisters is lustrous and warm. The chintzy carpet is thick and fleecy and held in place with gleaming brass rods. Tamir wants to show us one of the master bedrooms, and he radios down to Reception to see if it is vacant, while we fantasise about the kind of luxury we might find within. A walk-in humidor? A Jacuzzi? Alas, whoever has rented the master bedroom is making full use of it just now, and who can blame them?

So we wander out through something called the Ladies Smoking Room – a name it was apparently given in 1902, in deference to the suffragettes. It has a faint echo, in its gorgeous internal arches, of the Great Mosque at Cordoba; and then we are out on the balcony, and snuffing the perfume of the Euston Road. I look out at the traffic – flowing smoothly, I am pleased to note – and then back and up at the bonkers castellations of the hotel: the dormer windows ranged like a man-o-war's gunports in the steeply raking roof, the wizard hat conical turrets. You expect Tinkerbell to fly out, or possibly Dumbledore. It's as if King Ludwig of Bavaria had been invited to design a railway station hotel, and then come up with a collision between the Doge's Palace in Venice and the Grand' Place in Brussels. It is a prosciutto-pink brick fantasy in Victorian Gothic, and the history of this hotel is the story of London over the last 140 years.

We are not just here to have dinner. We are here for the purposes of research, to examine the glorious rebirth of a building that tells us a lot about the waxing and waning – and then re-waxing – of urban confidence. When the Midland Grand Hotel was re-opened in 2011 – as the Millennium Hotel, with luxury apartments on top – it was hailed as a masterpiece of restoration, that finally did justice to the plans of its creator, George Gilbert Scott. As it happens, it is a miracle that the building is there at all. For my entire lifetime – and for most of the twentieth century – it was shut, abandoned, derided and neglected; and in 1966 they announced that they were going to knock it down.

When the Midland Grand opened for the first time in 1873, it was meant to be the *ne plus ultra*, the most opulent and expensive of London's increasingly extravagant station hotels. There were grand pianos in the fancier bedrooms; Axminster carpets on the floor. Hand-operated lifts distributed coats and luggage to the rooms. There was a wine-cellar, complete with bottling plant and a laundry that could boil, dry and iron 3000 pieces of linen on a single day, with a special tube system to send the dirty sheets shooting around the place. Upon its opening, the *Builder* magazine reported that 'the whole building is most elaborately and lavishly decorated, apparently without the slightest regard to cost.'

Son of a Buckinghamshire parson, George Gilbert Scott (1811–1878) was a star architect, the Richard Rogers or Norman Foster of his day, and a man who believed fervently in the gothic idiom. This was not just a hotel. Every painted cornice, every spike or curlicue or otherwise pointless piece of decorative exuberance was a statement; and that statement was: This is us. This is us, the Londoners of the Victorian epoch. This is how we build our station hotels; imagine how we deal with our parliaments and palaces!

For a few decades the formula seems to have worked. The Midland Grand became the favoured venue for Sheffield cutlers, West Riding woollen merchants and Clydeside ship builders, and the clientele was courted with continual improvements. Electric light was installed in the 1880s. When residents complained about the noise of horse-drawn traffic, the hotel paid for the road to re-paved with wooden blocks set in rubber. One of the city's first revolving doors was installed in 1899, and even though there were too few ensuite bathrooms (of a kind they had the wit to fit at the Savoy), the place prospered until World War One.

Then on 17 February 1918 the cathedral-vaulted booking office was hit by a bomb dropped from a German plane. The explosion killed twenty and injured many others; but the first real rumbling of doom came in 1921. Times were tighter now. The running of the railways had been taken over by government, and rationalisation set in. It was decided that those stations served by St Pancras – Glasgow, Manchester,

Sheffield, Leeds and Nottingham – could equally be served by Euston. The Midland Grand became starved of custom. Its grandeur slipped imperceptibly away. By 1930 the place had become so rackety that a member of the visiting Australian cricket tem had his bag stolen. The painter Paul Nash recorded a wretched evening in the early 1930s, sitting in silence with a broken radio and being offered 'the most poisonous coffee I've ever tasted'.

In 1934 the chairman of the London Midland and Scotland Railway, Sir Josiah Stamp, mused aloud about tearing the masterpiece down. It was a hulk, an embarrassing reminder of Victorian pretensions the market could no longer bear. 'Will it be vandalism of the first order to destroy it?' he asked a dinner hopefully. In 1935 the hotel closed, and in theory the building became the office of the railway company. Such was the cost of upkeep that in practice large parts of the structure were deserted.

Children would sometimes penetrate the boarded-up doors and climb the soot-covered carpets and discover the portentous Victorian women still looking down on a London whose Industry and Forbearance had failed to match their expectations. Mark Girouard, the architectural historian, has recalled entering the building in about 1950, and finding dirty and empty rooms, and a ladder that took him out on to the roof of the western tower, with spectacular views across London. By the 1960s the electrification of the West Coast mainline sent most trains to Euston. St Pancras was downgraded, and in 1966 British Rail wrote their fateful letter to ask ministers to approve the 'necessary changes' – and to allow them to take the wrecking ball to the work of George Gilbert Scott.

Decrepit and humiliated, the former hotel was a metaphor for a culture and a society that had decisively fallen off its Victorian perch. It was a symbol of a city that had sustained a decline in self-belief, in relative wealth, and in global status. For the first time in more than two hundred years, London was now experiencing a substantial and unexpected fall in population. Ever since 1940, planners had been saying that London was too preponderant in the UK economy, and that its wealth-creating power should be somehow dispersed to other regions. Now the planners were getting what they wanted at last – but not in the way they wanted it.

The weird campaign began with the wartime Barlow Commission, which opined that London was over-dominant in manufacturing and trade. In 1941 Sir Patrick Abercrombie was commissioned by the London County Council to produce his famous plan; and by 1944 he reported. The plan had many good points. Abercrombie recognised the importance of London's old town centres and villages, and of improving transport networks. And yet the thrust of the Abercrombie Plan was to move 600,000 people out of London to 'new towns' or 'garden cities'; and though the intentions were doubtless good this forced exodus was often accompanied by the disruption of old ties of kinship and friendship, and the construction of unloved high-rise estates on the outskirts of the city.

Even in 1967, we can find traces of the Barlow-Abercrombie dogma, as the South-East Planning Council's first report repeated the essential demands – with what now looks like an insane attack on the city that had once been the powerhouse of the imperial economy and the workshop of the world. There should be 'major and sustained efforts to move out manufacturing industry … continued control of office development and every possible encouragement of moves to office centres away from London … there is a national interest in moving our manufacturing away from London'.

These words seem incredible now, in view of what was already happening to employment in London. The planners had called for London's riches to be taken and spread – like so much jam – over a wider area; and yet they fatally failed to predict the collapse of the docks, and the decline of traditional manufacturing.

In the year I was born, 1964, the docks were apparently flourishing. The West India Docks were the centre for sugar, fruit and hardwood trade, and for thirty miles downstream of London Bridge there were oil refineries, power stations, cold stores and vast industrial enterprises such as Ford at Dagenham. The London docks were still served by

11,000 vans or lorries every day, and goods of all kinds were loaded on and off 6,300 barges. Beneath the surface, though, all was not well with London's port.

The docks had long seethed with union activity: I will never forget the bitterness of the late and great Bill Deedes, who told me how the dockers had refused to load his landing-craft for D-Day, because they 'hadn't got the rate' for the job; and how his men had been obliged – with fatal consequences – to do the job themselves. The1947 Dock Labour Scheme had introduced rigidities not shared by other competitor ports. Flexibility was essential, because what did for the docks in the end was not the contraction of world trade, but its expansion.

The 1960s saw the dawn of containerisation, as goods started to arrive in London in metal cuboids 8 foot high, 8 foot wide and 40 foot long. The ships that brought these goods needed berths of 25 acres each. They didn't need legions of dockers and porters and stevedores and warehousemen with their complicated demarcations about who was allowed to do what. They just needed people who could drive the juggernauts. The old docks of London were immediately outgrown. London dock and St Katharine dock were sold to developers, and even the great sea-trenches of the late Victorians were finally obsolete by 1981. As Professor Jeremy Black has put it in his summary of post-war London history, 'the decline of London's relative position in recent years has been in part matched by the decline of London's docks'.

In obedience to economic necessity and the will of the planners, people left for Essex, St Albans, and other peripheral towns. From the mid-1960s onwards, the population of London was falling quite steeply. In 1939 the population was 8.7 m. In 1951 it was 8.19 m; in 1961 it was 7.99 m; in 1971 it was 7.45 m; in 1981 it was 6.80 m; in 1991 it was 6.89 m and in 1993 it was 6.93 m. Today there are about 7.6m Londoners, and it will be a long time before we get back up to pre-war levels. With all this destruction of traditional employment, and disruption of old and settled communities, it was perhaps not surprising that crime began to rise – trebling between 1955 and 1967 – and it continued to rise in the 1970s.

Radical plans to solve London's transport problems – notably with the 'motorway box' – were shelved amid protest from residents. So with rising crime, sclerotic transport, an official hostility to new office space and a declining docks it is perhaps no wonder that business and industry started to take flight. There was not only a 'British disease'. There was a 'London factor' – these commonly cited deterrents to investment and growth. I remember being a kid in London in the 1970s, and maybe you do, too. I remember some wonderful things: paying two pennies for a flake ice cream or a sherbet fountain, and endless mucking around with other children in the park and by the canal (and if we fought we used fists, not knives) and setting planks on a milk crate to do Evel Knievel jumps on our Chopper bikes and avoiding the oddly bleached white dog turds.

I also remember the chronic sense of economic crisis, the lights flickering and the pointless war between government and unions. I remember one dark afternoon going past King's Cross, and looking up from the back seat of our Renault Four at St Pancras and the morose Transylvanian mass of the former Midland Grand Hotel, and asking what it was.

Oh it was Victorian, said someone scathingly. In those days Victorian meant stuffy, risible, out-of-date. Had I gone inside, I would have found it even more pitiable than when Mark Girouard had entered twenty years before. The carpets had gone. The paint had peeled, and the floorboards had spanged up, and doors had come off their hinges. In those few rooms occupied by British Rail the chandeliers had been replaced by dangling fluorescent bars and the walls had been repainted that shade of municipal green favoured by primary schools and loony bins.

No one would take it off British Rail's hands; and though John Betjeman and others had heroically saved it from being destroyed – and even had it listed Grade One – there was no particular use for it, and certainly no demand from the hotel trade. For years the ex-Midland Grand Hotel stood on that corner as a memento mori, a reminder that great cities can go down as well as up.

Go to Detroit, which lost 58 per cent of its population between 1950 and 2008, and you will find plenty of bashed-up ballrooms in the tumbledown relics of formerly grand hotels. Go to Baghdad, and it seems hard to believe that it was once the most powerful and populous city on earth. *Seges est ubi Troia fuit*, as Ovid put it. There's a cornfield where Troy was.

The Midland Grand was passed desultorily from one quango to another; and then in the 1980s something happened. The decline of London began to be reversed. The population started to creep back up. Deserted dockland dumps became desirable waterside residences. Someone or something was responsible for helping to turn London around; and I know that any analysis of this phenomenon will be controversial.

The easiest way to get booed on BBC Question Time is to mention Margaret Thatcher, or the 1980s spirit of enterprise, or the boom in financial services. Her critics will certainly point out that whatever London experienced on her watch, it was not unique. New York went through a very similar resurgence, from a port to an economy reliant on banking and other service industries. Thatcher's supporters might say that London did even better than New York, and that the British government was even bolder in helping to create the conditions for one of the most extended periods of growth and dynamism that London has ever seen.

The government got rid of restrictions on high-rise office blocks, reversing the ban first imposed by Labour's George Brown. They promoted the 1986 Big Bang, and so created in London a new breed of powerful financial conglomerate. They unleashed the animal spirits of London's yuppies, with all their appalling vulgarity and greed and teddy bear braces. By 1996, London was back on the map, with New York and Tokyo, as one of the world's great financial capitals. Half of the trade in French and Italian shares took place in London, and 90 per cent of all European cross-border share trading. Half the world's ship-broking and half the Mergers and Acquisitions business was done in London. The growth of the City, and allied services such as law, accountancy and insurance, put more pressure on office space; and as values started to rise, people began to look around for bargains on brownfield sites.

In 1989 the former Midlands Grand Hotel was finally bought by a bona fide developer, and a plan was put forward to turn it back into a hotel. Alas the business proposal, even then, did not quite add up. There was one more change that needed to be introduced, and for that I believe the Thatcher government can surely take the credit, or at least some of it. It was transport infrastructure that had made sense of the new financial district they conceived in the docklands at Canary Wharf – the Docklands Light Railway and then the Jubilee Line Extension. And it was Thatcher who agreed with Francois Mitterrand that there should be a fixed link, under the Channel, between Britain and France; and in 1996 the Major government took the inspired decision to send the high-speed route from Europe, via Stratford, to St Pancras.

It was the new railway – and the total renovation of the station – that transformed the economics of the hotel. The catastrophe of 1921, when so many trains were routed to Euston, was reversed. Now St Pancras is the station of international romance, complete with the large glutinous bronze of a couple embracing. It is the gateway to Paris, and the Eurostar has helped to make London the fifth or sixth biggest French city in the world, with so many voters that the French presidential candidates deem it prudent to go to London to canvas.

Looking back now, it is clear that the middle years of the twentieth century were lost decades, not just for the Midland Grand Hotel, but for transport investment in London. The tube decayed. After the great Victorian spate of bridges, the only new crossing was at Chiswick in 1933, and nothing east of Tower Bridge until Dartford. With the population of London now climbing quite fast (certainly relative to the rest of the country) it is not a mistake we can make again. Transport for London's planners are looking at a second Crossrail, running from Hackney to Chelsea, partly to relieve the pressure on Euston from the planned high-speed link to Birmingham.

There are plans to extend the Northern and Bakerloo lines in south London, to introduce new river crossings in east London, and to extend the use of light rail and trams, such as the DLR and Croydon Tramlink; and this is on top of a neo-Victorian programme of putting in Crossrail from east to west, upgrading the tube, and building a gigantic supersewer running under the river, finally completing the work of Joseph Bazalgette. In the case of the Tube, these improvements are not so much an economic as a humanitarian necessity. As the new signalling allows the trains to travel faster, more kinetic energy is turned into heat and unless we lay on more capacity to meet the growing demand we will be asking people to travel in conditions that would be ruled inadmissible by Brussels for the transport of live animals.

Then there is one huge lesson we must learn from the sudden and shocking decline of the docks. It will be obvious from the foregoing that the problem with London's docks was not a shortage of demand. World trade continued to rise, overall, throughout the 1970s. London could conceivably have retained its position as a sea-port, an entrepôt like Felixtowe or Rotterdam. It was simply a question of infrastructure. The docks were too small for containerisation; and as London lost out there was a knock-on effect on manufacturing, investment, employment and confidence.

It is about one hundred years since Winston Churchill horrified his wife by getting up in a plane, then regarded as a new and insanely dangerous way to get around. Aviation is now not just crucial for business travel, but for the transport of goods. More than a third of world trade now goes by air, including 71 per cent of British pharmaceutical exports alone, and the proportion is rising. The Chinese are constantly opening or expanding airports in cities that many British people have scarcely heard of; and yet British business is relatively disadvantaged in connecting with these new markets. Every week there are 17500 seats on planes bound for mainland China from Frankfurt; there are 15000 on planes from Paris; there are 11000 from Amsterdam and only 9000 from Heathrow. China and India are both forecast to outgrow the United States in GDP – and yet we are making it harder for British busines people to get to the future megacities from London than from our competitor airports on the continent. If you want to fly to Chengdu,

Nanjing, Hangzhou, Xiamen or Guangzhou you can get there direct from one of London's continental rivals – but you can't get there from Heathrow.

The answer is surely not to expand Heathrow, where excessive noise already affects 250,000 people, and where the traffic impacts on the M4 and M25 would be disastrous. Even if a government were to be so ill-advised as to squeeze another runway in the west London suburbs, Heathrow would still be smaller than Amsterdam (6 runways), Paris (4) and Madrid (4). There is a growing body of support for a new hub airport, a 24 hour eco-friendly solution with four runways in or around the Thames estuary, where the bad effects on human beings could be minimised and where the birds would have little to fear.

Such a scheme would not only help to regenerate that part of the Thames Gateway so badly affected by Britain's maritime decline, from Tower Bridge to the Isle of Sheppey. It would help to cement London's lead, for generations to come, as the commercial capital of Europe. It is true that planes create greenhouse gases (and so, by the way, do ships). But one day there will be much cleaner planes, and it seems sensible to prepare for that day.

London became successful in the Middle Ages because of the port and the bridge, and because water offers less resistance than land to the moving of heavy loads. Air offers less resistance still. It is the transport mode of the twenty-first century. London suffered from having an aquatic port too small for its needs; and that is it is time to think big – to think neo-Victorian – about our airport today; not just because it is a good idea to import and export loads of club class business folk and Chinese tourists, but because mass transit improvements benefit the entire population. Apart from any other disadvantages, the present restrictions will drive up costs for people on modest incomes, and no matter how lovely London is, everyone deserves a holiday.

We don't build high-speed links to France just so that continental business people can luxuriate in swish hotels in St Pancras. We build these transport links because of the economic benefits they bring to hundreds of thousands of people in the area and beyond.

I have stressed the importance of these new connections by air, because at the end of this meditation on the lives of Londoners, I am struck by the huge importance of infrastructure of all kinds. If Aulus Plautus had not built that bridge, the city would not even have existed. It was the Norman keep of William the Conqueror that told the Saxons the facts of life – they were beaten – and created the peace and stability that led to the rise of mediaeval London.

Victorian trains and tube trains turned London into the world's first great commuter city, and the imperial scale of Bazalgette's drains made it possible for large numbers of Londoners to live together without giving each other terrible diseases. In a cold economic climate, such as today's, that strikes me as an important lesson for the future, and there are plenty of others.

You can see from the story that London has exhibited constant tension for thousands of years, between the moneybags and the politicians. Sometimes that tension has been creative, sometimes destructive; but it has always been important that London from very early on has been two cities – the City of London and the City of Westminster.

It is frankly hardly surprising that Londoners are now going through a period of bitterness towards the bankers and others whom they blame for the crash; and the story of London tells you that this is nothing new. History is littered with examples of resentment at the success of rich merchants, and especially foreigners. You can see it in the hostility towards the Rothschilds; you can see it in the murder of the Flemings and the Italian bankers in 1381 You could even argue that this animus against the moneymen is detectable in the Boudican rebellion, and the slaughter of an entire immigrant town. London has been a success because politicians have on the whole understood that they have to manage this conflict, and to do their best to bridge the eternal gap between rich and poor.

Sometimes the politicians have been on the side of the people, like Alderman Tonge allowing the peasants to cross the bridge and take the town. Sometimes they have been on the side of the merchants against the prerogatives of the King, like John Wilkes. Sometimes the merchants have behaved with selfishness and stupidity; and sometimes you have a banker who behaves with such wisdom and far-sightedness that his acts of charity have turned him into a name that echoes down the ages – like Dick Whittington. To anyone anxious about the future of western economies, the story of these Londoners seems to offer so many obvious consolations and points of encouragement.

It is plainly a city that can come back from almost anything – massacre, fire, plague, blitz; and it is clear that the genius of Londoners can sprout anywhere, like buddleia in a bombsite. There was no reason to think that the son of a Covent Garden barber would revolutionise painting and become the inspiration of the Impressionists. Sidcup railway station has many good points, but there if you go there you wouldn't immediately finger it for the birthplace of one of the world's greatest rock and roll bands.

If there is one thing that has changed the lives of these people, and sparked them off, it is the proximity of other Londoners. It is the cyclotron point that I have made several times now: that these extreme talents flourished because of the stimulus of other talent – the exchange, inspiration and competition you find in a great city. Shakespeare was a genius, but he surely wrote his *King Lear* with an awareness of the *King Leir* of Thomas Kyd, just as he wrote his *Merchant of Venice* with an awareness of Marlowe's *Jew of Malta*.

There is also something special about the environment of the city, the way London looks, and the way it works. I think back to that vision you would have seen, if you had ascended to the top of St Paul's in 1700 – a collection of villages, and I think of some wise words of India's great leader Mahatma Gandhi. 'The true India is not to be found in its few cities, but in its 700,000 villages,' he said. 'The growth of the nation depends not on cities but its villages'. This is a romantic and appealing sentiment, and as anyone who has lately been to India can testify, it is completely wrong. People who live in Indian cities have better healthcare, better education, higher per capita GDP and a lower carbon footprint than people who live in Indian villages, and that's why Indians are flocking to their cities. The same point can be made about Londoners, certainly in relation to productivity, which is about 30 per cent higher than in the rest of the country. But Gandhi's saying still appeals to something in our souls, doesn't it?

We yearn for the idea of the village, that Eden from which we were all expelled, a community of prelapsarian innocence and beauty. When we walk around London we can see that it is still a collection of 150 villages and town centres, now more or less effectively linked by public transport.

Cities are wonderful places to be anonymous, to seek pleasure, to make money; but sometimes there can something to be said for putting the village back into the city. That's why you will see huge efforts made by various parts of London government to bring communities together, to promote apprenticeships, as well as doing all sorts of things to improve the feel of the city – from planting thousands of street trees to encouraging people to take to the streets on big blue bicycles, a machine that we have seen was improved (if not, ahem, invented) in London.

When you look at London in the early twenty-first century it is hard to resist the conclusion that previous generations have done us proud. I know you would expect me to say this, and indeed it is my job to say it; but I also happen to believe it to be true, that a city with an illustrious past can have an extraordinary future.

London has the right time zone for a three way daytime conversation between New York and Shanghai, and we have the right language. In spite of the disasters of the credit crunch, we still have the largest financial services industry in the world – and even if people feel a bit 1381 towards foreign bankers, it is always worth remembering the cash and jobs they bring to London. Hollywood movies are edited and supplied with special effects in Soho. Apps for the world's Iphones are invented in Shoreditch. We export bikes from Chiswick to Holland. We export cake from Waltham Forest to France (let them eat cake, I always say, made in Walthamstow). We export increasing quantities of ballet shoes from Hackney to China.

A few hundred yards from my office they have almost completed the Shard; and whatever you think about Renzo Piano's design, it will be the tallest office building in Europe; and the Shard is nothing compared to the developments in the Olympic park, in east London, in the docks, and the potential for development in Battersea, Croydon, Earl's Court and elsewhere.

In a way the solution seems straightforward: sort out education, keep investing in transport, build more affordable housing, solve our aviation problems and get people into work by retrofitting tens of thousands of badly insulated homes then London will continue to lead the UK towards an economic recovery and to attract admiration around the world. Bygone Londoners have created this garden city, with its parks and plane trees and intricate solutions for bringing millions of people together and moving them around as quickly and comfortably as possible. Some of them were men and women of genius, whose ideas helped to shape the world. Most of them were obscure.

They have left us much more than a precious inherited conglomerate of buildings and views and mass transit systems. They have created that thing the Romans understood so well: a global brand.They have left the city with a reputation that makes people want to come here and tramp over London Bridge in search of money, food, fame, companionship – all the things that make a human being tick.

In the end, it is that 2000-year procession of Londoners that has created the city's worldwide brand and appeal. Or, as London's most famous poet and playwright put it, 'What is a city but the people?'

Acknowledgements

This book could not have been written without the generosity of Stephen Inwood, who has produced far and away the most readable, thoughtful and interesting one volume book about London and its development. In the course of a quick (vaguely Moroccan) lunch and a ramble around Cheapside he made all sorts of excellent suggestions – like the best sort of tutor – and sent me on my way. He also kindly agreed to speed-read the draft, though I should stress that any errors of fact, taste, judgment etc are entirely my own. Huge thanks to my fellow Brackenbury scholar.

I have truffled through far too many books to list them or acknowledge their authors, though it is only fair to direct readers to some that have provided particular pleasure or interest.

Anyone wishing to know more about Boudica should look at the work of Miranda Aldhouse-Green.

Richard Abels has written the most helpful and amusing book about Alfred the Great.

If your appetite has been whetted to discover more about John Wilkes, you should immediately get hold of the utterly brilliant biography by Arthur Cash.

Jack Lohman of the Museum of London allowed me to come at very weird hours to look at the books in his library, and I am most grateful to him and his staff for all their patience.

The polymath David Jeffcock once again supplied all kinds of tips and corrections. Andrew Roberts very kindly read the chapter on Churchill. Vicky Spratt did excellent research into many of the characters. Daniel Moylan pointed out the alleged connexion between Magnus Martyr and Magna Mater. Lara Johnson supplied some interesting tips about the origins of the police and Gina Miller helped with ping pong.

Jonathan Watt did heroic work throughout, and I am especially indebted to his compendious knowledge of mediaeval guild structures and bridge finance. Once again I am thankful that Natasha Fairweather is my agent, and above all I want to thank my publisher Susan Watt without whose enthusiasm and sheer maieutic drive this project could not have happened.